The Future of Governing

STUDIES IN GOVERNMENT
AND PUBLIC POLICY

The Future of Governing:
Four Emerging Models

B. Guy Peters

University Press of Kansas

Published by the University Press of Kansas (Lawrence, Kansas 66049),
which was organized by the Kansas Board of Regents and is operated and
funded by Emporia State University, Fort Hays State University, Kansas
State University, Pittsburg State University, the University of Kansas, and
Wichita State University

Library of Congress Cataloging-in-Publication Data

Peters, B. Guy.
    The future of governing : four emerging models / B. Guy Peters.
       p.   cm. — (Studies in government and public policy)
    Includes bibliographical references and index.
    ISBN 0-7006-0793-5 (alk. paper). — ISBN 0-7006-0794-3 (alk.
  paper)
    1. Public administration. 2. Comparative government. I. Title.
  II. Series.
JF1351.P393   1996
350—dc20   96-25429

British Library Cataloguing in Publication Data is available.

Printed in the United States of America

10 9 8 7 6 5 4 3

Contents

Preface

Change in the public sector is the rule rather than the exception. The quest for the perfect way of structuring and managing government has gone on as long as there has been a government, always to end in disappointment. The problem has been in part that no single definition of what constitutes perfect administration exists. Further, each solution tends to create its own new set of problems, which in turn will create a new set of reforms. Although this cycle of reform is beneficial for those of us interested in the process of change, it is less so for those involved in the process. Frequent changes tend to create cynicism about reform efforts both inside and outside the public sector. However, such efforts can be a politician's best friend, given that they are at times the only possible reaction to intractable policy problems.

Although change is a common experience in the public sector, the reform activity during the 1980s and 1990s has been extraordinary, not only in the number of reform initiatives but also in the fundamental nature of the changes being considered. In New Zealand, for example, it is not altogether hyperbolic to say that a revolution has occurred in the public sector. The traditional Westminster model of government in that country has been replaced by ideas drawn from public-choice economics and private management. Even countries that, according to other criteria, appear to be performing more than adequately have found it necessary to invest a great deal of time and effort in reforming their public sectors.

Perhaps because of the ubiquity and fundamental nature of change in these two decades, the administrative reforms being implemented are far from intellectually consistent. Although they sometimes parade under umbrella terms such as "reinvention," a number of different strands of thought about change are emerging. Further, these patterns are often inherently incompatible even though their advocates are implementing them as components of the same reform program. Thus it is crucial to understand the ideas that undergird reforms, not only intellectually but also for practical reasons. If a number of the reforms now being implemented are indeed incompatible, then they cannot be successful, and these probable failures can only exacerbate the already pervasive conception that government is incapable of doing anything right.

The ideas contained in these reform efforts may be incompatible, but it is significant that contemporary reforms are driven by ideas. Each of the four models of change I will discuss in this book has a set of ideas beneath the more practical reform proposals being implemented. Some of these models, the market, for example, have a substantially clearer intellectual basis than do the others, but all four do have some identifiable theoretical foundations. This characteristic distinguishes the current round of reform from some of the tireless tinkering that has tended to characterize administrative reform. Most discussion of the reforms has taken place in the context of individual countries or groups of countries, but it is important to look at the common ideas that have guided and motivated the transformations.

Although the focus is primarily on the ideas undergirding reform, another concern is with the manifestation of those ideas in different national settings. Context is extremely important for understanding politics and administration. The various political and administrative traditions of the developed democracies have provided a set of lenses through which to interpret contemporary ideas for making government perform better. These lenses sometimes produce confusion, with the same concept being interpreted quite differently in the various national settings. Despite that possible confusion, the differences are useful indications of the disparities among administrative systems and therefore can serve as the basis for interesting comparative analysis.

A comparative analysis could include almost the entire world and certainly the entire developed world. I will provide examples of reforms from a number of countries, including some in the developing world, but I will focus on examples from the English-speaking democracies. Ease of access to information is an obvious reason, but there is also more than a little intellectual justification for this focus. These countries have been innovators in a number of ways, and collectively they have reformed more extensively than have most other countries. Moreover, some of the Anglo-American countries were in need of more extensive reforms than were many other developed democracies.

There have been a number of people who have had a significant influence on the development of this book. Perhaps the individual to whom I owe the greatest debt of gratitude is Donald Savoie. Through Donald's good offices I have been able to develop a continuing relationship with the Canadian civil service and a large number of capable and dedicated civil servants. We have worked together as senior fellows of the Canadian Centre for Management Development (CCMD) for several years, a collaboration that has been crucial in developing my own thinking about government and public administration. Several other individuals at

CCMD have been extremely supportive of my research on public administration and have contributed to it. In particular Ralph Heintzman and Maurice Demers have encouraged and helped fund the research and have provided their own valuable insights into the practice of public administration.

A number of other colleagues have helped shape the ideas in this book, sometimes without being aware of how much they were contributing. Vincent Wright provided me with a visiting position at the Centre for European Studies, Nuffield College, Oxford. The opportunity to have several months of virtually uninterrupted time to think and write was crucial to finishing the book. Numerous stimulating, if sometimes rushed, conversations with Vincent also contributed to my thinking about contemporary administrative change. Jon Pierre and his colleagues at Forvaltningshogskolan at the University of Gothenberg provided a similar, if alas shorter, opportunity. Patricia Ingraham asked me to write a paper that became the foundation of this book. She and her colleagues at the Maxwell School, Syracuse University, also provided a number of interesting insights on the reform process at conferences in Washington, D.C., and in lectures in Beijing, China. Several colleagues in Norway, including Tom Christensen and Morten Egeberg, have provided interesting and important feedback on some of the ideas contained here. And many colleagues in Pittsburgh have helped me think through some of the ideas; others assisted (in their own way) by making it impossible for me to rush through the manuscript.

1
Changing States, Governance, and the Public Service

Governance is a scarce commodity. Governments have created a vast array of institutions designed to exercise collective control and influence over the societies and economies for which they have been given responsibility. Those efforts at institution-building have certainly provided comparative politics with an interesting array of data, but it is much less clear that they have moved any closer to solving the problems of regulating the behavior of people and organizations. If anything, these efforts at governance may be less successful now than were similar efforts in the past. There has been some loss of government's policy autonomy to external actors, such as international organizations and amorphous international markets, at the same time that an apparent popular resistance to being governed has sharply increased. Political leaders in the world today must ask whether what they do in their national capitals has much effect in shaping the lives of their citizens.

Fortunately, governments, government leaders, and their civil servants continue attempting to find better ways of governing. I say fortunately not just because these efforts keep students of the public sector occupied but also because there is a great capacity to do good for citizens, individually and collectively, through effective public action. It is now fashionable to malign government and the people working in it and to point out gleefully all their failures. Such skepticism and cynicism are cheap; great commitment and courage are required to continue attempting to solve problems that almost by definition exceed the capacity of any individual or private actor to solve. If the problems had been easy or profitable, they probably would have remained in the private sector, and government would never have been made to cope with them. Despite the popular mythology, government is rarely imperialistic, nor does it look for new problems to solve; governments are more likely to be handed the poisoned chalice of an insuperable problem.[1]

It remains crucial for governments, and the individuals who constitute them, to continue their search for innovative mechanisms for making government work better and to serve society better. This effort must be carried on even in the face of "ill structured" (H. A. Simon 1973) or "intractable" (Schon and Rein 1994) or "wicked" (Dunn 1988) problems and often in the service of a mass public that neither recognizes nor appreciates the effort involved. Contemporary public servants are neither martyrs nor saints, but they are individuals charged with continuing to make collective decisions and to enforce previous decisions on behalf of the public interest.

The leaders of government are also charged with reforming and improving the internal performance of their organizations. Many of the efforts at reform that I will discuss have been internally generated, an indication that the public sector is not resisting change, as many of its critics assume, but in some cases is actually leading the way for change (Tellier 1990; B. Peters and Savoie 1994; Derlien 1995). Of course, there are at least as many reforms that have been imposed from the outside, some of which have indeed been resisted vigorously by the entrenched civil service. There is no monopoly on virtue or vice in the world of administrative reform.

My purpose in this book is to examine the efforts that are being made to make government work better. Numerous efforts have been occurring all over the world since at least 1980. In most industrialized democracies these reforms have originated internally, but in many of the less developed countries they have been imposed by agencies of external aid as conditions of receiving assistance (United Nations Development Programme 1988). Even countries that appear to be extremely successful from the outside, such as Japan, have engaged in large-scale administrative reforms (Muramatsu and Krauss 1995), partly as a means of keeping pace with other countries.

The discussion will focus largely on the Anglo-American democracies, because generally these have been the most active and innovative reformers. I will, however, use examples from other countries if they can illuminate an analytic point. My intention is not so much to describe the numerous efforts at administrative reform—that has been done extremely well in a number of other places (Savoie 1994a; Zifcak 1994; *International Political Science Review* 1993). Rather, it is to look at the ideas that drive the reforms and that provide a diagnosis of the problems as well as the basis for prescriptions to remedy them. Given that purpose, and the ubiquity of reform, the focus on a smaller number of cases is not particularly damaging.

Understanding administrative reform in turn requires understanding the traditional model of governance that is the backdrop against which attempts at reform must be viewed. Rather than evolving from a set of intellectual principles, this model tended to evolve from practice and rarely has been articulated as a distinct model. Despite its lack of an intellectual foundation, the traditional model was once thought to be the way in which the public sector should be organized, and indeed it worked rather well for decades. During the height of optimism about government's capacity to solve social problems, for example, the 1950s through the early 1970s, the basic model for governance appeared to require little fundamental debate. The task then was to refine the model, make it more "rational" with techniques such as program budgeting (Novick 1965) and cost-benefit analysis (Mishan 1988), and then merely to let the governing system continue to produce effective policies and continued socioeconomic improvements.

Certainly some conservative politicians and thinkers did raise questions about the virtues of those (by then) traditional ideas about government and especially about the increased role of the public sector (Friedman 1962; Hayek 1968; Sawer 1982). For most people in and out of government, however, the parameters of acceptable public action then were broad and well established. There was a pervasive belief that government could regulate the economy through taxing and spending and that it had sufficient economic resources to ameliorate social problems such as poverty, sickness, and poor education. The fifties and sixties were the period of the "mixed-economy welfare-state," of "treble affluence" (Rose and Peters 1978), and of the promise of an ever-brighter future through public action.

The fifties and sixties were also the period of consensus politics (Kavanagh and Morris 1994) in most countries of Western Europe and North America, and both scholars and practical politicians proclaimed the "end of ideology" and the creation of a "post-industrial society" (Gustafsson 1979).[2] Even a conservative such as Richard Nixon would say, "We are all Keynesians now," and would attempt to create new social programs (Spulbar 1989) rather than roll such programs back as subsequent Republican presidents and congresses attempted to do.[3] Similarly, Christian Democrats in Germany could preach the virtues of the "social market economy" as a desirable alternative to unbridled capitalism (Peacock and Willgerodt 1989). Clearly something has changed in the economy and in the popular mind since that time, and with that change has come a change in the definition of what constitutes good government and acceptable public administration. Before looking at what has changed, however, I offer a somewhat more complete idea of the traditional model and some of its strengths and weaknesses.

TRADITIONAL PUBLIC ADMINISTRATION: THE OLD-TIME RELIGION

Dwight Waldo (1968) once wrote that public administration has had so many identity crises that in comparison the life of the average adolescent appeared idyllic. Waldo was discussing public administration as an academic discipline, but its contemporary practice displays much of the same uncertainty. Questions about its practice include such basic issues as the structure of government, management of those structures, and the proper role of public administration in governance (Harmon 1995). Many traditional certainties about government and the public service are now either totally altered or are subject to severe scrutiny.

Rather than being singular, the old model of public administration is actually a number of different concepts (Richards 1992), and at least six old chestnuts have guided our thinking about the public service and its role in governance (B. Peters and Wright 1996). These six ideas clearly are no longer as canonical as they once were.[4] The sometimes forgotten aspect in the discussion of alternative approaches to public management is that these principles evolved over a long period and generally represent responses to a number of problems that existed in public administration in earlier times. Indeed, there is a real chance that some of the problems for which the old chestnuts were designed may reappear once they are replaced with more modern conceptions about how to run government.

Reforms solve problems existing at one time, often in the process creating a new set of problems that may generate subsequent reforms (Kaufman 1978; Aucoin 1990; B. Peters 1995a). Moreover, a word of caution about administrative reform does not mean that the old ways of running government were necessarily better. The appeal to prudence simply points out that these approaches to public management did solve certain problems, albeit creating some additional ones. Overturning the older modes of administering, though solving some problems, may in the process revive older difficulties and perhaps even create new ones. If the potential costs of discarding the existing system of public administration are not recognized, then change may appear entirely too attractive.

An Apolitical Civil Service

The first of the six principles is the assumption of an apolitical civil service, and associated with that the politics-administration dichotomy and the concept of "neutral competence" (Kaufman 1956) within the civil service. The basic idea is that civil servants should not have discernible political allegiances and that they should be able to serve any master, i.e., any government of the day. The civil servant may have views about particular policies and is almost expected to, as a member of an organization responsible for making and implementing policies (Aberbach, Putnam, and Rockman 1981). But they are not expected to have partisan views that might lead them to be disloyal to a government of one complexion or another.

The principle of an apolitical civil service has been largely an Anglo-Saxon preoccupation, compared to administration in other industrialized democracies (Silberman 1993). However, even in countries with a more overtly politicized civil service, such as Germany and France (Derlien 1991; Bodiguel and Rouban 1991), the concept of competence ranks at least as high as political allegiance in the selection of civil servants. Similarly, the civil services of the Scandinavian countries tend to be less overtly politicized than that of Germany, but even there political allegiances are often known or assumed (Ståhlberg 1987). The characteristic common to these civil service systems is that objective qualifications are the first hurdle for recruitment, and political considerations follow those.

Although depoliticization of the civil service has been very much an Anglo-American concern, it is also a rather recent administrative value. In the United States, for example, the spoils system dominated recruitment until the mid-1880s, and even then the number of merit appointments under the Pendleton Act (1883) was rather small (Skowronek 1982; Ingraham 1995a). By 1904 only half of the total federal employment was under the merit system, and most of that was in lower-level clerical positions (Johnson and Liebcap 1994, 30–33). In the United Kingdom the merit system was initiated only slightly earlier than in the United States, although it spread throughout the administrative system more quickly (Parris 1969). The historical record in other Anglo-American democracies is not significantly different, as patronage appointments were either replaced by merit gradually under British rule from the end of the nineteenth century or as former colonies institutionalized merit systems quickly after gaining independent status (Braibanti 1966; Koehn 1990).[5]

Associated with the concern for maintaining an apolitical personnel system was the argument that politics and administration were, and more importantly, should be separate enterprises. In the United States this principle was stated first by Woodrow Wilson (1887) and restated more forcefully by Goodnow (1900). In the United Kingdom the argument was also advanced, first implicitly in the Northcote-Trevelyan Report (1853) on the civil service and then later in the Haldane Report (Machinery of Government Committee 1918) on the structure of government. In both countries the argument was that the job of the civil service was to implement the decisions made by the political masters and to do so without questioning the sagacity of the decisions.[6] Other Anglo-American political systems have had similar apolitical civil services and have encountered the same problems of increased politicization.

Despite the ideological advocacy of an apolitical civil service, it is increasingly clear that civil servants do have significant, if not necessarily dominant, policy roles in most contemporary governments (B. Peters 1992; Kato 1994; Plowden 1994). It is also clear to most analysts that governance is better, on average, because they do (Terry 1995). The policy role of civil servants is most obvious at the implementation stage, where the role of implementors in determining real policies occurred as early as the 1930s (Gulick 1933; Almond and Lasswell 1934). In addition to the policy that emerges from "street-level bureaucrats" (Lipsky 1980; Adler and Asquith 1981) dealing with individual cases, the public bureaucracy has a more systematic role in making public policy through implementation. The recognition of the empirical reality of the role of the bureaucracy in governance and of the benefits that arise from that involvement has not prevented the continuing ideological advocacy of separating politics and administration, however.

The manifest policymaking role of the public bureaucracy arises most clearly in the promulgation of "secondary legislation," "regulations" in the language of American government. Very few legislatures in the world are capable of writing laws that specify the necessary details for complex policy areas and thus depend upon their bureaucracies to fill in that legal and technical content. In the United States, for example, although Congress passes only a few hundred bills each year, something approaching 5,000 final rules are passed annually.[7] The accumulation of rules over the years has produced over 10,000 pages of them in the *Code of Federal Regulations* for agriculture policy alone (Kerwin 1994, 18–19). In other industrialized democracies the volume of secondary legislation appears no less; even in the European Union there are approximately ten times as many rules written as pieces of primary legislation adopted (Blumann and Soligne 1989).

The civil service also has a significant, if now threatened, role as policy advisers at the formulation stage. Although ministers may be elected to make policy decisions, they may lack the capacity to do so effectively (Blondel 1988). Even in countries where civil servants are generalists by education and career patterns, through experience they can gain greater command of the details of policy than can ministers who are in office for only a short time (B. Peters 1992). And the role of the civil service in policy formulation and advice is perhaps even more crucial within developing and transitional governments, in which the need for expertise and the demands for a "committed bureaucracy" are that much greater (B. Peters 1995a; Hesse 1993).

The problem then becomes how to structure government in ways that recognize the reality, and even the desirability, of the significant policy role for civil servants while simultaneously preserving the requirements of democratic accountability. This is a difficult balance for designers of government institutions to achieve, especially given the historical legacy of thought concerning the neutrality of the civil service and the current reality of public demands for enhanced accountability (Day and Klein 1987; Cooper 1995). Furthermore, political leaders have become ever more aware of the policy role of civil servants and in response often have attempted to minimize that role (Aberbach and Rockman 1988; C. Campbell 1993). Reducing the role of the civil service has been done partly for ideological reasons (they were perceived either as too far right or left) or simply for reasons of preserving institutional differences.

The struggle over competence and authority in making public policy is now more obvious to individuals working within government, as well as to citizens, than in the past. The politicization of the functions of the civil service, if not the members of the civil service themselves, may make the delicate balance of competent policymaking even more difficult to maintain. Years of one-party domination mean that current civil servants are often identified with the policies of that particular party. Further, the prevailing assumption, if not always the reality, is that civil servants must accept the party line of the incumbent government or face termination.

Hierarchy and Rules

The second significant change in attitudes toward the traditional model of government is the decline of assumptions about hierarchical and rule-bound management within the public service and about the authority of civil servants to implement and enforce regulations outside it. The neat Weberian model of management (Wright and Peters 1996) does not apply within public organizations as it once did, and in its place a variety of alternative sources of organizational power and authority are to be found. The market, as one example, is an increasingly significant standard against which to compare the structure and performance of government organizations (Lan and Rosenbloom 1992; Hood 1990; Boston 1991). Though it can be argued that the inherent differences between the public and private sectors are crucial to understanding governance (Savoie 1995b; Self 1993; Perry and Rainey 1988), even governments on the political left have implemented market-based reforms.[8]

For transitional and developing regimes the demands for greater economic efficiency in the public sector must be balanced against the needs to create some of the predictability, universality, and probity associated with Weberian bureaucracy. The changes being introduced in industrialized countries are based on the assumption that the employees implementing market-based reforms will have at least some of the public-service values that have informed the civil service. Without those values, market-oriented reforms run the risk of justifying corruption and becoming a publicly sponsored version of the excesses of capitalism. Those excesses to some extent have occurred already in the former Soviet Union and may well emerge in other transitional regimes. These aberrations, unfortunately, have not been entirely absent from the industrialized democracies in which market-oriented reforms have been implemented.[9]

There are other challenges to hierarchy. Alternative to the market model, as well as to traditional models of bureaucracy, is the "dialectical" or participatory organization. Scholars and reformers have discussed this model for a number of years, but government organizations are now being placed under increasing real pressure to accommodate the interests of lower-level employees, as well as those of their clients, into their decisionmaking processes (Barzelay 1992). This change in management is at once a manipulative mechanism for increasing efficiency and a genuine moral commitment to participation (Thomas 1993). Whether the participation is authentic or not, it is difficult for an organization to deny involvement and access to its employees and even to its clients.

Contemporary public organizations also must negotiate social compliance with their decisions and compliance with contracts for service delivery instead of implementing public programs directly through law and other authoritative means. The spread of network conceptualizations in the social sciences has been paralleled by a proliferation of network practices in governance (Scharpf

1991; Kenis and Schneider 1991). No longer can governments impose their wills through legal instruments and, if necessary, coercion; they must now work to achieve an outcome approaching consensus among a large group of self-interested parties who have some influence over the policy. Governing in most industrialized democracies has become a process of bargaining and mediating rather than applying rules (Kooiman 1993).

Civil servants increasingly are expected to make their own decisions about what constitutes the public interest, and they at times are compelled to make determinations diametrically opposed to the stated policies and desires of their nominal political masters.[10] If civil servants and other appointed officials are indeed to become entrepreneurial then they must become less dominated by the dictates of these masters. If this approach were practiced, it would alter fundamentally ideas of accountability as well as ideas of management in the public sector, especially in the Westminster democracies (G. Wilson 1994c).

Changes such as these make the role of civil service managers even more difficult than it has been and leave the role of civil servants within governments more ambiguous. Further, the general absence of a formalized normative structure in government may make preserving accountability increasingly difficult (*Public Money and Management* 1995).

For developing and transitional regimes these changes are even more problematic than for the industrialized countries. Bureaucracies in European and North American countries are searching for ways to become more entrepreneurial and less constrained by red tape, but governments in many developing and transitional regimes have different challenges. The problem for many governments in such regimes is in creating the Weberian and rule-directed bureaucracies that are now being supplanted in the industrialized regimes. Applying the earlier characterization of bureaucracies in transitional regimes by Fred Riggs (1964) as "prismatic," one of the challenges of public management in contexts of low universality of rules is to ensure equality and uniformity of those rules.

Permanence and Stability

The third change in the assumptions about governance and the public bureaucracy concerns the permanence and stability of the organizations within government (Kaufman 1976). Employment as a public servant is usually conceptualized as being a lifetime commitment, a "social contract," with civil servants trading a certain amount of income for secure employment (Hood and Peters 1994). Joining a public organization is sometimes seen as joining a Japanese corporation once was—as lifetime employment. The permanence of public organizations is frequently overestimated (B. Peters and Hogwood 1988), but it has been an important partial truth about government. Increasingly, this pattern of permanent organization is being attacked. The growing recognition of the dysfunctions of permanence and the realization that many significant social and economic problems currently exist within the interstices of public organizations have led to some discussion of alternative forms of government organization.

The character of the alternative organizational structures remains somewhat inchoate at present. In particular, ideas about task forces, "czars," interdepartmental committees, and similar structures have generated options for achieving more flexible governance.[11] Another possibility is the "virtual organization" as a means of linking a range of individuals, and with them institutional interests, to be employed across a range of government organizations. Given the spread of information technology, the necessity for people to be in a common setting in order to share the characteristics of an organization has diminished. Therefore, forming alternatives to traditional organizations has become practical.

For individual public employees, organizational methods would also be diverse, with contracting and consultancy arrangements, temporary employment at peak times (for tax and recreational employees, for example), and an increasing number of positions clearly not intended to be tenurable. In the senior civil service the idea of a distinctive career structure is now being questioned and abandoned, even in countries such as the United Kingdom, in which the civil service has been very much a group apart from other employment streams. The Treasury—long the homeland of the mandarin—has embarked on a process of reducing its own staff and thinking about how best to involve outside talent in its own work (HMSO 1993; HMSO 1994a).

The traditional sense of permanence in public organizations is being questioned from several perspectives. In one view, a change is simply a means of de-privileging the civil service during a time in which almost all organizations and employees are being confronted with downsizing and other threats to their existence. Another view holds that permanence and stability tend to ossify policy lines and to make coordination of policies more difficult. If temporary organizational structures were more common, the change could have two benefits. First, it would enable more organizational experimentation in solving problems (D. Campbell 1982) without the fear that a future dinosaur was being created (Kaufman 1976). Second, it could permit the creation of organizations with primarily coordinative tasks that could address a particular problem of interaction among programs and organizations and then disappear. The conventional wisdom would argue that government organizations would not disappear, but neither has there been much real attempt to create such organizations explicitly.[12]

Governments of developing countries appear even more affected by the permanence of public organizations and employment. Government is a major employer in these countries, especially for the relatively small professional and educated segments of the society. It is difficult for any government to dismiss existing workers, but it also may perceive the need to hire additional, politically loyal personnel. It may make sense to dismiss existing employees, however, if they have been compromised by their participation in a regime with serious human rights abuses (B. Peters 1995a). In any case, the tendency for public employment to be conceptualized as permanent presents real problems for these governments.

An Institutionalized Civil Service

The fourth fundamental assumption undergirding traditional public administration is that there should be an institutionalized civil service that is governed as a corporate body. This concept is a somewhat recent development in some industrialized democracies, with patronage or personal service to the crown or both being the older model for managing the state. For the intellectual father of contemporary bureaucracies, Max Weber (1958; see also Mommsen 1989), the development of authority and bureaucracy—beginning with charismatic and traditional authority using patrimonial organizations and ending with rational-legal authority employing bureaucratic organizations—represented the development of the modern state (especially in Germany). Although some analysts consider it central to political modernity, the concept of a distinctive and professional civil service has been brought into question in a number of countries seeking to establish a more committed and activist civil service.

In addition to the impermanent government organizations being created, the personnel commitments of government also have become less permanent. Government organizations increasingly expand and contract to meet variable demands for work, for example, in tax offices or recreation programs. Although this style of personnel management may save money, it produces several empirical and normative questions for public managers and policymakers. Temporary employment for a significant portion of the public labor force may produce even more difficulties for citizens than the presumed indifference of permanent employees. Citizens will have to cope with public employees who may lack the commitment to service and other public values that in most instances have characterized the career civil service. At a more practical level, temporary employees may lack the training and information necessary to do their jobs properly.

Even if the civil service system itself has not been challenged, the manner in which it traditionally has been managed is being questioned. For example, one of the common principles of personnel management in the public sector has been a uniform set of grades for personnel throughout the civil service, based upon their qualifications, the difficulty of their assigned tasks, or both, with relatively equal pay within each grade. Advancement was to be based upon merit, demonstrated either by performance on the job or by a series of examinations. It is now less clear that merit is to be measured within the context of the public service and the public sector, as forces and priorities of the market are being used to test the worth of individuals and of policies.

Internal Regulation

The fifth chestnut is that the civil service should be acquiescent and respond almost without question to policy directives issued by its nominal political masters. This demand goes beyond mere political neutrality. Many of the problems associated with government, and especially with public bureaucracy, are a function of controls imposed by political leaders seeking greater control and accountability (Kaufman 1977; Walters 1992a). Government organizations are generally among the most stringently regulated in any society (J. Wilson 1989), especially in Anglo-American democracies. Therefore, if the skills and entrepreneurship of public employees could be engaged more freely, then government is likely to be able to perform more efficiently and effectively (Osborne and Gaebler 1992).

It is less clear that deregulation is the most appropriate response to the needs of developing and transitional regimes. Certainly many of these governments have been characterized by extremely high levels of internal regulation (Beyme 1993) that have stifled creativity and produced problems in dealing with citizens. Further, in many instances international organizations and private-sector lenders are pressing for loosening restraints on government action. Still, deregulation may not be the most appropriate response for the governments of transitional countries. The need in these regimes generally is for greater predictability and accountability rather than for the increased entrepreneurship demanded in more developed regimes.

Equality

The sixth characteristic of the traditional model of governance and public administration holds that there should be as much equality of outcomes as possible. Personnel management stresses equal pay and conditions of employment for similarly qualified employees across the civil service. And there are strong norms that the decisions made by the public service with respect to its clients should be as similar as possible: clients with the same objective characteristics should receive the same benefits. In this Weberian conception of bureaucracy the civil servant applies the rules *sine irae ac studio* to produce equitable outcomes for all clients (Thompson 1975).

This conception of equality of services and outcomes is also being questioned, through several related types of reform. First, market-oriented reforms have tended to decentralize and disaggregate government departments and to provide an enhanced amount of autonomy to managers. The assumption is that these managers will still be obliged to follow the laws of the programs they administer. There does appear, however, to be much greater room for discretion, which is especially important if it is seen as possibly saving money for government. In this view the creation of differential levels and patterns of service creates a quasi market of sorts, so that citizens can exercise some choice over what they will receive (and perhaps what they will pay for) from government.[13]

The attacks on equality of services also arise from another quarter and are based on the participatory ethic in relationship to public services and public employment. The concept here is to empower lower-echelon workers in organizations and enable them to make more autonomous decisions about services. The argument is that the rigidity of bureaucratic structures designed to ensure greater equality of services for clients restricts the freedom of employees to "self-actualize" on the job and to make more creative and humane decisions about their clients. If the shackles of rigidity are removed, then public employees will be happier and will also deliver better services to their clients. Particularly for social services, programs that were intended to be humane and helpful have become bureaucratized (in the pejorative sense of that term) and frequently harm (if only in subtle ways) in addition to helping their clients (Smart 1991). Further, some proponents of the models of administrative reform argue for the empowerment of clients so that they can make more of their own decisions, a reform that may be diametrically opposed to the empowerment of the workers administering their benefits (see pp. 52–54).

The issue of equality also raises important questions about accountability and the law. Do clients want the outcomes of their demands for service to be contingent upon getting the "right" worker? Do other taxpayers want public employees to have so much latitude in delivering the services that are paid for with tax money? Is it legal (or ethical) for people with the same characteristics and the same rights to be treated differently by government, or are these other public values equally or more important than the values of empowerment? Unfortunately, these issues too often are not addressed in the contemporary debates about change in the public sector.

Rather than looking back to vestiges of past thinking about governance, I shall explore several alternative paths for the development of the public service. By examining the development of alternative models of the state that are emerging in practice, readers can look at the implications of these models of governance for the civil service. Except for the market model, they have not been articulated in a comprehensive form; they have appeared more clearly in government documents than in the academic literature. Thus they will have to be extracted almost as ideal types from academic and practical discussions of governing.

There is some similarity of analyses and prescriptions across the alternatives, although the meanings attached to the prescriptions may be quite different in each model. Most reforms have the effect, however, of "hollowing out" the state and making it, and particularly the career public service, a less significant actor in society (R. Rhodes 1994; Milward, forthcoming). Yet, interestingly, one of the approaches to changing government may have the (probably unintended) consequence of enhancing both the powers of government and of the civil service. Although the focus is on alternatives, one possible model is a vigorous restatement of the status quo ante. For many civil servants, and for some politicians, the "old-time religion" may still be the best way to run a government, even if they must face massive skepticism from the public.

WHAT HAPPENED?

The traditional system of administration persisted for decades and on the whole was extremely successful. It fought several world wars, produced and administered a massive expansion of social programs, instituted large-scale economic management for the public sector, and initiated a host of remarkable policies. This system has now, however, gone from "hubris to helplessness" (G. Downs and Larkey 1986). What happened to cause the large-scale rethinking of governance that occurred during the 1980s and 1990s? There is no single answer but a confluence of events that has resulted in this fundamental rethinking and in some attempt to move administration far from its roots. Although the changes can be seen most dramatically in the Anglo-American democracies, they extend into virtually all industrialized democracies, including Japan and other countries that are usually thought to be highly successful (Muramatsu and Krauss 1995).

One easy explanation for the change is that significant shifts in the economy forced governments to respond. The presumption is that as economic growth slowed or became less certain or both, government could no longer realistically count on the fiscal dividend of growth to fund increasing costs. Certainly any significant new programs were unlikely to be adopted. Further, if the costs of delivering existing services could be reduced by making administration more efficient, then by all means that should be done. The desire to be economically competitive in an emerging global economy (Savoie 1995c), it has been argued, began to outstrip most other concerns on the agenda of government so that any reductions in tax costs, regulation, and perceived public-sector inefficiencies were welcomed.

This economic explanation for the advance of governmental and administrative reforms is a bit too facile. Certainly there were economic problems, but in the recent past such problems might have been addressed by expanding the role of the public sector rather than reducing it; Richard Nixon's confession of his Keynesianism would appear to support that choice. Moreover, the economic problems were not as great as they had been at other times during the postwar period that produced a much less overt response from reformers, especially those within the public sector itself. What other influences, then, may help explain why the questions about the performance of the economy produced such massive responses?

One of the possible contributory factors is demographic change. The populations of almost all industrialized democracies are rapidly becoming older. Thus the level of entitlement expenditure for programs such as old age pensions and medical care is likely to rise rapidly and will have to be paid for by a declining number of working-age people. Reviews of these commitments, such as the Kerry/Danforth Commission in the United States (Bipartisan Commission 1994), have pointed to the rapid escalation of entitlement expenditures that will occur over the next several decades under existing law. Reforming public-sector management is unlikely to affect these problems per se, but it may result in reducing at least some of the total costs of government and in creating some greater capacity for future spending on entitlements. Further, making government appear better managed may be important symbolically if the people are to be asked for additional taxes.

The unease about entitlement spending is largely a concern of the political elite; relatively few people in the mass public are aware of entitlement obligations, apart from their own future benefits. The concern over governance, however, has not been just an elite phenomenon and indeed has taken on a manifestation approaching a populist uprising in some countries.[14] This populist reaction has a number of dimensions. On the political right there has been a reaction against taxation, public spending, and the degree of regulation imposed on business. Even many working- and lower-middle-class citizens who may be net beneficiaries of the public sector now oppose government spending and especially taxation (Petersen 1992; Sears and Citrin 1985). This reaction to the public sector has been the more common one, with demands that government simply shrink. The dominant assumption is that government cannot do anything well so should do as little as possible.

There has also been a populism of the left, although it has been less visible and less successful. It has attacked the large, bureaucratic structures that have been developed to deliver a range of social and economic services. The bureaucracies are attacked as insensitive, inefficient, and often as hostile to the very clients they were intended to serve (Smart 1991; Spicer 1990). Further, the left argues that government as a whole has become increasingly divorced from the people that it serves and is dominated by the affluent, the educated, and the powerful. In the extreme version of the argument, government is conceptualized as "regulating the poor" rather than actually serving them through social programs (Piven and Cloward 1993; Squires 1990). This version of populism is unsuccessful in part because it attempts to strengthen the positions of the poor and other groups who have relatively little political clout.

The cultural change manifested in populism has not been felt uniformly throughout the Western world. Even Sweden, Denmark, and some of the more successful welfare states have now undertaken administrative reforms that are derivative of the market model (Andersen 1994; Lundell 1994). Other countries such as Norway, however, have attempted to maintain the traditional values and even to increase the democratic and collective elements of policy and administration. Although Norway's wealth helps to explain some of the persistence of these values, the collective values being implemented also reflect their importance and the mass political participation within the culture.

Another explanation for rethinking governance is that the economies and societies that governments are meant to control and regulate have become less governable (Mayntz 1993; Kooiman 1993). This decline in government's capacity to regulate society effectively apparently results from several interrelated causes (Cohen and Rogers 1994). First, there is increasing social and political heterogeneity among populations. The role of the welfare state in rectifying market-based inequalities has been reduced, and income inequalities have been widening in most industrialized societies. Further, the ethnic and racial heterogeneity of these societies has also been increasing through immigration, with a related escalation of social tensions.

Second, the issues confronting contemporary governments seem to have shifted from being bargainable to being less so. Certainly economic issues remain at the center of the political debates in all societies and indeed have been returning to center stage in many. The general problems of sustainable economic growth, distribution, and employment are more important in the 1990s than they appear to have been at any time since the end of World War II. That having been said, however, the economic problems are now weighted with issues such as race, gender, participation, and equality that are more difficult to solve through the mechanisms of conflict resolution, created in postwar politics. The "post-materialist values" (Inglehart 1990) that undergird these conflicts tend to be absolute rather than marginal so that divisible goods such as money are often inadequate in the task of addressing them.

A closely related third point is the decline of stable organizations as the focus for government interventions as well as the source of input into governing. One of the most effective means of addressing economic policy issues during the postwar years was "corporatism," existing in its various guises throughout Europe and to some extent in North America (Schmitter 1989; Pross 1992). Thus when government attempted to cope with numerous economic demands and economic policy, a constellation of stable and reasonably well-structured interest groups existed with which government could bargain. Even in the most successful of these regimes, however, there has been some decline in the proportion of the work force represented by unions, and in the commitment of members to their unions, so that the bargaining partners of government are now less reliable.[15]

As soon as the public sector begins to have to make policy to address the postmaterialist issues, the constellation of interest groups becomes less stable and less able to deliver its members' consent to any deal. Members of "attitude groups" do not need to retain their affiliation, as do members of unions or employers' organizations, so if they disagree with the policies approved by their leadership there is little or no cost to their leaving and forming other organizations. Thus, the possibilities of making binding deals are more uncertain than in traditional economic policy negotiations, and governments may have a harder time framing the issues adequately, much less implementing effective policies.

VISIONS OF THE STATE AND GOVERNANCE

Few governments have remained untouched by the wave of reform that has swept through the public sector over the past several decades. The magnitude of reform undertaken in most political systems may have been unprecedented, at least during peacetime, but the reforms themselves also have tended to be extremely piecemeal and unsystematic (B. Peters and Savoie 1994a). The absence of clear visions and integrated strategies may partly explain why the results of the reforms have tended to disappoint so many of their advocates (Caiden 1990; Ingraham 1995b). Apparently, governments often have selected "off the shelf" reforms derived from one set of assumptions (implicit or explicit) at the same that they selected other reforms based upon quite different, or even directly contradictory, premises. The political and administrative leaders made these selections expecting all the changes to work well together. Yet it is little wonder that in practice the sets of reforms not only have not worked together in a large number of instances but that at times the interactions also have proven to be negative.

In this book, therefore, my task is to explicate several more integrated visions of possible futures for the state and its bureaucracy. The nature of each vision will, in turn, influence the manner in which governance, considered more broadly, would be practiced if such an administrative regime were to be implemented in toto. These reform agendas must not be considered in isolation from other political and cultural movements in society. For example, the emphasis on market models for reforming government represents but one strand of thinking about the need to inculcate the market approach into a whole range of social institutions, such as universities (Tully 1995). Likewise, the drive for making administration more participatory is but a part of a general ethos (largely contradictory to the market model) stressing greater opportunities for participation in the very same institutions.

If the implications of these alternative visions are more fully explored, understood, and contrasted with the traditional conceptualizations of governance, then there is some possibility of producing more effective planned change in government. There is certainly no guarantee of success even with more coherent programs, and the possibility that even the best-planned administrative changes will be diverted and subverted is inevitably present (March and Olsen 1983).

The practical significance of this exercise, however, will be secondary since my primary purpose is to enhance an understanding of what has been happening with governance as well as an understanding of the future implications of the alternative conceptions. Gaining a clear understanding of contemporary reforms is not easy. Speaking of the changes occurring in British government, Sue Richards argues:

> It is a confusing picture of changing patterns of behaviour, of informal and emergent rules, and of shifting power plays. We need greater clarity so public managers and other practitioners of public service may be assisted in their understanding, and so that a wider public may have better access to these changes (1992, 15).

It appears almost certain that the status quo ante is no longer a preferred option in the public sector, in Britain or anywhere, so it is essential to understand the patterns that are emerging. Academic and practitioner-analysts must explore the assumptions of those models, along with the particular proposals derived from those assumptions. Without that analysis and interpretation, it will be difficult to comprehend the emerging form of the state in society—both industrialized and transitional—and to think about the fundamental problems of governing in the twenty-first century.

A concern with alternative visions should not be read to mean that any of these schemes is superior to the traditional model of the civil service in governance. I tend to think that that is not the case, although certainly the traditional model is far from perfect and could be made to function better. I also assume that continuing reform in government is likely, or even inevitable in the current political climate, and if that reform is to occur it is more likely to be effective if the reforms are systematic and integrated. One should also remain cognizant of the internal contradictions inherent within some of these approaches to governance. It may be that, as in H. Simon's now classic discussion (1947) of the "proverbs of administration," there are also "proverbs of reform" that are equally contradictory (Kaufman 1978; B. Peters 1996). Current thinking about the complexities of the public service, even when guided by a relatively strong set of theoretical assumptions, tends toward constructing situational rather than systematic remedies. This emphasis can be seen most clearly in cycles of reform: centralization efforts follow decentralization followed by yet another round of decentralization.

Nevertheless, the context within which any particular vision of governance is to be implemented must be considered. For transitional regimes in Central and Eastern Europe perhaps a Weberian system of highly constrained administration may be the most suitable tool for restoring some legitimacy to government (Hesse 1993; Derlien and Szablowski 1993). The values inherent in that system may need to be institutionalized first, to be followed by the more marketized systems of administration. The politicization and extreme arbitrariness of the old system may have to be purged from people's minds before a more decentralized administrative system can be legitimate.

Yet some Third World regimes that have been dominated by a bureaucracy (perhaps in the pejorative sense of the word) may find the alternative models just as applicable and desirable as do the industrialized countries (Grindle and

Thomas 1991). One difficulty in the reform process has been that the advocates of reforms have assumed that "one size fits all" and that any government could be improved by the institutionalization of their preferred new pattern. Indeed, some of the problems with reforms, such as "reinvention" (Osborne and Gaebler 1992) in the United States, arise from the reforms being based on assumptions about government derived from the experiences of small local governments that may be inappropriate for central governments.

Through the development of these four alternatives to the traditional system of governance, the implications and prescriptions of each vision for several aspects of governing can be examined. Most basic is the diagnosis of the problem. Reform efforts imply a desire for change, and each of the four alternatives contains a clear idea about the source that is producing problems in the public sector. Thus, the models attempt to take the (often) vague sense of uneasiness and malaise that citizens feel about their governments and translate it into a specific cause-and-effect relationship. As with any attempt to impose such a construction on complex social and political institutions, this exercise often produces some oversimplification. The identification of a cause, however, also produces the clarity that may be needed to engage in the complex and difficult battles to reform government.

The other four dimensions of analysis are more specific conceptualizations of problems and particularly of alternatives to the status quo. The second dimension is structure: How should the public sector be organized? Governments have tended to be organized in a hierarchical manner, the principal format being large departments headed by a cabinet minister. This pattern remains the default option in most governments, but there is also a variety of alternative structures being introduced, more or less successfully, in almost all political systems. Thus, the structure of government is no longer the given that it once was, and scholars and practitioners should think about the options available and the relationships of structural decisions to the several emerging models of governance. Although some students of organizations tend to see structure as a relatively insignificant aspect of making an organization effective, I will argue that structure needs to be coordinated with other aspects of governance if the public sector is to be effective.

The third dimension of the models is management: How should the members of the public sector be recruited, motivated, and managed, and how should its financial resources be controlled? A clearly articulated model for personnel management has dominated thinking in the public sector. The thinking about structure has tended to question the conventional wisdom while largely retaining it, but in personnel management the dominant pattern has been to eliminate the old ways. These changes tend to replicate personnel management in the private sector and also tend to weaken the long-term commitment of government to its employees. Working for the public sector is now less different from working for the private sector, and one should think about the implications of those changes.

Similarly, there has been a dominant managerial ethos about the control of resources through budgeting and purchasing rules, which have tended toward the ex ante control of decisions by powerful central agencies. In this view management was largely a central function, with other actors following the direction of the central masters. There might have been some latitude for personal decisions by organizational heads, but the principal managerial tasks were carried out by conforming to rules rather than by exercising discretion. The emerging models of governing tend to shift the thinking about management toward greater autonomy and discretion for lower-echelon officials.

The fourth dimension focuses on the conception of the policy and the policy process: What should the role of the career public service be in the policy process, and more generally how should government seek to influence the private sector? These questions involve a variety of difficult issues about the procedures through which government should make its decisions as well as the content of those decisions. Too often, those two issues are conflated, with the assumption that certain actors (civil servants) will produce certain types of policies (interventionist). Therefore, more market-based instruments (vouchers, for example) that keep the bureaucrats out are preferable. Further, it is necessary to examine the impact of internal rules and regulations, such as civil service laws, in the policy process as the means that legislatures and judiciaries use to ensure that policies are made appropriately, if not always quickly.

These four emerging visions of governance each contain some conception of the public interest and an overall idea of what constitutes good government (see Table 1.1). The conceptions are often implicit in the models, but they are certainly apparent after a little reflection. Each has an answer to the question, "How should government govern, and what should it do?" This concern for the public interest is perhaps the most important component of the entire exercise, given

Table 1.1 Major Features of the Four Models

	Market Government	Participative Government	Flexible Government	Deregulated Government
Principal diagnosis	Monopoly	Hierarchy	Permanence	Internal regulation
Structure	Decentralization	Flatter organizations	"Virtual organizations"	No particular recommendation
Management	Pay for performance; other private-sector techniques	TQM; teams	Managing temporary personnel	Greater managerial freedom
Policymaking	Internal markets; market incentives	Consultation; negotiotion	Experimentation	Entrepreneurial government
Public interest	Low cost	Involvement; consultation	Low cost; coordination	Creativity; activism

that the fundamental question that anyone in government should be asking is whether the programs of reform adopted and the outcomes of the policy process are likely to benefit the public more than the system that is being abolished. All the reformers do believe that their changes will be for the best, although they often operate with very different conceptions of the public interest.

By way of preview, Table 1.1 highlights the four models and the four dimensions of evaluation. A careful look at the dimensions of change should enable readers to understand the strengths, weaknesses, implications, and interactions of the four models as well as of the specific reforms that are derived from them. A careful examination should also reveal why several of the contemporary packages of change have been disappointing to their advocates and have confirmed the suspicions of their critics. Changing the public sector, or any other significant aggregation of large organizations, is not an easy task. Perhaps with a more thorough and dispassionate examination, the difficulties, and the possibilities, will become clearer.

2
Market Models for Reforming Government

If there is a single alternative to the traditional model of public administration favored by contemporary politicians, academics, and probably the public it must be the market model. Instances in which this model has been applied, or claims made that it has been applied, are perhaps too numerous to list here.[1] The fundamental point is that the current Zeitgeist of reform in government is to use the market and to accept the assumption that private-sector methods for managing activities (regardless of what they are) are almost inherently superior to the methods of the traditional public sector. Whether administrative change is being considered in the most affluent country of Western Europe or the poorest country of Africa,[2] the operative assumption appears to be that the best or even the only way to obtain better results from public-sector organizations is to adopt some sort of a market-based mechanism to replace the traditional bureaucracy.

In the market view, the principal problem with traditional bureaucracies is that they do not provide sufficient incentive for individuals working within them to perform their jobs as efficiently as they might. Given this dearth of motivation, individuals will usually attempt to maximize other qualities in their job. One such quality might be "on-the-job leisure" (Peacock 1983), resulting in the familiar image of the slothful, indolent bureaucrat. A second view is that bureaucrats frequently maximize the size of their agency budgets as a means of enhancing their own personal power and income (Niskanen 1971; McGuire 1981). This argument raises the specter of the activist, megalomaniac bureaucrat—certainly the antithesis of sloth—and assumes further that administrators can gain personally from a larger budget.

A third concept is that bureaucrats and their organizations are sometimes overzealous, not about personal rewards but about the exercise of public policy, especially public policies that are alleged to damage industry and impose "internalities" on the society as a whole (Wolff 1988; Booker and North 1994). Once created and granted a mandate to regulate a certain area of policy, an organization may become difficult to control. Bureaucratic drift may occur (Shepsle 1992), in which the organization tends to move increasingly further from original legislative intentions and toward its own definition of good policy. This regulatory activity is usually conducted with good intentions, but for the regulated industries, such activism is generally unwelcome.

The market model is assumed to be able to cure this set of complaints concerning traditional public administration. The problem is, however, that these diagnoses are based on rather different, indeed contradictory, perceptions of the failings of the old model of administration, yet this single type of reform is expected to be capable of correcting them. The characterization of internal contradiction is perhaps somewhat unfair, given that the market model itself is to some degree significantly differentiated and comprises several components. Still, this observation does expose the strong element of ideology in almost all efforts to improve the public sector, and extreme thoroughness is necessary in evaluating any claims being advanced. Enthusiasts for the various models have not always worked through all the empirical implications of their ideas, a critique true not only of the market model but also of the other approaches to reforming the public sector (R. Moe 1993; 1994), including the ideological argument used by some advocates of the traditional model (Goodsell 1995).

THE IDEAS OF THE MARKET MODEL

There really is no single market model, only the basic belief in the virtues of competition and an idealized pattern of exchange and incentives (King 1987; LeGrand 1989). The market model as it has been applied to public administration has several intellectual roots. Just as there is an internal variation in the thinking about government, so too have the programs for change derived from these strands of thought been diverse. Therefore the explicit and implicit ideas involved in market-based changes must be extracted from both the academic literature and from practice. Those ideas can then be related to the administrative changes being imposed in the real world of government. In some instances the linkage between ideas and action is clear (or at least meant to be so). Margaret Thatcher once advised her ministers to read William Niskanen's work on bureaucracy and then to follow its advice (Hennessy 1989). Yet in the Reagan administration and the Mulroney government, for example, any relationship of actions to ideas was probably accidental (Savoie 1994a).[3] As Peter Self wrote, the ideas of Reagan and his principal advisers appeared "too shallow to be debited to any respectable theorist" (1993, 71).

The Efficiency of Markets

The fundamental intellectual root of the market approach to changing the public sector is the belief in the efficiency of markets as the mechanism for allocating resources within a society. Advocates of the market model, basing their ideas on neoclassical economics, believe that other forms of allocation, i.e., through bureaucracies or law more generally, are distortions of outcomes that would be produced by a free market. Therefore, society would on average be better off (at least in economic terms) if the market or analogous competitive institutions were allowed to rule. This assumption tends to beg questions about the distribution of those resources among individuals (LeGrand 1991a)—that is one of the problems that public intervention commonly is designed to remedy. The advocates of the market also assume that there are no significant costs of production (pollution is the classic example) that are not included in the price of the product—the familiar externalities problem (Coase 1960)—that would cause social cost and market cost to diverge.

Any number of critiques have been written about the assumptions contained within the neoclassical economic model.[4] The approach here, however, is to consider what the adoption of this model as the standard for efficient social allocation does for the role of public bureaucracy as it has been developed in most industrialized democracies. The quick answer is that the acceptance of the market tends to require advocates of any deviations from distributions produced by competition to justify those positions. Justifications have been made through the recognition of externalities, the recognition of the social desirability for some redistribution of income (Commission on Social Justice 1994), and the existence of public goods that cannot, by definition, be allocated efficiently through markets because of their nonexcludability characteristic (Atkinson and Stiglitz 1980). Other analysts, however, want to use market mechanisms to solve externality problems such as pollution.

Even when the deficiencies of the market as a mechanism for social allocation are recognized, bureaucracies and formalized legal instruments may not necessarily be the best, or even the better, means of government intervention. The advocates of the market tend to assume that the closer that instruments of public intervention come to the market, the better the collective outcomes will be. Therefore, the traditional direct mechanisms for intervention will often be characterized as an inefficient "tool" for the public sector to use (Hood 1986; Linder and Peters 1989). Rather, more market-based mechanisms such as contracts, incentives, and tax expenditures emerge as preferable instruments under those assumptions (Hula 1990; K. Walsh 1995). For example, many policy analysts prefer market-based incentives for pollution abatement over the command-and-control mechanisms usually used (Schultze 1977; Oates 1995).[5]

Bureaucratic Monopolies

The second intellectual root of market-based reforms stems from the analysis of the failings of conventional bureaucracies by scholars such as Niskanen (1971), Tullock (1965), T. Moe (1984; 1989), Ostrom (1986), and a host of other advocates of public-choice analysis (Bendor 1990; McLean 1987). These scholars have argued that because of the self-interest of the members of the organizations, especially bureau chiefs at the apex, public bureaucracies tend to expand at an unjustifiable rate and to charge their sponsors (read legislatures) too much for the services produced for the public. The permanence of bureaucrats, and especially their monopoly on information, it has been argued (Banks and Weingast 1992), places them at a competitive advantage in dealing with the legislature. The basic cause of the failings in the public sector, when visualized from this perspective, is the self-interest of bureaucrats.[6]

Interestingly, another school of economic analysis argues that bureaucracies undersupply certain goods and services (Breton 1974) because of the self-interest of the bureau chiefs. The claim here is that bureaucracies have the choice of creating public or private goods through their budgets. Given the indivisibility and nonexcludability of public goods, they are not usually perceived as conferring any particular benefits on individual members of society. Private goods, on the other hand, do benefit particular individuals and thus have a much higher political payoff for the bureaucracy and for their political masters. Therefore, bureaucracies (assuming they have the available latitude) will undersupply public goods and oversupply private goods to their clients. Using similar logic, Anthony Downs once argued that the public budget would tend to be too small in a democracy (1960), a conclusion that today appears startling if not heretical.

Other scholars (Dunleavy 1985; 1991) have argued for a "bureau-shaping" approach to understanding the maximizing behavior of public bureaucrats.[7] Not all expenditures are equally valuable to the personally ambitious bureaucrats; transfer money that simply passes through the bureau to grant recipients outside, for example, generates work but produces few appropriable benefits for the bureau chief. Therefore, rational bureaucrats will attempt to maximize the "core budget" of the bureau, i.e., that portion of their budget that funds their own staff and operations, rather than attempt to expand the total budget. The rational bureaucrat would expand the core budget at the expense of other forms of expenditure, perhaps even total expenditures. In this view of behavior, bureaucrats will attempt to develop methods of maximizing their nonpecuniary rewards of office, given that their salaries and benefits tend to have been determined by fixed scales. With the shift to performance-pay and differential-pay policies for public employees (see 34–36; Eisenberg and Ingraham 1993), however, it now makes more sense for civil servants to be concerned with their personal salaries.

These perspectives on the public bureaucracy in the economics literature are clearly views in which the individual bureaucrats are personally ambitious, or at least self-indulgent, and attempt to use the monopoly powers of their bureaus to maximize their own personal self-interest (Egeberg 1995). These officials are able to exercise this power in the budgeting process partly because they have better access to information, especially about the true cost of production of the service, than does their sponsor. If there were effective bureaucratic competition to provide the same service, so the argument goes, the bureaus would have an incentive to hold down their production costs in order to drive their competitor out of business. This is the same competitive mechanism presumed to work in the private sector, and it supposedly would result in minimizing the costs of delivering the services.[8] Even if overt competition did not work, in the instance of multiple agencies, the sponsor might be able to play one agency off against another, having them reveal their true production costs (A. Downs 1967) and then using that information to control public spending.

The problem with this analysis is that one of the canons of public-sector management (and even in the private sector within a single firm) is that there should be minimal redundancy of functions (but see Bendor 1985; Landau 1969), thus preventing any effective competition among agencies.[9] The need to minimize redundancy is certainly true in the regulatory arena, where citizens and corporations complain about multiple and conflicting requirements (Duncan and Hobson 1995; Mastracco and Comparato 1994). Even that regulatory redundancy, however, might be efficient from the perspective of a sponsor seeking to gain information both about the performance of the bureaus and of the regulated organizations.[10]

Even in service provision, however, there are many demands for one-stop shopping for social benefits (Jennings and Krane 1994). The integration of services is presumed to provide for greater efficiency, both for the client and government. Yet it may conflict with an emerging emphasis on providing customer satisfaction with government services. People do not want to have to go to several locations to receive their services, but they also want to have their case considered by a knowledgeable civil servant who can make a decision. Too much emphasis on one-stop shopping and on cross-training employees can create as much dissatisfaction as too much (organizational or geographical) division of services.

Moreover, competition does not appear to be an effective solution for the problem of the undersupply of public goods through the bureaucracy. The sponsors would have many of the same incentives as the bureaucracy to attempt to please their own particular clients and to spend less on public goods in order to be able to provide more private goods. In the case of a mixed bureau providing both public and private goods, budget-shaping of a different sort might permit managers and sponsors to shift resources from public to private goods. Indeed, the incentives for the sponsor to provide private goods may be higher, given the need for reelection (Fiorina 1989; G. Miller and Moe 1983).

The strength of these incentives for the sponsor will vary somewhat, depending upon the structure of the legislature. Legislative structures such as that of the United States, with numerous committees responsible for oversight of administrative agencies and with the members of those committees having a pronounced political interest in the activities of the bureau, will be particularly susceptible to the oversupply of private goods and the undersupply of public goods. Proportional representation systems that limit the direct connections between individual legislators and particular constituencies (geographical if not always functional) would appear to reduce these incentives for bureau-shaping by legislative sponsors.

Several other difficulties arise from the assumption that monopoly powers of bureaucratic agencies generate inefficiencies. First, some of the services delivered by government may be delivered more efficiently as monopolies rather than through competition. Williamson (1985) specifies some of the conditions for monopoly (whether public or private), including the conventional criterion of natural monopoly. This efficiency is almost certainly the case for publicly owned utilities, such as gas and electricity in Europe. Even if privatized, these services tend to retain their monopoly status and must be regulated by government (Wiltshire 1988; Richardson 1984).[11] And many public services already have substantial competition from the private sector, e.g., private education, private health care even in government-dominated systems, and the numerous private courier companies competing with postal services. Very few public services continue to enjoy a monopoly of provision; thus there is already a great deal of effective competition, with little capacity for government agencies to escape the pressures (B. Peters 1995c, 35). Moreover, government provision or regulation or both may be justified when the social risks involved are too large and too difficult for reasonable private contracts to be negotiated (Perrow 1984).

There is already a good degree of competition over the allocation of resources in government through the conventional budgetary process. Even if an agency is not directly competing with another public agency delivering the same type of service, they are competing with all other agencies for resources at budget time. This competition plays a crucial role in the survival of an agency and is indeed very competitive. In addition, the budgetary process is used to elicit a good deal of information from the agencies for the "sponsor" (Savoie 1990; Wildavsky 1992), especially when the sponsor is well structured to exercise such oversight through budgeting (Schick 1990). Indeed, sponsors tend to be quite effective in gaining information through the budgetary process and in using it to gauge the success of public management and to punish the less effective.

The market-oriented view of government and its bureaucracy supposes a good deal of autonomy for agencies within the public sector. In this view agencies are capable of engaging in a variety of ploys that mask their activities from their sponsor's effective scrutiny. The problem with this analysis is that such a degree of agency autonomy exists in very few governments, and even in those few cases there are numerous mechanisms designed to restrain autonomy. In essence the Niskanen model of government is patterned after structures existing in the United States, with a highly fragmented government and consequent difficulties in exercising effective control (B. Peters 1992; Goodin 1982). Other countries such as Sweden and Norway (Christensen 1994; Petersson and Soderlind 1992) also permit their agencies a great deal of autonomy, albeit within the constraints of a well-articulated legal and budgetary framework that produces adequate coordination without direct control.

Most of the world of government, however, does not permit such great autonomy for its agencies or for the civil servants within them. Either through ministerial structures with stronger internal controls, through the strength of central agencies, or both (C. Campbell 1983; Savoie 1995b), agencies are forced to conform more to the wishes of their political and administrative masters. Interestingly, however, some of the market-based reforms now being implemented (see 31–33) are creating just the type of agency autonomy that Niskanen assumes to be one cause of much of the difficulty. The change is now being implemented in the name of "entrepreneurship" and "efficiency," but the results may be similar to the effects that occurred when autonomy was granted to enhance the policy-making powers of the agency—if indeed that was ever a conscious choice to enhance agency autonomy in the United States—or to provide Congress greater control over policy.

In this public-choice view, bureaus also derive some of their power through their influence over the agendas of government (Altfeld and Miller 1984). This power is dependent partly upon the relative level of information enjoyed by the bureaucracy. Perhaps the strongest agenda power for an agency is negative: the capacity to prevent an issue from being considered. This "second face of power" (Bachrach and Baratz 1962) derives from the close contacts of most agencies with their policies as they are being implemented and their knowledge of problems emerging in an existing program. If this information is suppressed, then the capacity of either the minister in charge or the legislature to intervene to correct the problem is limited.

Public bureaucracies have substantial control over one aspect of the policy agenda, the issuing of secondary legislation, or "regulations" in American political parlance. When legislatures pass any major piece of legislation, they tend to leave a great deal of the elaboration of specifics to the bureaucracy. Legislatures cannot specify all the particulars that may arise and so delegate substantial authority to their bureaucracies (Schoenbrod 1993). The agencies then have the power to pick and choose among the options and thereby shape policy.

Given the amount of legislation in force in developed democracies, agencies have substantial capacity to determine their own agenda and to initiate regulatory action. This action can provoke their sponsors to respond since bureaucracies sometimes issue regulations not anticipated by the legislature. Some legislatures have sought to control secondary legislation through devices such as the legislative veto (Foreman 1988) or through committees that scrutinize secondary legislation (Byrne 1976). In other cases the executive also attempts to control perceived bureaucratic aggressiveness through mechanisms for "regulatory review" (McGarrity 1991) or the examination of the costs and benefits of regulations issued and the rejection of the more costly one. Nevertheless, bureaucracies often can set the terms of the conflict between institutions and therefore determine at least part of the agenda of government.

Bureaucracies are also agenda-setters in other, less obvious, ways. The public-choice literature on bureaucracy and its role in policy has focused attention on the capacity of an agency to make policy proposals that establish the terms of debate in other institutions (Tsebelis 1994; Altfield and Miller 1984). Analysts also have explored a set of presumptions about the unit costs of providing public services (Bendor, Taylor, and Van Gaalen 1985) as a part of the agenda-setting process. Although rational-choice analysts discuss this behavior in terms of the ability of agencies to manipulate their sponsor, this power could simply be a function of their command of the details of relevant policy issues. Their technical expertise and associated organizational perceptions enable them to force particular definitions of the policy problems onto the rest of government.

Generic Management

The third intellectual root of the market approach to governance is found in generic management and its ally, the "new public management" (NPM) (Pollitt 1990; Hood 1991; Massey 1993). This corpus of analysis is founded upon the assumption that management is management, no matter where it takes place. In such a view the creation of a separate discipline of public administration with a distinctive ethos would be seen as mistaken.[12] Proponents of this approach argue that the instruments used to organize and motivate personnel are as applicable in the public sector as they are in the private (Linden 1994). Advocates of the approach then deny the relevance of most aspects of the traditional model of administration.

In its most aggressive form, NPM literature argues that much of the infrastructure that has been created around public management was a means of justifying the inefficiencies and the privileges inherent in that system. Part of the goal of the managerialist reforms is to "deprivilege" the civil service (Hood 1995) and to open up a traditionally internal labor market to greater external competition. By using the techniques and motivational devices from the private sector, advocates argue that good managers can produce (in the optimistic language of the Gore Report in the United States) "better government for less money." Government can be made to work better if only the managers are allowed to manage and are not caught up in the rules, regulations, and other constraints on management that have typified the civil service.

The views of the new public management become most evident when confronted with issues of accountability and the special obligations of the public sector. As Ranson and Stewart argue:

> By overemphasizing the individual to the exclusion of the needs of the public as a whole, consumerism has neglected the inescapable duality of the public domain which defines its unique management task, that is, the requirement of achieving public purpose (1994, 5).

Rather than deploring the absence of a sense of the public interest as a guide for policy action—as the public-choice literature often appears to do—the generic management approach to the public sector assumes the lack of meaningful differences between the two sectors. In this view, if the incentives are structured properly, private and public interest can be made to coincide. Further, in the NPM conception of government, values that tend to dominate the private sector—efficiency most notably—should become more important in the public sector, and the shift toward a managerial perspective will be essential in producing a public sector that will truly serve the public interest. It may be that in this view, the conception of the public interest is so radically different from the traditional one that it appears to be absent to people accustomed to the older view.

On a relatively higher intellectual plane the recommendations of this variant of managerialist thinking can be based upon the ubiquity of principal-agent relationships in public policy (T. Moe 1984; Shepsle 1989) and the application of transaction-cost analysis in organizations, whether public or private (Williamson 1975; Calista 1989; Alexander 1992). At a lower level of academic development, generic management is often the accepted doctrine of outsiders who want to export their favorite management techniques—strategic planning, Management by Objectives (MBO), Total Quality Management (TQM), and so forth—to the public sector.[13] At both levels of conceptualization the generic approach has been criticized by insiders (scholars and practitioners alike) who consider management in the public sector as a distinctive undertaking rather than simply as running another organization.

Another implicit, and sometimes explicit, consequence of the new managerialism is that the role of public servants becomes defined in terms of their managerial tasks. These are certainly important, and in the past at times have been ignored or at least given only secondary emphasis. The role of senior civil servants has been defined largely as policy advisers to their ministers (Plowden 1994). Now managers must manage, and politicians are attempting to take over principal responsibility for making policy decisions. Taking the policy reins once in office is sometimes more difficult for politicians than they had realized, and advice from the public service remains crucial to making good policy in most areas (Rose 1974; Kato 1994). The ideological shift to managerialism, however, has reiterated the familiar politics-administration dichotomy (C. Campbell and Peters 1988) and made the involvement of civil servants in policy appear even less legitimate than it had been.

How do these various intellectual arguments about the place of the market in governing work in practice, and what practical solutions have been derived from the ideas? The connections between ideas and practice may be vague at best, but the reformers believe that their actions are derived from a coherent set of concepts and principles. In particular, reformers working from the market perspective believe that their methods emulate so far as possible the workings of private markets within the public sector. In their view, using the market as a model provides a moral claim for the reforms as well as the more practical claim that government will work better. Thus it is important to remember that the reformers often do believe that they are working in the public interest, even if their critics generally perceive them to be philistines desecrating the public temple.

STRUCTURE

Advocates of the market approach assume that the principal problem with the traditional structure of the public sector is its reliance on large, monopolistic departments that respond ineffectively to signals from the environment. Indeed, most of the critiques argue not so much that these organizations have difficulty in responding but that they do not want to respond. The departments are conceptualized as being self-guiding and concerned with the personal advancement of participants, particularly that of their leaders, rather than as serving the public at large or their political masters. Self-aggrandizement is a familiar stereotype of public bureaucracies, but public-choice theorists have been able to put some analytic flesh on the ideological and anecdotal bones of that perception.

Students of the public-choice approach see the size and complexity of government organizations, combined with their delivery of unpriced goods and services, as the root of much perceived government inefficiency and ineffectiveness. In the absence of signals and constraints coming from the market, hierarchy has been used to control organizations. The structural difficulties are accentuated by the emphasis on formal rules and authority as guidelines for action within public organizations (see chapter 5). In the view of the critics, formalized rules insulate decisionmakers from the need to make choices, result in too many preprogrammed decisions, and limit the entrepreneurial possibilities for managers. Rules further exacerbate the tendency of large organizations to respond slowly and cautiously to environmental changes and may make error detection difficult.

Even if a smaller public organization emerging from reform cannot be subjected to direct competition, it is argued that some advantages exist simply from being smaller and concerned with delivering a single product. In his analysis of the presumed inefficiencies of the public sector, Niskanen (1994, 106–12) argues that the multiservice bureau is less efficient and more costly than several single-purpose organizations delivering the individual services would be. Therefore, splitting large organizations into as many smaller ones as there are product lines would reduce costs even in the absence of effective market signals for the pricing of their products. Further, if single products were provided by an organization, it should enhance the capacity of the legislative sponsor to monitor the organization's behavior.

These ideas about the structure of government departments are mirrored in much contemporary thinking about the organizations in the private sector (Weir

1995). Business firms in the 1960s and 1970s tended to create huge conglomerates that were engaged seemingly in any and all economic activities, but the tendency in the 1980s and into the 1990s was to differentiate product lines within large firms and to disaggregate some of the conglomerates. Some of this thinking about the structure of the firm revolves around the need to serve the customer better, who becomes extremely difficult to identify within large conglomerate organizations. Therefore, even when businesses remain large and diversified, their structures tend toward the M form (Lamont, Williams, and Hoffman 1994), with more autonomous subunits acting almost as firms within the firm.

The structural prescriptions for this diagnosis of the problems in public organizations should thus be clear. One central element of the reforms is decentralization of policymaking and implementation. The most fundamental way to break down large government monopolies is to use private or quasi-private organizations to deliver public services. Privatization has been practiced widely in Western European countries and in the Antipodes, which previously had significant levels of public ownership (Wright 1994). However, this structural shift toward privatization has frequently produced the need for regulation to control inherent problems of natural monopolies. For many European countries, imposing regulations on economic monopolies was an unfamiliar policy, so that at least in the short run substantial inefficiencies in the delivery and pricing of products resulted (Foster 1992).

Decentralization also has been achieved through splitting up large departments into smaller agencies or through assigning functions to lower levels of government. This method is particularly applicable when the goods or services in question are in principle marketable. In extreme versions of this approach, government would create multiple, competitive organizations to supply goods and services, with the expectation that the competitive mechanisms presumed to work in the private sector would also work for the public sector. In the more probable case government would create a number of smaller organizations, each with a particular service to deliver, these agencies replacing the traditional multipurpose ministries.

The practice of dividing large departments into smaller segments has been accepted in a number of developed democracies such as the United Kingdom, New Zealand, and the Netherlands (Davies and Willman 1992; Boston 1991; Kickert 1994) and has been established in the Scandinavian countries for decades. Beginning in the late 1980s, New Zealand, for example, corporatized its former ministries into a large number of autonomous or semiautonomous organizations to supply public services. The policy functions remain in a number of much smaller ministries, with the entire policymaking system continuing to be dominated by the Treasury and the activists who initiated the changes (Boston 1991, 255; State Services Commission 1994).

A similar structural change has been undertaken in the United Kingdom under the rubric Next Steps (Hogwood 1993). This reform represented a major departure from the conventional wisdom in British government, which had favored the large ministerial department linking policy and administration. Since the Ibbs Report appeared (HMSO 1988) almost 100 executive agencies have been created. Agencies range from small organizations, such as the Wilton Park Conference Center (thirty employees), to the Benefits Agency, which employs approximately 70,000 people and is responsible for delivery of most social service benefits in Britain (Greer 1994, 32–44). These agencies tend to be single-purpose and are more responsive to market forces and other direct means of performance assessment than were the ministerial departments. Their leadership has been drawn from within the civil service and from the private sector, and they are meant to be managed like private-sector, or at least quasi-private, organizations rather than like strictly public organizations. Executives, for example, tend to be on performance contracts, with possibilities of dismissal for poor performance.

New Zealand and the United Kingdom are the most extreme examples of movement toward the model of decentralized service delivery except for the Scandinavians, from whom the system was largely copied (Petersson and Söderlind 1994).[14] There are, however, other experiments under way in implementing such structures. The Netherlands has launched an effort to create a number of agencies (Kickert 1994; 1995). Canada also has begun to experiment with Special Operating Agencies to deliver some services (Canada 1991; Wex 1990; I. Clark 1991), although the long-standing instrument of the Crown Corporation in Canadian government has some of the same features as agencies (Laux and Malot 1988). These various structural experiments serve as compelling examples of attempts to address the familiar problem of government inefficiency and ineffectiveness.

Implementing such a system of market-oriented organizations assumes a capacity to monitor effectively and measure adequately the performance of the decentralized bodies created. Thus, this organizational pattern appears applicable to the "machine" functions of government (Mintzburg 1979) but probably less so to the complex social and developmental tasks that governments must also perform (but see Romzek and Dubnick 1994). Administrative reform needs to be matched carefully to the needs of a society and to the characteristics of the tasks being reformed, not routinely applied in a simplistic and mechanical fashion. The unwise adoption of market-based reforms in some cases has brought those attempts into some disrepute.

The penchant for breaking up larger organizations and making the resultant ones more entrepreneurial is a case in point against applying the market model slavishly. Arguably, the Next Steps initiative and similar structural changes have gone further to create the world that Niskanen was decrying than any other administrative changes before or since. First, the breaking up of the departmental structure, if anything, has tightened the grip of each organization on its policy area. Second, the entrepreneurial element and the loss of civil service rules mean that growth in the budget of the agency (admittedly now often more earned revenues along with income from the budget process) is more directly linked to the perquisites of office than ever before.

The market approach to reform has some structural recommendations at the microlevel within organizations as well as at the macrolevel of entire departments. The emphasis on entrepreneurial activity and individual responsibility pushes toward relatively flat organizations with little of the layering that traditional public organizations tended to consider essential for control and consistency in decisions. Advocates of the approach presume that organizational leadership, as well as the bottom line resulting from the organization's dealings with the external environment, will be more effective than hierarchy in producing appropriate decisions (but see Jaques 1990), an observation that points to the importance of integrated and consistent, as opposed to piecemeal, reforms. The structural changes without associated changes in management behavior are unlikely to produce the benefits presumed theoretically.

Finally, decentralization sometimes also means territorial decentralization and giving local governments more power over policies. Especially in unitary governments there has been a tendency for central governments to dictate policies to subnational ones. Even in federal regimes the financial resources of central governments have sometimes produced a "priority inversion" in which local priorities are squeezed out by central concerns (Levine and Posner 1981). The logic of geographical decentralization is similar to that of creating agencies. First, it reduces hierarchy and places control over organizations somewhat closer to the public. Second, it reduces the monopoly that single organizations may have had over services so that experimentation or "voting with one's feet" or both can produce different types of controls over organizations.[15]

MANAGEMENT

The managerial implications of the market model should now be clear. If public-sector employees are considered to be much the same as private-sector workers, then the same managerial techniques should work in government as elsewhere. This assumption also would imply that some cherished traditions of personnel and financial management within government would have to be modified. To generic-management advocates such changes would be long overdue, assuming that the public sector has been able to maintain its rather arcane system of civil service management for too long already. The generic-management gurus would tend to argue, as would the public-choice proponents, that the distinct public-sector management system has been used primarily to shield people in government from the real world and to enable them to extract excessive personal benefits.[16]

Among the clearest manifestations of the ideology of introducing private-sector management into the public sector were exercises such as the Grace Commission (United States) and the Nielsen Commission (Canada). These two programs brought a large number of private-sector managers to the two national capitals and assigned them the task of finding mismanagement (B. Peters and Savoie 1994a). The results were reports with thousands of recommendations for managerial change. Especially in the case of the Grace Commission, many of the recommendations were totally out of touch with the realities of the public sector (Kelman 1985; B. Peters 1985), partly because the executives who came to Washington apparently did not take the career public servants seriously. The Canadian report fared somewhat better (S. Wilson 1988); it had at least some representation from the public service. The simple (or simplistic) assumption that guided these exercises was that public and private management were really the same.

In addition to some of the general managerial trends occurring as a result of the implementation of market-based ideas, I will discuss more specific changes in several areas of public management—personnel and finance in particular—and attempt to identify their probable impact on government. These reforms are themselves not exceptionally coherent, and some of the changes appear to be at cross-purposes with other transformations already implemented as a part of the market-reform process.

Personnel

The market-oriented reforms are already under way in a number of areas of public personnel management, most obviously in the reward provided public officials for their participation in government (Hood and Peters 1994). One tradition of public personnel systems has been that individuals in the same grade of the civil service are paid the same, with any differentiations based largely upon seniority. In this traditional personnel system merit and ability to perform the tasks were proved prior to entry and constituted the basis for promotion. The assumption was that all people in each grade within a uniform system were equally meritorious and therefore should be paid almost exactly the same.

Although there was some attempt at least to link movements of public-sector pay to wage movements in the wider economy, the market level of wages was only an indirect indicator of what pay in government should be.[17] In Germany, for example, pay for working for the state was governed by the principle that someone in that significant social position should be paid well enough to live accordingly (Derlien 1994). For Anglo-American societies, working for government was expected to provide other tangible and intangible benefits—including some genuine financial perquisites such as early retirement—so that salaries could be less than comparable positions in the market would command. Given that some of the benefits of government employment, such as tenure, are being jeopardized by other reforms, pay becomes a more important factor in public employment.

This rather rigid payment scheme is being replaced with a merit principle based on the argument that people should be paid salaries comparable to those they could earn in the market and that better performance should be rewarded with better pay, regardless of differences that might emerge among employees. The implication is that the traditionally uniform civil service system should be replaced. Although there certainly have been some economic motivations among the members of the system, there were also strong commitments to the service as an organization and to public service as an ideal (B. Peters 1995b; Schorr 1987). These amorphous, yet real, values and incentives are being replaced with monetary reward as the principal means of recruitment and motivation.

The emphasis on differential rewards for differential performance is especially important at top-management levels of government. One of the earliest schemes for differential rewards, for example, was the bonus system for members of the Senior Executive Service (SES) in the United States (Ban and Ingraham 1984). By law, SES members would have been eligible for bonuses of up to 20 percent of their annual salaries. The same legislation that established the SES (the Civil Service Reform Act of 1978) also called for extending merit pay, whether through bonuses or differentiating base pay, to middle managers in the federal government. Ultimately, the failure of Congress to fund these bonuses adequately and the difficulties in developing the measures to judge meritorious performance have rendered the merit-pay system only a hollow echo of its original intent.

Merit pay, or pay for performance, is now being spread across a range of political systems (Eisenberg and Ingraham 1993). It is most common in small, relatively autonomous agencies created as a part of the market approach to governance. In several reward schemes already implemented, managers are hired under contracts that contain specific performance standards. If the agency manager and the organization achieve those standards, the manager is eligible for full pay and perhaps bonuses. If the organization does not reach these goals, then the manager may lose pay or be fired.[18] In this model managers are individual entrepreneurs responsible for what happens within their agencies and are rewarded accordingly. Lower echelons within these organizations may be rewarded under similar contractual arrangements based on performance standards.

These schemes for differential rewards depend upon the capacity of government to measure the performance of employees and their organizations. Any number of studies have demonstrated the severe difficulties encountered in attempts to perform the seemingly simple managerial task of measuring individual contributions to the performance of large, complex organizations and policy-delivery systems (Boston 1992; Sjölund 1994a). The problem is especially difficult if performance is to be measured at the output or impact level rather than merely at the activity level (Carter, Day, and Klein 1992). This dilemma means that either performance contracts and effective managerialism will be limited to the relatively few agencies providing marketable and otherwise directly measurable services or that the scheme must depend upon inadequate or even specious measures of performance. In either case the capacity to implement this aspect of the market vision of the public sector appears at least a little suspect. The suspicion grows when there is a political element involved in the evaluation of employees.

These managerialist trends are not neutral in their effects on the role assigned to the public service. Measuring performance is substantially easier for the managerial and service delivery functions of the civil service even though it is not without difficulties. It is much harder to measure for the policy-advice functions. As a result, adoption of managerialist pay schemes tend to contain some implicit bias toward a managerial role over a policy role for civil servants. This result may occur because of changes in the signals coming from evaluators and because of decisions by the evaluated that they can maximize their own rewards by playing the managerial game.

Performance-based management and reward techniques run counter to many other ideas motivating reform in the public sector. In particular, one of the increasingly popular means of motivating workers is to allow them greater self-determination on their jobs. These participatory ideas are becoming even more important through the empowerment approach to reform (see 63–64). If, however, performance measures are being used to judge individual contributions to organizational goals, then participation and team-building will be difficult to achieve (Behn 1993b). Team concepts and individual foci of management are still difficult to reconcile empirically or normatively. Thus, promoting reform must be done carefully, and all the good (and not so good) ideas floating around cannot be implemented at once.

Financial Management

As a part of the drive to introduce generic management, financial management is being reconsidered and changed drastically. These reforms have been going on for some time in countries such as Britain (Pliatzky 1989) and Australia (Department of Finance 1987; C. Campbell and Halligan 1992) and show little sign of abating. The new ideas are also being spread to a number of other countries. Financial-management reforms have ranged from simple changes, such as better cash management and tighter controls over public loans, to some fundamental rethinking of the manner in which the public-sector budgets and considers the costs of providing public services. As with personnel management, some of the reforms have been well conceived and implemented, but others appear virtually to have missed the point of government's purpose and methods.

One of the several market principles underlying the financial reforms of the public sector is the separation of purchasers and providers and the creation of internal markets (OECD 1993). In traditional public administration such a reform was irrelevant, or perhaps even inconceivable, given that the old model was one of hierarchy and unitary services. In contemporary systems, however, this reform is an important mechanism for ensuring that market principles pervade the public sector. For example, in the National Health Service in Britain the purchasers and providers had been managed as part of one corporate entity. That unified structure has now been replaced with a quasi market in which Area Health Authorities purchase services for their customers (citizens) from providers (hospitals and so on). Likewise, budget-holding general practitioners will begin to negotiate with specialists for their services on behalf of patients. In this management system the separation of the two functions is intended to reduce costs and increase efficiency (Ranade 1995), although there has been substantial public and academic criticism about the real consequences of the changes (Harrison, Small, and Baker 1994).

The government of New Zealand has undertaken a similar separation of purchasers and providers throughout the entire government. Under the Public Finance Act (1989) the purchaser-provider dichotomy is intended to pervade a good part of the public sector (Pallot 1991). In this system, government, through its central agencies, in essence becomes the purchaser of the output of the departments actually producing the services (Boston 1993). Those services are meant to be costed fully, including factors such as interest, taxes, and capital depreciation that frequently have been excluded from the internal pricing of goods and services in public-sector budgets. In this approach to public finance, virtually all public-service providers essentially become public corporations with even more stringent financial controls than usually have been applied to public corporations.

Even the Swedish government, long the model of the welfare state and of skepticism about the market, has begun to think about introducing market reforms into government. A plan for separating purchasers from providers in the health service, similar to the system in the United Kingdom, has been implemented by the counties, and a greater choice of physicians for citizens has been introduced (Burkitt and Whyman 1994; Forsberg and Calltorp 1993). Given that the health-delivery service tends to be concentrated at the county level and the purchasing through insurance is quasi-public at the national level, the institutional structure for separation was to some degree already established. Similar market-based management schemes are being considered and implemented in a number of other publicly controlled health care systems (Jerome-Forget, White, and Wiener 1995).

The Financial Management Initiative (FMI) in the United Kingdom (A. Gray and Jenkins 1991) and the Financial Management Improvement Programme (FMIP) in Australia (Keating and Holmes 1990) are two of the principal programs designed to change financial management in central governments. These two reforms have some common elements. The most important is the attempt to identify within government the "cost centers" associated with the delivery of services and to allocate total costs of each service more accurately than in the past. For example, the overhead costs of government—central management functions, information technology, and so on—are sometimes difficult to attribute to particular programs so that the programs that consume a great deal of these overhead services tend to be subsidized by those programs that do not.[19] With the financial management improvements that have been implemented there has been an attempt to assign true costs more fairly to each program, which results in better judgment of the relative efficiency of programs.

Following from these attempts the British government has undertaken a number of other efforts to change the manner in which funds are allocated to programs. There are now active proposals to implement "resource accounting and budgeting" in government (HMSO 1994b). The idea behind these reforms is to account for public money not just in current costs but also in terms of the opportunity costs of the uses of the resources (Mellett and Marriott 1995). This reform is designed to reflect more accurately the real impact of the public sector on the economy. Australia meanwhile has resumed the practice of program budgeting so popular during the 1960s. This return to rationality also reflects an attempt to capture better alternative uses of resources within the public sector.[20]

Interestingly, these changes, which are largely rationalistic in their motivations, are being implemented during a period of attempts to reduce overall public spending more radically. This trend is perhaps most evident in the United States—witness the proposed balanced budget amendment and the radical changes in the budgetary process, such as the Budget Enforcement Act of 1990 (LeLoup and Taylor 1994). In virtually all countries, however, the same desires to reduce public expenditure and to balance public budgets have required cutting exercises that tend to be carried out across the board or by some other less than fully rational method (Tarschys 1981; 1986). The simple economic motives of the market advocates thus at times appear to conflict directly with their own attempts to create greater economic rationality within government.

Finally, the increasing stress on financial management in industrialized democracies has produced an increased emphasis on auditing, though not of the old-fashioned financial sort (yet certainly the search for "fraud, waste, and abuse" continues in all these regimes). Auditing is now directed more toward the three E's: economy, efficiency, and effectiveness—in addition to financial probity. Some government auditors, such as the General Accounting Office in the United States (Mosher 1979), have a history of performance and effectiveness, but the doctrine has been spreading around the world. Auditors have now been transformed from their green eyeshade image to being integral parts of the reform and accountability process in many contemporary governments.

Market-Testing

In addition to the series of structural changes already outlined, the reform of central government departments in the United Kingdom has proceeded to another round, this time focusing more on management. The principal component of this attempt at marketizing government is "contracting out" (Ascher 1987), or more recently, "market testing" (Oughton 1994). The idea of this reform is that virtually all functions performed within government should be subjected to some form of competitive bidding to determine whether the private sector is able to perform the task better, more cheaply, or both. This requirement was imposed on local authorities earlier (1986), under the terminology "compulsory competitive tendering" (J. Painter 1991). The concept more recently has been extended to the central government as well through a White Paper, "Competing for Quality" (HMSO 1991). It has been followed by the closely linked idea of "fundamental reviews," which is a test of whether the public sector should be in any way involved in a policy.[21]

The United Kingdom is far from alone in attempting to impose this form of market discipline on its public-sector organizations. Indeed, requirements for competitive bidding for government work have been around for some time in a number of governments. In the United States, Office of Management and Budget (OMB) Circular A-76 in the mid-1970s required at least 10 percent of all work performed by an agency to be subjected to bidding from outside contractors, with consideration of how much additional work could be performed outside more efficiently. More recently the General Services Administration (GSA), which once had a monopoly for providing services such as office space and automobiles to federal agencies, now must compete with private vendors for over 90 percent of its business (interview, 16 October 1994; GSA 1993). In Australia and New Zealand requirements for subjecting government programs to external bidding have been established for a number of years (Keating and Holmes 1990). In all these cases the government agency can establish the conditions of the bidding, and to some extent therefore it gains an inside track in the competition. There have been some good-faith attempts to determine just how money might be saved, however, and whether the usual criticisms about inefficiency within the public sector are correct.[22]

At least in the United Kingdom, critics argue that this change has undermined the reforms undertaken in the earlier program, Next Steps (Jordan 1994; Richards and Rodrigues 1993). Although supporters of Next Steps apparently argue that if the structure is changed then efficiency will follow, market testing requires that assumption to be proven. Almost before most of the agencies have had any opportunity to settle into a working pattern, they are being forced to develop bidding processes and then prepare their own bids. The employees of the agencies believed they had paid the price for keeping some functions public but now find that they are again required to justify their existence within the public sector. Although some management analysts argue that constant change is a function of organizations, the people who are living through it do not find it so beneficial.

Perhaps more fundamentally, the competitive tendering process and the documents that have established it seemingly lack any definite sense of which activities are clearly public functions and therefore not potentially subject to contracting out. One important case is policy advice: should it be contracted out, or should it remain an internal governmental activity (Boston, 1992b; Australia

1992)? Of course, a certain amount of policy advice has been contracted out in almost all political systems, with consultants, interest groups, political parties, and even academics providing reports and recommendations too voluminous to catalog. Still, governments have retained a dominant in-house capacity to sift through the outside advice and then generate directions to ministers. Should that function be contracted out to the private sector, or is it sufficiently vested with the public interest that it should remain a governmental activity?

As befits an approach attempting to make government more like the private sector, the market perspective on governing places a great deal of emphasis on "improving" management (I use quotation marks because there is less than universal agreement that the changes being implemented are indeed positive). For many people committed to the traditional civil service style of running the public sector, proponents of these changes have misread the nature and purpose of government. The assumptions behind generic management, for example, seem to undervalue seriously public administration and its distinctiveness. Yet clearly there can be no return to the (presumably) glorious past of civil service government, so some accommodation between the traditions and the innovations will emerge if government is to move forward.

POLICYMAKING

The third aspect of the marketized vision of the state is the conceptualization of how public policy should be made and, in particular, the appropriate role of the career public service in making it. A fundamental contradiction appears to reside at the heart of the role that this vision of governing assigns to the bureaucracy. On the one hand, the market approach advocates decentralizing bureaucratic functions to multiple, "entrepreneurial" agencies that would be authorized to make autonomous decisions, which presumably would be based upon either signals received from the market or simply the judgment of the organizational leadership. Breaking the (supposedly) stultifying bonds of bureaucracy is meant to liberate decisionmaking and to produce greater risk-taking and more innovative programs in the public sector.[23]

On the other hand, the practitioners who have advocated this approach have expected these quasi-autonomous organizations to comply with the policy and ideological directives coming from above. One consistent observation concerning the Reagan, Thatcher, and Mulroney governments and other similarly purposive regimes is that they have attempted to impose their own views on the civil service (Savoie 1994a). Bureaucrats were seen as too committed to the growth of their own organizations and to serving their narrow clientele instead of the public interest. They and their organizations therefore should be made to follow the directives of their political masters (as embodiments of the *volonte generale*) rather than their own interests.

To many people in government the pressure to conform to prevailing policy doctrines was an attempt to politicize the public service and policymaking. Such efforts are by no means new but appear to have become more overt during the 1980s (Meyer 1985). Politicization has been seen by defenders of the traditional view of government as the erosion of one of the most important features of merit systems and the civil service. In some ways, however, these demands for conformity merely reaffirm the traditional view (at least in Anglo-Saxon regimes) that civil servants should be "on tap but not on top" and that political leaders should be responsible for policy. Whether it is part of the traditional conceptualization or not, there is an inconsistency, and civil servants are faced with a set of perhaps irreconcilable demands and expectations.

Even if the inconsistency could be resolved, additional problems for policy-making would arise from the market approach. One of the most important is the difficulty in coordination and control that decentralization presents. As one commentator has said, "The ship of state has become a flotilla," and the creation of many small organizations presents significant problems if government hopes to speak with a single voice. The radical decentralization of policymaking to more autonomous organizations provides relatively little opportunity for either senior bureaucrats or political leaders to coordinate policy effectively (Boston 1992b; Jordan 1994, 96–136).

In applying some of the market advocates' economic logic to examine their own recommendations for reform, several interesting questions arise. For example, one of the justifications of the large firm in the private sector is the reduction of transaction costs (Williamson 1975), or the costs imposed by the need to interact with other parties. Much the same should be true for the large executive department in the public sector. If a number of smaller organizations are operating with substantial autonomy, then (all else being equal) there will be substantial transaction costs when they must cooperate to deliver a set of services to the same clients (Calista 1989). Indeed, the transaction costs may be borne by clients rather than within government itself, given that the services may not be rendered in an integrated and coordinated fashion. The clients would be forced to go from agency to agency seeking the full range of services they need.

Another point is that decentralization is to some degree centralizing. Conferring decisionmaking autonomy onto a number of independent organizations that previously had been coordinated through a ministry does not diminish the need for coordination. The only remaining locus for the coordination is at the top of government, whether that is through central agencies or through cabinet and prime minister. Thus, as Wildavsky once argued about program budgeting (1969), once individual organizations are forced to set priorities, then some superordinate organization will be forced to choose among the priorities.

One critique of the traditional approach to governance has been that the independence of the bureaucracy actually thwarted consistency across policies and often produced destructive competition among organizations over budgets and policy (Allard 1990; Smith, Marsh, and Richards 1993). The market approach appears to exalt that competition and its potential inconsistency—so long as the actions taken correspond to the ideology of the current political leaders and do not require additional public spending. It is perhaps too much to believe that leadership of autonomous agencies would be content to be managers of these organizations and would not become concerned with the policies being implemented by their organizations (T. Rhodes 1995). The inconsistency and redundancy produced by applying the market model are bad enough in wealthy societies but may be particularly undesirable when the model is exported to less affluent developing countries, as it so often is by management consultants and international organizations.

At a more conceptual level, there is the problem of the changing role of the citizen. The market model tends to categorize the recipients of government programs, and the public more generally, as consumers or customers (Pierre 1995a; Behn 1993a). This definition is simultaneously empowering and demeaning for the public. Seen as a beneficial change, this definition of citizenship is intended to provide citizens with the same expectations of quality services that they have when dealing with a private-sector firm.[24] Although usually considered to be components of participatory reforms, changes such as the Citizens' Charter in Britain and PS 2000 in Canada contain many of the elements of consumerism (Lovell 1992). Just as earlier consumer movements attempted to rectify the balance between private-sector organizations and their customers, this movement seeks to redress that balance between public organizations and their clients.

Yet citizens have been made into little more than consumers, and their role as the holders of rights and legal status vis-à-vis the state appears diminished (Pierre 1995a; Lewis 1994). Government may be concerned with more than buying and selling and almost certainly should be. If governing is reduced to the level of mere economic action, then citizens become less significant figures in political theory than they should be. Moreover, this shift in conceptualization of the public is important because it conflicts with other movements in contemporary political life. Most significant of these is the trend to think of politics as being about rights (and even obligations) rather than merely about money.

Although the public's shift to "post-materialist values" (Inglehart 1990; Inglehart and Abramson 1994) may have been overstated, there have been changes in people's expectations of government and in the values they want to see maximized through public action. One of these values is participation (see chapter 3); another is the special claims of groups such as ethnic minorities and women. This transformation has been under way even longer than the shift toward an acceptance of an enhanced role for market mechanisms in public life. Thus, although ideological forces are driving toward an economic rationale for policymaking, forces are also resisting that change and driving toward policies determined by much "softer," humanitarian values. The market and economic values appear to be in ascendance at the moment, but the triumph may be only temporary.

THE PUBLIC INTEREST

The final component of the market vision of governance is its definition of the public interest. Although generally not clearly articulated, the market vision definitely does contain such an idea. The primary element of the definition is that government should be judged on the basis of how cheaply it delivers public services. Fundamentally, the market model asks which services should be public. Much of the market model's indictment of government claims that it is overly expensive and inefficient. To achieve the goal of lower costs, government may have to undertake its activities in rather unconventional ways, for example, through creating multiple competing service providers; but in the long run the public—in their role as taxpayers—is better served by government acting in this more businesslike manner.

A second component of this definition of the public interest is that government should respond to market signals, so that accountability—a fundamental component of the public interest in any democratic system (Day and Klein 1987)—is more difficult to identify than in the traditional system. Rather than being defined as progressing upward through ministers to parliament and then to the people, accountability is defined increasingly in market terms. In this emerging definition, instruments such as parliamentary oversight and judicial reviews become less important than the financial bottom line. Indeed, along with rules and hierarchy, these formalized mechanisms are often indicted as the means through which government organizations have avoided meaningful accountability.

In the market model, accountability would depend upon output measures to replace the process measures used in the traditional model. As with several other aspects of the market model of governing, this version of accountability appears to beg a number of questions, the most important being the measurement issue. Can we measure the performance of public organizations, even in their marketized format, sufficiently well to be able to use nonprocedural devices for defining accountability effectively (Glynn, Gray, and Jenkins 1992)? Even if analysts could make those measurements effectively, could they attribute differences (whether across time or across organizations) to the management of those organizations? What level of performance is "good enough"? The "new evaluative state" (Henkel 1991) runs the risk of attempting to fire its analytic cannons before they are fully loaded.

The third component of the market vision of the public interest is that citizens should be conceptualized as consumers as well as taxpayers (Lewis 1994).

Therefore, in addition to providing guidance for policymaking, the public interest can be served by allowing citizens to exercise freer choice in a market for public services. This autonomy would replace the system of forcing citizens to consume a package of services determined by the legislature, the bureaucracy, or both. The enhanced choice for "consumers" can be created either by breaking up the monopolies that traditionally have provided most public services or through increasing the wherewithal of citizens to exercise freer choices among service options.

The options for citizens exercising their choices can be expanded through several means. One is to permit private firms to enter into competition with services that traditionally have been public monopolies, as has already happened in the case of postal services, for example, where private courier services have taken over a large share of the most profitable end of the market. Private providers have also been able to compete in most countries in the field of education for a number of years. Services that were thought to be the peculiar concerns of government, such as managing prisons (Black 1993; Goodman and Loveman 1991) or providing personal social services (Llewellyn 1994), are now considered appropriate targets for private-sector providers.

Choice can also be created by providing vouchers for services such as education and perhaps housing (J. Chubb and Moe 1990; Adler, Patch, and Tweedie 1990). If the argument is correct that one of the principal reasons for the perceived failings of education in many countries—especially Anglo-American countries—is that the state holds a monopoly over education, then the creation of competition through vouchers may be a useful mechanism both for improving education and leveraging private resources for it.[25] The limits to voucher plans for social and educational programs are not yet entirely clear, however. The Conservative government in Britain, for example, has considered a plan to convert virtually all primary and secondary education in the country to fee-paying systems supplemented by vouchers. Nor is it clear what role public education should play in a democratic society, especially in the United States, which has relied on public education as a major component of the system for enculturating immigrants.

The choices available to the public may also be increased simply by providing information to citizens about the service options that are obtainable. One feature of bureaucracies, especially those that also have a professional component, is that they tend to deny autonomous choices to clients. Such denial is in the perceived best interest of the client, who is assumed to be incapable of making informed choices about complex legal or technical matters or both, in medicine, for example. Proponents of both the market and the participatory models of reform argue for greater openness and more real choice for the public. No matter how individual choice is to be enhanced, the idea of creating a genuine market for the goods and services that have been provided through monopolies (whether bureaucratic or professional) is the central element in the market model's prescription.

The market vision has become the most popular alternative conceptualization of the state and government. This view perceives traditional public bureaucracies more as instruments of personal aggrandizement by civil servants than as instruments for unselfish service delivery to the public. Its proponents also believe that public-sector agencies face the same managerial and service-delivery tasks as do organizations in the private sector and, therefore, are as amenable to the same techniques for managing those tasks. Advocates of the market argue that an acceptance of the models of traditional public administration is little more than a means of protecting bureaucrats against control and accountability. Market-oriented analysts assume that if the rule-based authority structure usually associated with public bureaucracy is removed, or at least deemphasized, then a flowering of the creative and administrative talent of individuals working in the public sector can occur.

Although usually associated with the political right, some devotees of the market approach believe that its successful implementation would result in a more effective and efficient public sector, whether delivering defense or social services. Indeed, one of the strongest test cases for this approach has been the experiment in New Zealand by the Labour party (P. Walsh 1991). Moreover, several elements of a market approach have been introduced into Scandinavia by governments of the political left (J. Olsen 1991). There appears to be a Zeitgeist that pervades contemporary thinking about government and that has pushed many governments in the direction of reducing public-sector controls on the private sector and toward using more market-based instruments within the public sector.

Although the market perspective is extremely popular with politicians and with many people in the mass public, the questions of how well it describes the failings of the old system and what possible avenues of positive change it offers must be asked. Doubts about the market are not simply a knee-jerk reaction against change in government but represent an attempt to understand better just what possibilities exist for improving the performance of government. Such reflection may lead to a recognition that the old system was not entirely bad and indeed did some things rather well.

Moreover, most proposals for movement away from the old system will be far from costless. All the reform proposals have substantive as well as transitional costs for government, which employees within public bureaucracies will certainly bear, and the clients of programs may also pay. Some programs may be eliminated entirely, and others may be reduced and their delivery streamlined in ways that many clients may find undesirable. Therefore, in deciding to make the move to new forms of government, those costs and the losses of positive features of the older administrative system must be understood and weighed against the potential benefits of the reformed system.

The market model—despite its emphasis on exercising choice through vouchers—tends to provide little real choice for citizens about whether to search out new levels or varieties of service provision (Scott-Clark 1995). In this view of the "policy marketplace," the dynamic element seems to be lacking, and impersonal forces rather than human agency appear to make the policy selections. Further, the choices offered in the policy market are often about implementation rather than about the existence of a program itself. This more basic choice is apparently within the province of the participatory model of change, to be examined next.

3
The Participatory State

The second alternative approach to reforming governance—participation—is almost the ideological antithesis of the market approach. The political ideologies that most of its advocates use to justify their concept reject the market and search for more political, democratic, and collective mechanisms for sending signals to government. Participation is one of the dominant political themes of the 1990s. Bill Clinton gained substantial political advantages by having town hall meetings and riding across the country in a cavalcade of buses. British prime ministers now find it politically desirable to go among the people to legitimate policies, if not always to seek advice on what those policies should be.[1] Consultation and citizen involvement in policymaking have become central components of Canadian government, including the budgetary process (Lindquist 1994). This is clearly an age in which government finds it difficult to legitimate its actions without active public involvement.

Despite their ideological differences, in some instances the analysis and recommendations derived from the participative and market approaches appear remarkably similar. Perhaps most common in their views is the belief that conventional bureaucracies are an impediment to good government and that if nothing else is changed there must be new ways to deliver services. These common strands in thinking, however, have been the source of substantial confusion in the administrative reform literature as well as in practice. One of my principal purposes is to identify more clearly the differences among the four approaches to change in the public sector as well as where and when they are and are not compatible.

While monopoly appears to be the principal villain to proponents of the market model, hierarchy is the evil most directly addressed by advocates of the participatory model. The assumption is that the hierarchical, top-down style of management in traditional bureaucracies restricts the involvement of employees in their own jobs. The lack of involvement alienates them and reduces their commitment to the organization. Advocates of the market and the economics of organization also argue against hierarchy, preferring a set of contracts that can structure behavior within the organization (G. Miller 1992). They further argue that hierarchy imposes enforcement costs on government that voluntary contracting would not. Hierarchy within a single organization appears more acceptable to that group of scholars, however, than does monopoly within a set of organizations.

I am calling this second approach the participatory state, but it has been discussed under a number of different names.[2] An alternative characterization might be the empowerment state, in which segments of organizations and societies (presumably) excluded under more hierarchical systems are permitted greater organizational involvement (Kernaghan 1992; M. Clarke and Stewart 1992). Very much like the market and the deregulatory approaches, the participatory approach considers the hierarchical, rule-based organizations usually encountered in the public sector as severe impediments to effective management and governance. However, unlike the market model, the participatory approach does not concentrate attention on the upper echelons of managerial leadership in public organizations, who are conceptualized as the protoentrepreneurs within government. Rather, it pays much more attention to the lower-echelon employees as well as to the clients of the organizations.

✷The fundamental assumptions informing this approach are that a great deal of energy and talent lies fallow and underutilized in the lower echelons and that the workers and clients closest to the actual production of goods and services in the public sector have the greatest insight and information about the programs. It is assumed further that if those ideas and talents were harnessed adequately, then government would perform better. The general prescription for making government function better, therefore, is to foster greater individual and collective participation within segments of government organizations that commonly have been excluded from decisionmaking.

For some advocates of the participatory approach, increased participation should be structured to include the mass public in addition to, or even instead of, individuals directly benefiting from a policy. The argument is that bureaucratization has produced segmentation of the public sector, with only consumers and producers within the particular policy area having influence over policy or implementation (Muller 1985; Tonn and Feldman 1995). Further, the bureaucratization and segmentation of policies limit the capacity to coordinate programs and to produce coherent policy regimens that span multiple policy areas. Thus, very little attention is given to the overarching concerns of the public in their roles as citizens and taxpayers.[3] Proponents argue that participation may not result in an undivided benefit but that it has virtues contingent upon how it is structured, even in a democratic regime.

Somewhat predictably, advocates of the participatory approach tend to be associated with the political left (Bachrach and Botwinick 1992). Yet some theorists from the political right, concerned with empowerment, community, and self-management by clients as instruments for enhancing efficiency, also advocate versions of this approach.[4] Moreover, in the domain of mass politics, the manifestations of the participatory approach often appear from the political right. Except for true elitists, participation is a value that can be embraced by the entire ideological spectrum within a political democracy. This broad acceptance of the concept leaves only the problem of sorting out just what is meant by participation within those different political camps.

IDEAS ABOUT THE PARTICIPATORY STATE

The intellectual roots of the participatory approach are diverse, indeed substantially more so than those of the market approach. The manner in which participation has been conceptualized varies from pragmatic attempts to motivate public employees through enhanced involvement in their jobs to more complex, philosophical statements concerning the true meaning of democracy in a mass society (Pateman 1970; Pennock and Chapman 1975). These various conceptions of participation are bound together by their common concerns with minimizing hierarchy and technocracy (Fischer 1990; Meynaud 1969) in governing. Four interpretations of participation are relevant here to the management of public organizations and to the role of those organizations in the governing process. These four ideas about participation are not entirely managerial, however, but are concerned with broader questions about the relationship between state and society and the opportunities for involving the mass public in decisionmaking.

The idea of enhancing participation in government organizations is hardly new. In fact, it has been one of the recurring themes both in administrative and more general reform efforts for the public sector. A number of countries already had made significant advances in improving participation in their administrations prior to the contemporary round of reforms. A number of attempts have been made to enhance the involvement of workers within their organizations and to make the climate in public organizations more participatory. The Scandinavian countries and Germany developed principles of workplace democracy and codetermination some years ago in both the public and private sectors (Hancock, Logue, and Schiller 1991; but see Werth 1973). Even extremely modest participatory programs, such as flexible working hours, apparently have had substantial positive impact on morale and productivity. Although the ideas are not new, the extremes to which several of the model's contemporary advocates appear willing to extend them are.

Participatory Management

At its simplest level, participation in this analysis means involvement of employees in the organizational decisions that affect their working lives and a substitution of collective decisionmaking for some aspects of hierarchy. A large body of literature argues that involvement and participation are the most effective means for motivating individual employees, even if those practices do have the potential to become manipulative (USGAO 1995a). The literature argues that most employees desire greater scope to exercise their own initiative and to make independent decisions on the job and would be willing to invest more time and energy in the organization if they were granted a greater level of personal involvement (Perry 1994; Garvey 1993). Employee involvement and job expansion have been dominant themes in management in both the public and private sectors for a number of years. Identification, analysis, and advocacy of this style of management go back at least to the famous Hawthorne study (Roethlisberger and Dickson 1941) and have been carried forward by a long line of management scholars, including Argyris (1964), Likert (1961), and Follett (1940). These scholars have advocated "organizational humanism" as the best way to promote both efficiency and morality in organizations.[5]

In American public administration one of the milestones of thinking about participation in public organizations was the Minnowbrook Conference and the New Public Administration (Marini 1971). This volume reflected the beliefs of a cadre of younger scholars of public administration whose ideas have been shaping transformations of both theory and practice. The initial work was followed by a number of other works advocating and analyzing greater opportunities for participation in public organizations (Dvorin and Simmons 1972; Frederickson 1980). More recently, Robert Golembiewski (1995) has argued that one of the major contemporary challenges for public administration is managing diversity or simply the differences that exist among employees and clients of public organizations. He sees traditional administrative structures as impediments to meeting that challenge.

These analyses correspond to what Stillman (1991) refers to as the "stateless tradition" of bureaucracy, especially within the context of the United States. Stillman argues that this more open approach to governing searches for means of delivering public services in ways that are not destructive to human values for either employees or clients. It is in contrast to traditional hierarchical bureaucracy, which is seen as destructive to those values. That view of hierarchy, of course, may itself reflect the negative, "stateless" Anglo-American view of bureaucracy as contrasted to a more positive conception of both government and bureaucracy commonly held in much of continental Europe.

Although many of the ideas about job expansion and organizational participation are old, they have been rediscovered and dressed up in the new language of empowerment. The idea is simply that if the workers within an organization, especially a white-collar one, are empowered then a number of positive outcomes will result. In addition to the humane aspects of permitting people to have more control over their own lives, this change in management style, it is argued, will also produce substantial benefits for the organization (Romzek 1990). As the older analyses of organizational participation argued, workers will be more productive if they are more involved in the organization and more empowered to make decisions. More empowered workers should be willing to work harder, share more ideas with management, and treat their clients more humanely since they are themselves being treated better.

One of the more commonly cited contemporary manifestations of the empowerment concept is Total Quality Management. As with many of the managerial practices in the market approach, TQM has been borrowed from the private sector, indirectly from Japanese management to be precise (Deming 1988). TQM is a participatory program, however, rather than a market-based idea.[6] The basic idea is to inculcate in employees the concept that the quality of their product is their major consideration. Producing a quality product involves several requirements (in this view). One is that all members of the organization must be committed to quality. Another is that the members of the organization should work together as a team, not be linked only through hierarchical authority and the division of labor. Moreover, the ideas of all members of the team are valuable so long as they can contribute to quality and organizational productivity. The organization therefore should create mechanisms through which participation and communication in all directions, not just from top to bottom, are encouraged.

There is some question about whether TQM is really suitable for the public sector, but doubt has not prevented numerous attempts at implementing the system. During the Bush administration, for example, a Federal Quality Institute (FQI) was established in Washington.[7] Its mission was to spread the idea of TQM and quality throughout the federal government (Brockman 1992; Burstein 1995). Following that, the National Performance Review (NPR—the Gore Report) emphasized similar issues, albeit couched in rather different terms (Kettl and DiIulio 1995; Ingraham 1995b). Because of the NPR, and for obvious political reasons, the Federal Quality Institute was terminated early in the Clinton administration.

The quality movement has been even more influential at the state and local levels of government in the United States than at the federal level (Durant and Wilson 1993). The former levels have been at the heart of the reinvention and quality movements, and they began implementation well before the federal government began to do so. The quality program has been enhanced partly because of its use in services having outputs and impacts that are somewhat easier to quantify than those on the federal level.

Skeptics question whether TQM is really suitable for the public sector (Swiss 1993; Walters 1992c). In the first place, there may not always be the latitude for involvement and job-shaping in the public sector that is found in the private sector. The duties and obligations of public employees are shaped by law, so that they simply cannot decide that doing a job differently is a good idea (G. Gilbert 1993). Certainly for some routine activities such latitude may be available, but for actual delivery of services it most often is not. Second, definitions of quality may also be more contestable in the public sector, when any clear bottom line is lacking to assess whether a program has been a success. Measurement of quality and success is a general problem for all service producers (Bowen and Schneider 1988), but the problems are exacerbated in the public sector.

The argument also can be made that quality in the delivery of public-sector services depends to some extent upon cooperation in production rather than on government employees simply delivering the service (K. Walsh 1991). Although this may be true to some extent for most service industries, it is particularly true for the public sector. If social service programs are to be effective, for example, beneficiaries must ultimately want to change some of their behaviors—either economic or social—and no amount of social service delivery will be successful without that value change. This perspective on quality parallels the direction of the emerging communitarian emphasis on coproduction of services. In this view, the only really effective and efficient service programs are those that demand participation rather than passivity from the clients.

Empowerment has been an appealing idea for politicians and for civil servants. Indeed, one of the reform documents most clearly stating the case for empowerment—PS 2000 in Canada—is largely the work of the civil service itself (Tellier 1990) rather than an idea forced down their collective throats. This reform is a marked contrast to many of the market reforms that have been implemented (B. Peters and Savoie 1994a). For the public service the concept of empowerment provides a means of fighting back against several decades of imposed market reforms. It further reinforces the sense of collective identity within the public service that has been threatened by more individualistic methods of evaluation and reward. In this style of managing, members of the public service can work together instead of perceiving themselves to be in competition.

Street-level Bureaucracy

Another body of literature on participation and empowerment argues that the lower echelons of public organizations are central to the effective functioning of those organizations and as a simple empirical reality the role of street-level bureaucrats needs to be recognized (Lipsky 1980; Prottas 1979; for France see Dupuy and Thoenig 1985). Whereas the empowerment literature previously discussed exalts the potentiality of the lower echelons of organizations for improving performance, the literature on street-level bureaucrats attempts more to recognize and describe the powers that these employees already possess. It then attempts to identify the consequences of this bureaucratic power for individuals who come to public organizations seeking benefits from government. One common finding is that workers often begin to identify with their clients and to debureaucratize agencies as well as to provide clients services to which they might not formally be entitled (Goodsell 1981b). The debureaucratization in turn provides clients an important locus of participation within the administrative system.

Just as the participative management literature has deep intellectual roots, so too does street-level bureaucracy, as revealed in some of the earliest empirical studies of public administration (Lasswell and Almond 1934; Blau 1960). After that initial research, there was a great deal of interest in involving clients in decisions that affect them, especially in programs such as Urban Renewal and Model Cities (Rogers and Mulford 1982). Although the evidence is strong that these well-intentioned efforts at democratization of programs were largely unsuccessful and even counterproductive (Moynihan 1969; Millett 1977), the values of participation and programmatic democracy continued to be espoused. Indeed for some clients, such as middle-class parents concerned with their children's education, participation is considered absolutely essential to successful service delivery.

In considering the outcomes of governing for individuals, it is important to think about whether they receive the benefits they sought or not. There may be other consequences as well, and they may be of greater significance to the bureaucratic system itself than they are to the clients. The face-to-face contacts between public employees and the public help to define the relationship between state and society (E. Katz and Danet 1973; Goodsell 1981a). For most citizens government is a relatively amorphous entity. They may see pictures of leading politicians on television and may respond to certain national symbols, but government is something that happens somewhere else and involves somebody else.

Nevertheless, the public has a number of encounters with representatives of government, most of whom are street-level bureaucrats. These contacts range from relatively mundane encounters with postal workers, schoolteachers, park rangers, and the like to more serious and potentially threatening ones. Citizens in financial distress must interact with social workers who have a decided impact on their immediate economic well-being. Citizens from time to time also must interact with policemen, whether as crime victims, speeders, witnesses, or in some other capacity. Even the most honest citizens may have their tax returns audited and be required to justify their interpretations of the forms and their rights. In short, citizens do see government face-to-face and often develop their impressions of it from those encounters (E. Katz and Danet 1973).

The good news is that most of these encounters are positive, at least for the industrialized democracies.[8] Most of the empirical studies available report that citizens are satisfied with the way in which they are treated by their public servants, even in some of the more threatening circumstances, such as in tax offices. There are, of course, exceptions that frequently make the newspapers, but the average encounter between the bureaucracy and its public is a positive one—on average as good as with private-sector employees. Now for the bad news. The positive encounters with public employees do not appear to add up to a positive impression of government in general. Paradoxically, a remote and inefficient administrative structure apparently is composed of pleasant and efficient individuals (Bodiguel and Rouban 1991). The Zeitgeist is such that public bureaucracy is a popular object of abuse even though its individual members seem to the public to be perfectly decent people.[9]

In contrast to views of participation and empowerment as normative and ameliorative, street-level bureaucracy as an approach to participation has somewhat less of a reformist zeal, but the implications for change are clear. If government is to be effective, then a good deal of attention needs to be paid to the work of these bureaucrats. They are already participating in reality, but that participation is not very well structured or even understood (OECD 1987). Moreover, their participation is often conceptualized almost as illegitimate and as if their appropriating authority is not rightfully theirs. The problem may be that the responsibility is indeed theirs, but it has not been designed in a way that empowers them. Instead it makes them appear, and feel, that they are operating on their own, without any support from their masters above or even from their clients below.

Another way to link participation and street-level bureaucracy is to think of participation as a means of overcoming the problem of "contravention." As Dexter (1990) has argued, the politics within an organization is at least as important, and contentious, as that among organizations; and there is a need to persuade the members of an organization to work together effectively.[10] A basic tenet in any organization, public or private, is to ensure that all members of the organization will act in approximately the same manner when faced with similar stimuli from the environment. That is, all regulators should find the same objective conditions in a factory either in or out of compliance with the environmental laws, and all social workers should give clients with the same objective criteria the same answers concerning their eligibility for benefits. Adequate participation within an agency cannot guarantee that, but it can help.

Discursive Democracy

Besides describing and improving management within government organizations themselves, the participatory model is also concerned with managing the participation of citizens and the relationship between state and society. In its simplest form participatory government is plebescitarian, with the public being asked to decide all manner of policy issues by a direct vote. State and local governments in the United States have something of this character (Cronin 1989), as does Swiss government (Kobach 1993), and there has been an increasing use of referenda for policy issues in other European countries (*Economist* 1995; Butler and Ranney 1994). Although broadly inclusive, referenda tend not to permit the public to make more than a "yes" or "no" choice about a decision that has been set for them by political elites.

At a somewhat higher intellectual level, and with a more intensive conception of public participation, various bodies of literature on "discursive democracy" (Dryzek 1990), "associative democracy" (Hirst 1994), "strong democracy"

(Barber 1984), and other similar ideas call for reforming government fundamentally. These ideas offer a much broader conception of participation and democracy than conventional representative democracy. The argument presented in these scholarly works calls for enhanced participation by clients, workers, and especially the public at large in the identification and clarification of problems within government as a whole as well as those dominating particular public organizations (Handler 1986).

The fundamental concept behind this version of participation is that the experts in a bureaucracy do not have all the information, or perhaps even the right type of information, for making policy (Majone 1989). Therefore, isolating important decisions from public involvement will generate policy errors. "No single actor, public or private, has all knowledge and information required to solve complex dynamic and diversified problems; no actor has sufficient overview to make the application of needed instruments effective" (Kooiman 1993, 4). Although pharmaceutical regulation in the United States, for example, is far from perfect (Roberts 1995), the openness of the system to a variety of interested parties appears to help minimize errors.[11] In contrast, the relatively secretive system of drug licensing found in the United Kingdom (*Observer*, 7 May; see also Harrigan 1994) and several other European countries does not permit that error correction.

The deliberative models contain an implication at least that representative democratic institutions are far from perfect in transmitting the wishes of the public into policy. This is hardly a new thought (Rose 1974), but what distinguishes this perspective from others is the assumption that more direct democracy can be made to work in even complex modern societies. In this view, therefore, there is a need to involve a wider range of citizens in the shaping of issues, in the formulation of responses, and perhaps also in the implementation of programs once they are adopted; this style of governing has come to be known as *Burgernahe* (closeness to citizens) in Germany. Government should be forced to become more open to a range of views, it is argued, not just to those of the policy experts and bureaucrats managing the program.

This manner of thinking about democracy and governing is often associated with continental social theorists such as Jurgen Habermas (1984) and Niklas Luhmann (1990). Habermas, for example, has developed the concepts of the "ideal speech community" and "communicative rationality" to describe the conditions under which participation would be most effective. In such an idealized setting there would be no hierarchy of individuals or of ideas. Rather, in this open forum all ideas are equally valuable and should be voiced in order to ascertain the true range of opinion within the community. Clearly, decisionmaking in this model would not be easy or quick. But the democratic virtues of participation, as well as the chance of developing innovative ideas about how to solve policy problems, would justify the extra expenditure of time and energy (S. White 1988, 70–71).

In many ways this vision of democratic governance is similar to the somewhat older ideas of participative management already described (49–52). The major difference appears to be in the scope of the discussion that would be permitted under each model. In the participative management or empowerment mode of thinking, the discussion would be primarily about how to administer a program that was already accepted as policy.[12] Further, it would be chiefly among the members of the public organization charged with delivering that service. For the advocates of discursive democracy, however, the subject matter and the types of participants involved would be much broader; the discussion would be about what should be done as well as about how it should be done. Public employees would be involved, but members of the community at large also would be, including perhaps some citizens with very different ideas about what constituted good policy.

Critics of this conception of governing can readily point to the practical problems that it raises. The public wants to be involved in making decisions, but they also want government to be able to act swiftly and decisively. Would not participation simply be another form of red tape that would bog down a system already perceived as being too slow? Does the public at large really have much useful information to add to a discussion about the details of complex policy issues? It sometimes appears that the experts have sufficient problems reaching any consensus on issues without involving a whole host of amateurs whose ideas may only waste time. There are also a number of legal constraints on government to prevent it, and other participants in the policy process, from simply doing what it wants to do, when and how it wants to do it.

Governments are further constrained by the practical point that often the only way that they are able to make difficult decisions is to limit participation rather than to foster it. In order to close military bases that became unnecessary at the end of the cold war, the American government, for example, had to create a base-closing commission and to limit the capacity of politicians and other potential participants in influencing the decisions (Koven 1992b). Likewise, both New York City and more recently Washington, D.C., have had to establish financial boards of control to limit the growth of deficits created through more participatory, democratic government. Even that strategy has not been fully successful in producing fiscal restraint, but there is more chance of achieving the goals if participation is minimized.

If one moves away from the ideal version of the model and examines some empirical examples, one can see that many industrialized democracies are attempting to construct patterns of policymaking that approximate the requirements for dialogue and discourse (Handler 1986). They have been doing so without necessarily building in the practical constraints that would so severely restrain the capacity to reach decisions in a timely fashion. "Issue network" and "policy community" frameworks for understanding policymaking are two examples that have become popular over the past decade (R. Rhodes and Marsh 1992;

Sabatier 1984; Jordan 1990). Although it is unclear whether these structures have always existed and social scientists have just discovered them or whether they truly have been developing, their increased prominence in the discussion of policy does provide a more participatory cast to that discussion.

The basic idea underlying these frameworks is that surrounding each policy area is a host of interest groups, professional associations, scientists, activists, and so on, all of whom have something to say about the policy. The trick for government then is to structure discussions in a way that permits maximum input but that still allows making decisions in a timely fashion (Barker and Peters 1993). The balance that is struck may be a function of cultural factors: the Scandinavian countries, for example, are generally willing to tolerate longer delays in order to gain maximum participation (Meier 1969), and the Anglo-American countries are much less concerned with full participation than they are about making a decision. Yet even in the less consultative regimes, political pressures are now forcing much more complete public consultation before a policy can be made legitimately.[13]

Government must make related decisions about how broadly to cast its net in seeking and accepting input from groups and individuals when making policy. At the extreme, corporatist systems of participation might limit participation to a few selected interest groups, thus obviating the real meaning of public participation in the eyes of many discursive theorists (Schmitter 1974; Micheletti 1990). Other methods, such as public hearings, town hall meetings, and teledemocracy, permit broader participation but present real difficulties in reaching policy decisions (Pierce 1992; Etzioni 1993). The task for government then is to balance the need for timely decisions with the need for participation and to develop some criteria for the probable relevance of input from prospective participants.

In thinking about public administration as the focus of much of the reform activity in government, it is interesting to note that in some ways the decisions made by these (presumably closed) organizations are in some ways more open to public participation than the decisions made by representative institutions. For example, in the United States, the Administrative Procedure Act (1946) mandates that each regulation (secondary legislation) issued by the bureaucracy be subjected to one or another mechanism for public input into the decision. The simplest is "notice and comment," through which the public has a certain number of days to respond to a published notice about a proposed regulation (West 1985). Other types of regulations and licensing rules will require open public hearings before a decision can be made. These mechanisms are far from perfect and depend upon an attentive public (usually only interest groups respond to notices), but the system is indeed more open than might be expected.

There are movements to make the regulatory process in the United States even more open and consultative. The principal device in this quest is "negotiated rulemaking." As the name implies, this method would permit the actors affected to negotiate among themselves and with the agency the nature of the rules that would become law (Harter 1982; Pritzker and Dalton 1990). The system is in-tended not only to enhance the democratic nature of the process but also to im-prove the quality of the rules adopted. Given that all or most affected parties would be participating in the negotiations, the probability of capture might be less than under other systems of regulatory decisionmaking.

The access of the public to rulemaking in the United States is far from per-fect, considering that relatively few average citizens have the desire to read the *Federal Register* on a regular basis, but it is better than in many other countries. Yet even more open systems of participation in rulemaking exist in the Scandi-navian countries. Public agencies there are required to circulate a request for opinions about proposed legislation (primary or secondary) prior to its being is-sued. This method tends to involve primarily the interest groups, but given the large number of groups sent the "remiss" requesting opinions and the organiza-tional intensity of Scandinavian societies, most segments of the population will be contacted.

Even simple changes in political life can be used to enhance participation and the influence of citizens over policies. Decentralization in favor of local gov-ernments, for example, is a part of the agenda of market reformers, but this struc-tural change can also enhance participation. Local governments, by their very size, make participation more meaningful. Moreover, local governments tend to use more mechanisms that permit direct citizen involvement than do national or regional governments. The famous New England town meeting in the United States (Elder 1992) and the annual meetings in some Swiss cantons are perhaps more striking examples (Frenkel 1994), but all manner of procedures, such as open meetings of governing bodies, public zoning hearings, and citizens' advisory bodies, enhance participation at the local level in ways that would probably be impractical for national governments.

Communitarianism

The development of the set of political ideas usually labeled as communitarian is important for understanding the emergence of participatory models of govern-ment (Etzioni 1993; Spragens 1990). The basic thrust of communitarianism is that the individualism implied in the market, as well as in some of the preceding ideas on participatory government, is misdirected. Rather than thinking about individ-ual gain and individual power in formal structures, one should think first about the impact of policy on the community, however defined, and about how the com-munity can be more directly involved in the production of services. Communi-tarianism denies the central importance of bureaucracies in the delivery of public services and instead looks for means of coproduction and personal involvement as the way to make government work better (Koven 1992a). Bureaucracies may still be necessary for some functions, but the people themselves can play a larger role in the system (see Racine 1995).

Communitarianism is sometimes discussed as a means to revive the glory days of the political left and to replace the market-driven ideas of the 1980s with a more humane vision of governing for the 1990s and beyond (Mulhall and Swift 1992). This view is certainly accurate, but only partially; there are some communitarian strands of thinking representing the political right as well. At the level of mass political activity, the "conservative populism" manifested in the Swedish elections in 1991 (Taggart 1995), in the Canadian elections in 1993 (Lemco 1995), and in the American congressional elections in 1994 can be seen as a form of communitarian revolt against big government and its bureaucracy. Unlike most earlier populist movements (Kazin 1995), this manifestation conceptualizes big government as one of the enemies (Boyte and Riessman 1986), if not the major enemy of the people. In the past, populists had envisioned the public sector as a solution to the economic and social problems caused by big business.

At the more elite level some conservative thinkers visualize that communitarianism will revive volunteerism as an alternative to social and educational services provided by government (Willetts 1994). Their view is that the expansion of the mixed-economy welfare state has stifled all forms of individual and collective initiative so that alternative forms of provision—including the family—that once flourished are now moribund. If community action and involvement can be given a moral claim on people's time and energies, then there will be less need for government as well as better and more caring public services (see Jenkins 1995). This version of communitarianism, like that on the political left, appears somewhat utopian, but it is also appealing to large numbers of people.

Whether attached to and promoted by the political left or right, communitarianism would emphasize the growth of the "third sector," meaning nonprofit organizations other than those in the public sector, as a solution to many problems of contemporary society. The way to reform government, therefore, is to use its power to foster the creation of more groups in this third sector. Interestingly, the actions of the market reformers in creating more autonomous agencies, and especially in creating the now famous "quangos" existing between the public and private sectors, may be a step in the right direction from the point of view of communitarians.[14] The structures needed for some of their reforms are thus already established. The only requirement left is to inculcate those structures with the desirable communitarian values, and the problems of governing society will be solved.

In this light it is interesting to note how little attention students of public administration have paid to the third sector and its relationship to government. It is less true in the United States (Kearns 1996) than in Europe, given the power of the volunteer sector in areas such as social services; but even in the United States apparently these organizations often have been perceived as the competition rather than as the potential allies in solving problems (see Anheier and Seibel 1990). In some ways public/private partnerships with business have been more successful than relationships between government and nonprofits (Pierre 1995a).

Economic realities as well as ideological changes seem to be encouraging a change in the relationships between the sectors.

The participative approach to reforming the public sector is not short on ideas. They are rarely as clear as those that have animated the market model, however, and approach the problem of government at several levels of abstraction. Nevertheless, there is a rich lode of concepts that can be and has been applied in thinking about how to make government perform better. "Better" here has a meaning quite different from the one held by the advocates of the market approach. Yet some of the ideas, such as consumerism in the market approach and empowerment of clients in the participatory mode, are not totally opposed. Indeed, both models target large institutions as a source of the public's perceived problems in coping with government, and both propose that the remedy is to break them down.

How does the participative approach deal with the issues of structure, management, policymaking, and the public interest? Given that there are at least four versions of this (presumed) approach to change in government, there may be some internal contradictions in terms of specific reform ideas and recommendations for change. The recommendations, however, will be held together by their common search for a way to involve more people—lower-echelon workers, clients, and the public at large—in the governing process and to break some of the bonds of conventional bureaucracy.

There will also be some contradictions to the market approach, which is to be expected, given the different ideological and philosophical roots of the two models. The contradictions are significant because specific reforms based on each group of ideas are being implemented simultaneously within the same governments. The failure to understand the logical basis of reforms and to make them compatible is a prescription for defeat, perhaps even worse. That is, implementing incompatible reforms can lead to negative synergy more easily than to positive synergy and thus to an actual reduction in the effectiveness of government.

STRUCTURE

The structural implications of the participatory approach to reform are somewhat less clear than those of the public-choice approach. Participation as a guide to reform appears to focus more on process than on the structures within which the processes take place. At one level, formal organization may be irrelevant if other opportunities are available for the workers and clients to participate in decisions. There are, however, structural reforms that may make their participation easier; thus this approach is not entirely silent on the design of public organizations. In considering both participation and decisionmaking it is necessary to note the extent to which enhanced participation by one group—either lower-

echelon employees or clients—may minimize the capacity of the other to participate effectively. The model's advocates talk as if there were an endless supply of
opportunities, but the supply may in fact be a limited commodity in a "zero-sum
game."

The most obvious implication for structure is that, much like the public-
choice approach, public organizations would become much "flatter" and have
fewer tiers between the top and bottom. If the lower echelons are perceived as
having a great deal of insight and expertise to offer in decisionmaking and are
highly motivated to provide good services, then hierarchical levels of control are
merely impediments to good performance in an organization. Further, if this
shift in the locus of decisionmaking is going to occur anyway, then eliminating
the middle-management tier is a good way to save money. This flattening of organizations clearly has been happening in the private sector under the rubrics of
"delayering" and "downsizing," and the pressures on the public sector to save
money through the same techniques are at least as intense.

The alternative implication, however, is that if clients and lower-echelon employees are to be permitted substantial involvement in making decisions, greater
control from above may be needed to ensure adherence to public laws and financial restraints. The need may be especially great if values of public service and
accountability are not well institutionalized in transitional systems. The street-
level bureaucracy literature points to the extent to which employees may become
advocates for their clients instead of administering the law *sine irae ac studio*.
Therefore, empowerment might produce a countervailing need to look over
shoulders rather than to assume that all is going well.

These possible implications point to yet another of the contradictions in the
mind of the public and experts about government. On the one hand, people want
government to be decisive, efficient, and less burdened by red tape. On the other,
people want to ensure that public employees are adequately controlled so that
they do not waste money, violate laws, or assist the wrong people. It is difficult to
have it both ways, and thus a constant battle persists between these two forces in
the design of public organizations and the processes that control them.

Another implication is the possible need for a variety of structures to channel participation. This is especially true for clients but may also be for lower-level
employees who have not been as involved in decisionmaking as is envisioned in
this approach. As governments have begun implementing programs of participation for both clients and workers, a variety of councils, advisory groups, and the
like have come into being. As with so many issues surrounding contemporary administrative reform, a number of points about the involvement of clients in organizations remains open for contestation.

First, who are the clients? The question is analogous to that asked about customers in the market approach. Are they the individuals who are being served
directly by the program? Are they those who are indirectly affected by the program? Are they the public at large? Each of these possibilities, all of which have

some validity, implies different structures for channeling the participation. In many countries there are already well-developed mechanisms for handling the input from the immediate clients of programs, although to some critics these systems remain oriented toward a top-down explanation of policies and decisions and do not permit authentic input from the clients.

Second, it is interesting that much of this definition of the rights of participation, albeit construed as citizenship rights, in practice means the rights of consumers of public services. This consumer characteristic again brings the participatory approach closer to the market approach than might be expected, given the political ideologies of each model's typical adherents. The development of charter rights, even for consumers, may be especially difficult to bring about in transitional and developing societies in which there is not a strong tradition of involving "customers" in government decisions or even the right to complain about decisions once they have been made. And among the developed democracies, marked differences may exist in the more participatory cultures of North America and the more quiescent public consumers in Europe.[15]

A third point is that most existing programs of participation in the public sector operate as ex post rather than ex ante controls over government. That is, government is much better organized to deal with the complaints of citizens about the poor quality of services than it is to involve the public in the design of programs (Lewis and Birkinshaw 1993). Although it is difficult to argue against the desirability of effective complaint procedures, it is also hard to accept on democratic grounds that complaining is the best form of participation. This is especially true in dealing with services, such as health, that produce outcomes that may be difficult to reverse.

The Citizens' Charters in the United Kingdom provide an example of a mechanism that operates largely ex post (Doern 1993; Connolly, McKeown, and Milligan-Byrne 1994). These statements of consumer rights for government services are mainly about the redress of grievance, as are devices such as alternative dispute resolution (Manring 1994), the ombudsman, and administrative tribunals. The Citizens' Charters were promulgated with much input from the public about what the people wanted from the services, but the charters were themselves top-down instruments (Tritter 1994). There have been increasing attempts to involve citizens in the creation of charters in Britain, as can be seen by the growing number of local charters put forth by individual hospitals, schools, community-care facilities, and the like (Department of Health 1994).

Some devices, such as public hearings, public inquiries (Barker 1994), and *remiss* proceedings in Scandinavia (Petersson 1989) do permit greater public involvement at the policy-formulation stage, but these mechanisms are less prevalent than those designed to handle administrative failures. As important as the redress of grievance is, certainly it would be better for a democratic government to prevent the grievances in the first place.

The final structural implication of the participatory approach has been the creation of a number of new structures that complement, or circumvent, traditional structures of government, especially local government. The new structures are more concerned with a single policy; local governments tend to be multipurpose. The reasoning behind the single-purpose authority is that it can focus attention on the issues in the one policy area more effectively and will not get bogged down in issues that cut across policies. Thus it will involve people in the community who might not be interested in an array of public issues but who do care about a single issue, very often education or the environment.

There may be political reasons as well for wanting to circumvent existing local authorities. In the United Kingdom, for example, many local authorities have been controlled by the Labour party even during a period of Conservative dominance at the national level. Therefore, creating new single-purpose authorities may reduce the political control of those local services; moreover, the performance of the former is easier to identify and measure. The creation of quangos and other bodies permitting appointment by central government also allows for evasion of powerful local authorities.

MANAGEMENT

The participatory approach to governance contains somewhat more obvious implications for public-sector management than it does for structure. The basic premise is that government organizations will function better if the lower levels of the organizations, and perhaps the clients of the organization, are included more directly in managerial decisions. At one level this involvement might be considered manipulative, with top management exchanging a little bit of participation for greater productivity and loyalty from workers. Although early human-relations management had some of this manipulative character, the contemporary advocates of participation have been more ideological and believe in the human as well as the organizational importance of participation. Nevertheless, there can be a manipulative element in thinking that overall social governance can be enhanced through permitting and encouraging greater social discourse in the process of making decisions.

Perhaps the most important feature of the participative approach is its attempt to involve social interests in governance explicitly. One should remember, however, that these managerial ideologies are by no means the first theoretical justifications of enhanced participation. The neocorporatist and corporate pluralist literature represents another strong strand of thought about how to gain the advantages of the knowledge, and the quiescence, of social groups (Olsen 1986). The difference may be that this level of legitimate involvement of social interests is now becoming popular in countries with an Anglo-American political cultural legacy as well as in countries with a continental legacy. Thus, although the market model may denigrate the role of the citizen, this model appears to enhance that role and to attempt to induce democratic participation through means other than voting.

POLICYMAKING

There are several implications of the participatory vision of governance for policy-making, to some extent because of the internal differences in the approach itself. Clearly there is a preference for a bottom-up versus a top-down version of the policy process.[16] That is, this vision favors decentralized decisionmaking over the use of relatively rigid hierarchies, like that of the market to some degree. Thus the lower echelons of organizations would have substantial, if not determinate, impact on policy decisions and the organizations themselves would have a great deal of control over the decisions that determine their own fates. The assumption here is that decisions made in this manner will be objectively better, given the presumed higher levels of information possessed by the lower levels of the organization. In its emphasis on decentralization the participative approach shares a good deal with the theorists, if not always the practitioners, of the public-choice approach.

Because of its concern for involving lower-echelon workers, the participative approach is almost silent on the involvement of top-echelon bureaucrats—those usually referred to as at the decisionmaking level—in policymaking. One possible implication would be that political leaders, having greater involvement with the public, might be more suitable conduits for participatory inputs than senior public servants would be. On the other hand, if communications within organizations are even moderately efficient, the lower echelons should be able to send messages that then influence policy through their organizational hierarchies. In either case, on the question of design for participation, one must ask, how can the employees who are usually excluded from decisions influence them? There is no simple answer.

Another perspective that the participatory model may offer on policymaking is the observation that lower echelons of the bureaucracy do have a major impact on policy in almost any political system (Lipsky 1980; Adler and Asquith 1981). Most governmental decisions are not made by the political leadership or even by the upper echelons of the civil service. Rather, by far the greater numbers are made by the lower echelons—the policeman, the social worker, the tax collector, and other street-level bureaucrats—who must make numerous decisions about particular cases every day. The available evidence indicates that these lower-echelon workers already possess a great deal of discretionary power in making decisions about individual clients so that little enhancement may be necessary.

The level of discretion available to street-level bureaucrats is especially evident in settings such as welfare offices, police stations, and sometimes schools, situations in which the clients themselves have little power. The argument has been advanced that policies are designed and implemented to control disadvantaged members of the public in these settings rather than to assist them (Piven and Cloward 1993; Spicer 1990). Therefore, instead of concentrating on empowering lower-echelon officials in these organizations, some critics instead search for additional means to hold them accountable. One essential difference between the public and private sectors is that in the former the client usually has some capacity to appeal against decisions as a matter of right.[17] If lower-echelon workers are empowered too much, they may be able to escape the legal constraints that would prevent their acting in an "arbitrary and capricious manner."[18] Thus, administrative discretion must be balanced with appropriate levels of accountability and responsibility.

Not only are those decisions crucial for the actual determinations of citizen's claims for services, but they also are crucial for popular perceptions of government. For most people government is the policeman, or the tax collector, or the safety inspector, and the interactions between citizens and state representatives shape the public's ideas about what government does and what it thinks about its citizens (Rouban 1991). Thus, more participation may make government more popular with clients, if not necessarily more efficient in delivering services.

One of the prevailing ideas about reforming public management is that the public will be better off if there is greater decentralization of existing hierarchies. The idea is held both by the market reformers, who want these new organizations to be entrepreneurial and responsive to market signals, and by the participatory reformers, who want to allow clients and employees greater involvement in the decisions of organizations. Decentralization may mean different things to different people, but to most contemporary critics of the public sector, its centralization and hierarchy require attention.

The market approach, with its recommendations to create many small and possibly competitive organizations to provide services, clearly results in coordination problems. They may be exacerbated by the simultaneous invocation of participatory ideas. If workers in organizations are empowered to make more of their own decisions, these probably will be more variable than if hierarchy and the imposition of a common pattern held sway within the organization. This variability, in turn, will make coordination and coherence more difficult to achieve.

Furthermore, if the ideas about "dialogical democracy" are implemented, then coordination of programs and organizations will become even more problematic. If there is wide-scale consultation about decisions, then once those decisions are made they will be difficult to change. Coordination among organizations, however, often requires that the organizations involved be able to bargain among themselves to produce a package of policies that the relevant actors can accept. This in turn requires some flexibility by the leadership of the organizations when they negotiate with one another. In short, although consultation and dialogue may produce greater happiness within an organization, they may ultimately produce increased incoherence within the world of policymaking organizations and simply move the locus of imposed decisions, as opposed to bargained ones, to another level within the political system.

Thus if workers and clients do participate in making policy for the organization, through devices such as Total Quality Management, then their decisions will have ideological as well as practical importance. That is, by virtue of their being created through an open political process established as a result of the participative methods of management, decisions become the collective property of the organization. Coordination with other organizations that may not share the same view may become more difficult, even if the organizations serve the same clients. Studies of coordination among organizations, for example, point out that organizations with different values or different orientations toward clients—even if existing within the same policy areas—have difficulty coordinating (B. Gray 1985).

Organizational change and policy change may also become more difficult if there is a group commitment to a decision. This possibility suggests some of the arguments of the new institutionalism (March and Olsen 1989), in which institutions invest their own processes and the decisions that emerge from them with particular meaning and thus resist imposition, or even bargaining, from the outside. If, as in the world of communitarianism, groups and individuals are coopted into programs, then they will have even more internalized meaning attached to them and change will be yet more difficult.[19] In short, participation can be a great strength, but it also can be a weakness when flexibility becomes important.

There appear to be several ways to address the problem of coordination. Chisholm (1989), for example, claimed that there could be "coordination without hierarchy." He argued for coordination in the context of transportation systems that, to serve the public well, needed to be well coordinated. Unfortunately, the formal structures providing these services were themselves not well coordinated. Chisholm discovered, however, that informal mechanisms of coordination developed to compensate for what the formal structure could not do. In this case the relatively decentralized structures, rather than developing cultures that were internally directed, developed ones that were more service-oriented and hence solved the interorganizational problems instead of exacerbating them. One must question, however, the extent to which this outcome is simply fortuitous or is this kind of development a general feature of the cultures existing in more decentralized, empowered organizations? If it is not, could it be developed?[20]

Similarly, Scharpf (1989) argues that there are mechanisms available for producing coordinative outcomes among any set of organizations, although he places a great deal of emphasis on unanimity rules that appear more likely to emerge as the basis of interorganizational bargaining.[21] These rules, in his "confrontational style," present real barriers to effective coordination. In his "problem solving" style, however, Scharpf argues for the presence of positive-sum games that can be used to create more positive forms of coordination (see also Mayntz and Scharpf 1975, 145–50). Even in the confrontational style, though, there would be options for side-payments and issue-packaging that could ameliorate some of the barriers of coordination.

THE PUBLIC INTEREST

Advocates of the participatory state assume that the public interest is served by encouraging employees, clients, and citizens to claim the maximum involvement possible in policy and management decisions. Involvement can occur through at least four mechanisms. First, citizens and employees should have the right to complain if they believe that they have not been served properly by government or if the system as a whole does not appear to be functioning properly. In order for this right to be effective, they first need to know what is occurring in the public sector. Thus, one of the requirements for effective citizenship and participation may be more open government, not necessarily in the radical sense of the dialogical theorists but at the more basic level of making policy-relevant information available to the public and even to other formal decisionmakers (Overman and Cahill 1994; Ashton 1993).

Many countries have already made substantial strides in opening their governments. The Scandinavian countries have had extremely open systems for a number of years. The Swedish Press Law, for example, permits access to almost any government document that is not explicitly classified, and it also makes classification of documents difficult. The United States passed the Freedom of Information Act in 1974 and, despite some limitations and difficulties in implementation (Cate and Fields 1994), it has served as a landmark in opening government to greater scrutiny from the press and the public. Other countries, especially those derivative of the British tradition, have found creating open government to be difficult, but difficulty may be a prerequisite for meaningful participation (Plamondon 1994). Moreover, as governments begin to employ the market philosophy as a part of reform, information may become less available as it is subjected to a variety of user fees or is privatized outright (Victor 1995).

One aspect of openness often overlooked is that for many services the public may not know what to expect and what constitutes "quality." It is easy to tell if the trains run on time or if garbage is collected when it is supposed to be. For more complex services, such as medicine or education, however, is the average citizen capable of determining a high quality of service? Even for the more mundane services, it is still difficult to say what is "good enough." Circumstances will inevitably cause some trains to run late. Indeed, if the trains are late for safety reasons, that may signal a higher quality of service than if they are on time but taking inordinate risks. Good services for some citizens (travelers wanting to get through customs quickly) may not be good for all citizens (those wanting protection against smuggling). How do people know when they are being served well by the public sector?

Government is making a number of attempts to establish standards for adequate performance by public services. In the United Kingdom, the Citizens' Charters—over twenty separate ones exist—(Doern 1993) are means of enumerating service standards so that citizens can identify instances when the standards have not been met and then complain and perhaps receive compensation. At the very least these standards can serve as diagnostics for public organizations. In a sense they can substitute for signals from the market, which guide decisions in private-sector organizations. Other countries are implementing or considering programs designed to resemble the citizens' charters (T. Rhodes 1995), but several of these programs contain almost as much about the duties of citizens as they do about the service-delivery responsibilities of government.

One interesting aspect of citizens' charters and a number of other similar participatory mechanisms is that they have been mandated from the top down (Hood, Peters, and Wollman 1995) instead of coming from the bottom up. An uncharitable characterization of this practice would be that public officials are telling citizens what quality they should expect when it is in the officials' self-interest for the public not to expect very much. Although this is not true of the Citizens' Charters in the United Kingdom, it is for almost all similar exercises in drafting service standards for the public sector (Barnes and Prior 1995). Public involvement tends to be permitted and encouraged only after the basic goals of the service have been decided, not when the more fundamental questions are being asked.

For employees of public organizations, the second mechanism for effective participation can occur through their enhanced capacity to make independent decisions and to influence the policy directions taken by their organizations. This concept of governance is sometimes discussed as a means of conferring power on street-level bureaucrats and to make policymaking a bottom-up process (B. Peters 1994). This openness to influence from the bottom is assumed to make the decisions of government objectively better, given that they will reflect the knowledge of participants in the organization who are most closely in touch with the relevant environment. Even if the decisions are not objectively superior, they will seem better to the people who made them, and then at least their implementation should be smoother.

But who is the public in this version of the public interest? Apparently, for most adherents of participation, the public is narrowly defined as the direct producers and consumers of the benefits of the programs, not the public at large. For many citizens, this narrow range of public involvement would most certainly not be an acceptable definition of the public interest. They, the taxpayers, would be required to fund the programs but would no longer be able to exercise control through the mechanisms expected to function in a democracy.

The average taxpayer would see this constrained version of participation not as a democratic process but as merely serving another special interest. It could be, in fact, that this clientelistic approach to governance might be retrograde in terms of how democratic systems are managed. At the extreme it would become almost a re-creation of the patron-client relationships about which Western analysts have commented in such unfavorable terms concerning the less developed world (Roniger and Ghuneps-Ayata 1994; Crook 1989). Thus, for the many definitions of participatory democracy currently in vogue, there should be included a means by which the public at large can scrutinize government decisions, either by political oversight or administrative auditing.

The third meaning of the public interest in the context of enhanced participation in decisionmaking is a more political one. In this version of the participatory state, advocates argue that public decisions should be constructed through a dialogical process permitting ordinary citizens to exert a substantial influence over policy (Linder and Peters 1995). The public interest thus will emerge through the creation of processes that enhance the rights of citizens to say what they want from government. Citizens should be able to bargain directly with other citizens who have different views about the appropriateness of public policies as well as able to bargain directly with government bureaus. This "discursive" view stands in clear contrast to the "decisional" approach more characteristic of traditional representative and bureaucratic government institutions (March and Olsen 1995). In the decisional view the capacity to produce decisions, rather than the ability to create consensus, is the characteristic mark of governance.

The fourth mechanism for involvement within the participatory state is one that depends upon citizens themselves being included in making many choices about policy and even in delivering those services. The participatory state is similar in this respect to the market state, given that both strategies recommend allowing citizens to make more consumer choices and giving them more direct control over programs. The manner in which consumer choices would be exercised in the participatory state is, however, more political than that of the market approach. Rather than voting in the marketplace with dollars or vouchers, citizens would vote through a political process. It might be in referenda on policy or through localized political structures, exemplified by parental involvement on school-management committees in Chicago (Vander Weele 1994) and in the United Kingdom (Levacic 1994). One fundamental point is that for advocates of greater participation in governing, better decisions (procedurally if not necessarily substantively) are made through public participation rather than through relying upon bureaucracy and technocracy.[22]

The United Kingdom has gone perhaps further than most other industrialized democracies in institutionalizing mechanisms for choice within the public sector. Although critics of British government, and especially local government, point to its seemingly undemocratic nature in some dimensions (W. Miller 1988), it has been able to implement a number of direct participatory mechanisms within particular policy areas. In education, for example, schools may opt out of local-authority control and attain grant-maintained status, which gives school governors (often parents) more real capacity to control the quality of education provided (Leonard 1988). It must be said, however, that this decentralization is occurring in the context of the simultaneous imposition of greater central controls over education funding, a national curriculum, and an increasing impact of the school inspectors, which minimizes the real autonomy of the school governors.

The housing sector has also been tapped for enhanced participation and self-management in the United Kingdom (Malpass 1990). The United States has engaged in some experiments with tenant management of large public-housing projects (Hula 1990), but the efforts in the United Kingdom have been more extensive. Although the scheme for Large Scale Voluntary Transfers in the Local Government and Housing Act of 1989 is in many ways just one more form of privatization, it does permit tenants some control over whether their housing estates will be transferred from local-authority control to alternative forms of management. In at least two instances tenants have been successful in blocking proposed transfers (Pollitt 1995).

The coproduction of public services (Hupe 1993; Gurwitt 1992) and the use of voluntary action as a complement to or substitute for government activity is also emerging as a mechanism for thinking about the public interest. To some extent coproduction is not a new idea at all but reflects traditions of community involvement and participation in service provision. These ideas have been displaced by professional public services in most industrialized democracies but remain in operation in some. Corporatist political regimes, for example, often use interest groups to implement the policies they previously helped formulate (Cox 1992). The "militia bureaucracies" of Switzerland exemplify the widespread use of people and of organizations as a means of effecting policies and involving the public in government (Germann 1981).

Communitarians tend to consider voting and other political forms of participation as necessary but not sufficient to change the nature of governing in service-delivery systems that have become highly bureaucratized. The more fundamental requirement, communitarians argue, is a shift toward greater personal involvement in the life of the community, helping out in school, for example, or at the extreme, home-schooling. Communitarian participation would mean not counting on government to care for the homeless and needy but engaging in cooperative efforts to feed, house, and reintegrate fellow citizens. Although critics consider many ideas of communitarianism utopian, its advocates argue that implementing its concepts is the only way to recapture society from alienation, bureaucracy, and ultimately decay.

The participatory model may seem to be less clearly articulated than the market model of administrative reform. Actually, the problem may be that it is too well articulated, with a number of different versions of the one basic approach competing for attention. Even with its internal differences, it is possible to extract several common implications of this vision for the role of the civil service in governing society as well as for the nature of governance itself. Ideologically, the participatory model is very different from the market model and the public-choice concepts that undergird market interventions, and it is built upon quite different assumptions concerning human behavior within organizations. Perhaps most fundamentally, this approach assumes that individuals are motivated in their organizational and political lives by "solidary"—participation—incentives rather than by "material"—pay and perquisites—incentives (P. Clark and Wilson 1961).

Despite the differences, the prescriptions for institutional design coming from the two approaches are not altogether dissimilar. In particular, the principal prescription is for decentralization and some transfer of power to the lower echelons of organizations as well as to the clients of the organizations. Moreover, most versions of the participatory model recognize the central role of the bureaucracy in making public policy just as does the public-choice approach, although advocates of the former consider this involvement more positively. If nothing else, the bureaucracy is a channel for participation by interest groups, the general public, or both, whether or not that participation is designed to bolster the position of agencies.

Although some prescriptions from the participatory approach are similar to those from the market model, the meaning attached to those designs for governance are markedly different. Rather than creating competition among service providers so that a market can develop and function, decentralization in the participatory model is intended to channel control to a different set of bureaucrats or to the clients of organizations. This transfer could be seen as the "regulatory capture" that the public-choice model seeks to avert (Macey 1992). Involvement of lower-level bureaucrats in decisions is considered as a positive, with domination by upper-level bureaucrats preferred over that of political leaders. Nevertheless, in the participatory model, both of these elites are considered to be equally antithetical to the interests of clients instead of as competitors for power, as in the market model.

4
Flexible Government

The third alternative to the traditional model of government, flexible government, is the least clearly articulated of the four models, yet it captures several important realities of public complaints about government and contemporary proposals for reform. At the basic level, a flexible government is capable of responding effectively to new challenges of surviving in the face of change. A number of governments in Eastern and Central Europe, as well as many others in the developing world, have failed that test recently. At a more refined level, flexibility refers to the capacity of government and its agencies to make appropriate policy responses to environmental changes rather than merely responding in habitual ways to inherently novel challenges.

Flexible government can also be considered as the antithesis of patterns of public-sector management in the recent past. Joining a government organization has been conceptualized in many countries as accepting lifetime employment (Walters 1992a), assuming that the employee wants to remain in government.[1] Likewise, forming an organization in the public sector conventionally has been considered as creating a permanent entity, no matter how transient the reasons for forming it may appear (Kaufman 1976). The permanence of both public employment and organizations frequently is overstated, but these suppositions still tend to shape a good deal of thinking about the formation and management of public-sector organizations. In particular, government leaders, the media, and the (moderately) informed public have begun to advance proposals for decreasing the permanence of budgets, organizations, and employment in the public sector.[2]

The dysfunctions of permanence in government, both for individual employment and for public organizations, are widely recognized. Governments have begun to address them even though permanence and institutionalization are more familiar as solutions than as problems to most of these bodies. The flexible approach to reform makes several viable proposals for changing the status quo in the public sector. It also represents a less ideological approach than the first two models. Meanwhile, ideas and suggestions for practicing its reforms, derived from the basic assumption about permanence in the public sector, do appear to be emerging in a number of governments.

As with most other diagnoses and prescriptions, the critics of permanence in government have somewhat conflicting views about the dynamics of the problems and therefore about the remedies required to produce a better public sector. On the one hand, permanence has come to be considered not only as the source of excessively conservative policies but also as the source of employees' commitment to their organizations instead of to the policies administered by the organization.[3] Employees may be more concerned with keeping their jobs and the organization healthy in budgetary terms than with effecting policy. On the other hand, organizational permanence may institutionalize the liberal social programs of the past.

In addition to causing management problems, a commitment to the existing structure tends to institutionalize prevailing conceptions of policy, even policy problems, so that policy change becomes much more difficult (Hogwood and Peters 1983; Rochefort and Cobb 1993). This immobility exists even when the objective environmental conditions confronting the organization and its policies change radically. The organization provides a conceptual lens and a stable and sufficient resource base that allow its members to dismiss the changes if they so desire.

Some of the more extreme versions of this conservatism have been encountered in military and international affairs, for example, the persistence of the horse cavalry into the twentieth century and the failure to learn lessons in foreign affairs (Etheredge 1985). The same sort of locking-in to the ideas of the past is encountered in domestic organizations, also. Agricultural policies, for instance, are apparently fixed in a model of a highly regulated and subsidized market while most other industries have been privatized or deregulated or both (Skogstad 1993). Furthermore, most public organizations responsible for labor-market policy continue to operate as if the phenomenon of globalization had never occurred (King 1995). Few organizations (public or private) are willing to invest in change while they are still viable, and the conceptual lenses provided by the organization may even distort collective perceptions of viability.[4]

Although it is conventional to think of organizational permanence as something of a mortmain on creative, activist policy initiatives and as an assurance of incremental change (Hayes 1992), some critics from the political right believe that permanence has rather different policy effects. In particular, the political right tends to consider virtually all existing public organizations as committed to big government and to the perpetuation (and even expansion) of programs developed during past liberal regimes (Aberbach and Rockman 1976). These continuing programs have produced (at least in the eyes of their critics) the "excessive" public spending perceived to characterize contemporary mixed-economy welfare states (Cook and Barrett 1992; Taylor-Gooby 1985). The programs are also blamed for other problems, such as continuing public-sector deficits.

The critics of public bureaucracy tend to conceptualize existing organizations as defending their policies not so much in the interest of their clients but more in their own self-interest as the producers of services (Egeberg 1995). In this now-familiar negative view of bureaucracy, the institutionalization of government structures has produced a perpetuation of policy priorities and governing styles that have had serious negative consequences for the society. Critics argue that these self-perpetuating structures are especially out of touch with the current mood of most industrialized democracies in which the public is seeking mechanisms to reduce the size and influence of the public sector.

This conservative conceptualization of government is similar to Niskanen's views and the views of other market advocates, but in this case the principal dynamic force (an oxymoron in this context?) creating difficulties for the public sector is permanence.[5] In budgetary terms a permanent organization may be a source of increasing expenditures, even if spending increases only gradually and incrementally.[6] Some earlier techniques for reforming government, such as Zero Base Budgeting (Schick 1978), have attempted to eliminate the upward pressures on expenditures associated with permanence, but for a variety of reasons they have been unsuccessful. So long as government organizations exist they will require care and feeding, and if politicians are incapable of making the difficult decisions required to terminate them (Bothun and Comer 1979), then an ever-increasing public budget is likely.

Thus, from the perspective of critics of permanence, the easiest and most effective way to generate a significant transformation of the public sector and its policy priorities will be to shake up the organizational universe that makes and implements those policies. Reforms such as Next Steps in Britain and the "corporatization" of government in New Zealand clearly had their major intellectual roots in the market, but they also had some justification in the simple desire to force the system of government to change (Boston 1991; Hogwood 1993). Some advocates of administrative reorganization, as well as some who advocate reorganization of firms in the private sector, have argued that change can be in itself positive (Hult 1987). In the case of the reforms in Britain and New Zealand, however, clear policy targets were associated with the desire to transform the organizational universe.

THE RELEVANCE OF STABILITY

One should not, however, be too quick to dismiss the virtues of stability and permanence in either public or private organizations. Long-standing organizational structures can help to guide policy choices along positive, if well-trod, routes. The assumption that all old policies are bad is almost certainly as fallacious as an as-

sumption that all existing policies are good.[7] The challenge then is to find mechanisms for identifying and discarding the overly mature policies while retaining
the effective ones. This choice is, of course, dependent largely upon policy values
(Mansbridge 1994) rather than on the existence of unambiguous standards for
measurement.

The negative characterization of stability assumes that the civil servants who
are members of public organizations desire only a quiet life and lifetime employment. Yet it may be that these employees actually are professionals, whether self-
defined professional administrators or members of other more well-defined professions, such as engineering and medicine. With these backgrounds the
employees will maintain contacts with professional organizations and generally
attempt to improve the policies they administer, often in the face of political opposition. In the present conservative political climate such policy advocacy—
whether for professional reasons or only for reasons of institutional protection—
may be considered as even more negative than excessive stability, but advocacy by
professionals does point to the need to avoid facile condemnations of permanence.

Moreover, stability is an important source of organizational memory, and
with it comes some of the institutionalized capacity of organizations to avoid expensive error (E. Stein 1995; March 1991). Ministers may resent being told that
"we tried that before and it didn't work" when they have a bright idea for a policy
innovation (at least to them), but this simple statement by their (permanent) civil
servants may save the public a good deal of time and money (Theakston 1992).
The policy process certainly requires important judgments about whether the
persistence of memory serves to hinder needed change or to preserve some necessary stability during times of rapid social and political change.

Clearly, from a more theoretical perspective the organizational memory is
simultaneously a repository of prior learning and a potential barrier to future
learning (Olsen and Peters 1995). There is always the danger that organizations
(or individuals) may learn one set of lessons too well, and those lessons may then
inhibit their learning newer and more relevant lessons (March 1991). If it is at all
possible, memory and organizational routines press an organization to encode
any new events and challenges as merely repetitions of older happenings. This
characteristic of memory enables the organization to use existing responses it
deems appropriate. The failure to recognize the new for what it is inhibits the
ability of organizations to adapt.

ORGANIZATIONAL PERMANENCE—FRUSTRATION AND FUTILITY?

Despite some obvious and important attractions, permanent government structures present significant problems for effective and efficient governance, at least
in the view of those advocating flexible governing. The dinosaurs that still roam

the landscape of government are a source of expense and may constitute barriers to policy innovation. Many existing policies and programs are valuable, but none should be allowed to persist without effective testing and evaluation. Some politicians and scholars believe that making government organizations less permanent has virtues as a goal in itself, regardless of how well or how poorly they may be functioning. Simply forcing organizations to rethink their values and policies on a regular basis may be a spur to more effective government.

In addition to public recognition of the dysfunctions of organizational permanence, the changing nature in the problems of governance has resulted in movement away from permanent structures. An increasing number of the significant problems governments confront are cross-cutting and fall between the stools of existing organizations. In some cases these issues produce only simple coordination problems. For example, although the United States has a Drug Enforcement Agency, numbers of other agencies—the Coast Guard, Department of Defense, Customs Bureau, FBI, state and local government police, and so on—are involved in the war on drugs. Coordination here is conceptually simple but politically is often extremely difficult, even with a drug czar to try to bring it about. Being willing to engage in that coordination may imply a loss of turf by one organization in favor of another, and with that, a loss of budget, prestige, and perhaps even organizational survival.

In other cases, the coordination problems are more complex. In making drug policy, for example, law enforcement agents often must become involved with the health and education aspects of the problem so that treatment "confronts" law enforcement as the better remedy (Sharp 1994). These coordination issues require some fundamental thinking about what the policy of the government is and what it should be. Coordination involves some turf fights, but the encounters are more often so fundamental that the territorial issues are subsumed under questions about the nature of the problem being solved (Rochefort and Cobb 1993). Shaping the nature of the issues and policy problems is a basic aspect of the policy process, and the fundamental coordination issues arise from conflicts over ideas rather than from organizational interests.

This widened involvement of multiple agencies in almost all policies has created a fourth or fifth or nth branch of government that attempts to coordinate and control existing organizations and policies (Fournier 1987; Derlien 1991). The "policy space" and the organizational space for governments are already well populated (Hogwood and Peters 1983), and there is a rapidly increasing need to coordinate actors and actions within that space. Because of real changes in policies, changes in the international environment of public policies, and greater awareness of the multiple interactions of policies in the society, the coordination problems appear to have become exacerbated over the past several decades. No longer is economic policy a concern just for economists and central bankers; it must also involve departments responsible for education, unemployment assistance, agriculture, labor market policy, international affairs, and probably many others.

Furthermore, the Zeitgeist for contemporary administrative reform is to devolve the functions formerly performed by one large department into a number of smaller organizations, bearing names such as "executive agencies" or "special operating agencies." Although some efficiency may be gained from the disaggregation of larger organizations, significant losses may also occur, including losses to overall efficiency within the public sector. One of the more important sources of such loss is a reduction in coordination (see 32–33). These executive agencies have been designed to some degree to be flexible and creative, but like other organizations, they quickly become permanent (or at least begin to feel and act as if they were permanent). Hence, they soon require some form of coordinative action from above. The need is even more evident, given that these organizations were designed to be creative and entrepreneurial. These two qualities match those of the market motif underlying the formation of the organizations rather well but make the governmental character of their activities more difficult to reconcile with traditional values such as elimination of redundancy and enforcing accountability.

The need to coordinate across the range of public organizations may itself vary across time. Economic policy departments, for example, may have a paramount need at one time to coordinate with foreign policy departments on issues of trade. That problem may be solved, or at least move down on the agenda (A. Downs 1972; Peters and Hogwood 1985), and the same economic policy departments may then need to coordinate more with education, training, and unemployment-insurance departments. Having created a permanent coordinative structure for the first problem might represent an inappropriate locking-in of priorities, and a more flexible structure, in practice, would be more appropriate for the needs of the public sector. There may then be a role for the coordinators of coordinators if government cannot respond more creatively to its needs for coherence in policy and programs.

It should be noted that the idea of using temporary organizations in the public sector is not new. They have been a common means for addressing the rapidly expanding and contracting administrative needs of wartime and other emergencies. All governments have from time to time developed task forces or other (presumably) temporary organizations. Governments in France and Germany, for example, have used formats such as *projets de mission* and *Projektgruppen* to address policy areas that they believed could be solved by short-term but intensive government action (Timsit 1988). The efforts to generate quick solutions were far from universally successful, but the structures did represent an attempt to prevent the creation of more permanent organizations.

Some scholars have argued that organizational permanence borders on futility and does not present a real problem. The formal structure may remain the same, they claim, but the capacity to control the society is not sustainable. The argument is that society is "autopoetic" (t' Veld 1992), or self-organizing. And other scholars discuss organizations as self-designing systems (Kiel 1989). As government organizations institutionalize their instruments of control, the regulated segments of society will find ways to minimize their effects. Thus, a flexible approach to regulation and a set of flexible organizations ultimately will produce better outcomes than will a more rigid and permanent structure. Further, flexible governance will be more legitimate, its advocates argue, because the regulated will believe that they have more influence over policy outcomes.

Another factor resulting in impermanence in government organizations is the fundamental transformation of the labor market in most industrialized societies (Borjas 1995; Dicken 1992). The transformation is partly a consequence of profound technological change as well as a function of the internationalization of economies (Savoie 1995c). With those changes have come a decrease in full-time and permanent employment and increasing levels of part-time and temporary employment. The assumptions that most workers have held about being able to prepare for one type of lifetime employment simply do not hold true any longer. Most people can now expect to change jobs several times and also to be retrained for different types of employment during their working lives.

Government has already begun to adjust to these broader economic changes and has found that offering part-time employment is a way of saving money and enhancing organizational flexibility. There may be no reason, at least in terms of efficiency, to keep employees who are needed only for peak workloads or emergencies. Some government organizations, such as parks and recreation and conservation organizations, have always operated in this manner but could depend upon a stock of interested, even dedicated, temporary employees available on a seasonal basis. Other public professions, such as teaching, have reserves of employees who tend not to be employed on a seasonal basis but who can fill in for full-time employees who must be absent for a day, a week, or a term. In these instances professionalism and commitment substitute for continuing attachment to an organization and its values. It is not clear if that model is generally applicable, however.

Market advocates point to the need to use outsiders in government to eliminate its separation from other actors and values in society. One standard complaint about government is that its employees are not aware of the problems of the real world and thus make decisions that appear nonsensical to business or other private-sector actors. If there were greater rotation of personnel through the public sector, then perhaps its employees would understand better the needs of the rest of the economy and society.[8] Some governments, for example, that of the United States, have always been more open to temporary employment,[9] but that model is now being considered in a range of other countries (OECD 1990).

Thus, even when there is a permanent public organization, its members may themselves be transients. This is certainly a shift from the tradition of government employment, and the permanent civil servant would no longer be the backbone of government. This change has important managerial and policy implications, but even more important, it would have implications for public accountability, responsibility, and responsiveness. Strict economic efficiency is but one of many values that government should seek to uphold; and flexibility, especially in employment, may undermine many other important values.

THE IMPACTS OF THE FLEXIBLE MODEL OF GOVERNING

Such then are the problems the model of flexible government is intended to ameliorate. As do the other three emerging models, this one has a number of specific implications for how government is, and should be, practiced. Although perhaps less well articulated and integrated than those arising from the other three perspectives, they provide an interesting and important perspective on how to push the public sector to perform better. This approach to reform requires some collective thinking about why specific public organizations exist and why government employs as many people as it does as a part of the career public service. The market model assumes that feedback from society will make that determination, but the flexible model appears to require a somewhat more "rational" consideration.[10]

STRUCTURE

The fundamental advice that the flexible approach offers is to use alternative structural arrangements within government. Rather than relying on traditional departments, agencies, and bureaus that perceive themselves as having virtually a permanent claim on a policy space, this approach seeks flexibility and frequent termination of existing organizations.[11] Frequent termination is intended to prevent the ossification that often can afflict permanent organizations, and greater flexibility might allow government to respond more rapidly to changing social and economic conditions. There might, for example, be less resistance to creating organizations to respond to novel circumstances if there were some assurance that they would be terminated when their task was completed.

The ability to create and destroy organizations appeals to fiscal conservatives who argue that permanence and bureaucratic monopolies create excessive costs along with rigid policies. Indeed, the organizational universe emergent from the flexible approach might be somewhat similar to the agencies already being created by market advocates. However, the agencies can assume an air of permanence rather quickly, but organizations created through an attempt to enhance flexibility would be subject to rapid change. Further, the market approach prefers to use market tests to evaluate performance of programs and organizations, but the flexible approach tends to look at flexibility almost as a benefit in itself. Therefore, its advocates want to establish the principle of uprooting organizations rather than relying excessively upon evaluations that can always be rigged in favor of an existing organization.

Another organizational option appears to the extension of the "quango state" that is already being created in the United Kingdom (D. Wilson 1995), with analogous structures reportedly spreading in many other political systems (Kettl 1993; Hood and Schuppert 1989; Masa 1990). Although exact definitions and classifications differ (Hogwood 1995), the basic concept here is that under pressures to reduce the apparent size of the public sector, governments have begun to use increasingly nondepartmental bodies and quasi-governmental organizations to conduct business. Given their somewhat less formal structures and small staffs, these organizations apparently are a viable means of providing public services while maintaining organizational flexibility. In practice, however, they seem to have substantial survival power themselves. Thus there may be no simple structural answer to the problem of permanence but a need to address the perceived problems with procedures, management, and political will.

As well as being structurally impermanent, these organizations might not be populated to a large degree by full-time employees who (at least in the United States) would spend most or all of their careers within the same organization. This change in career patterns is already occurring in government. The proportion of total work hours logged by federal employees has been gradually creeping up since the 1960s and appears likely to continue to increase. The predictions of almost all studies of the labor market is that the trend toward temporary employment will continue in nearly all segments of the economy. The trend may be applauded by fiscal conservatives who want to save money in the public sector, but it potentially damages other conservative values about the accountability of the civil service and its stability as a source of advice and values in an otherwise rapidly changing government.

The discussion to this point has focused on the structure of "line" organizations actually providing public services. Another aspect of creating flexibility lies in the management of coordination and the interfaces among organizations. Some countries already have a well-developed system of committees and task forces that coordinate existing agencies and ministries. France, for example, has coordination devices existing at three levels within its administrative apparatus (Fournier 1987), and central agencies elsewhere, such as the Office of the Prime Minister and Cabinet (Australia) and the Kansli (Sweden), also perform these coordinative tasks (M. Painter 1981; Larsson 1986). The problem is that central agencies tend to be even more ossified than the organizations that they attempt to coordinate so that the coordinative structures can outlive their utility even more readily than the coordinated structures.

Central agencies usually can evade hierarchical controls that would tend to force their own reorganization, with the major exception of elections and new governing political parties. Therefore, they must find methods for institutionaliz-ing their own responses to change or they become barriers to effective govern-ance. One possible solution to this problem of reforming the reformers is the idea of the "virtual organization" (Bleeker 1994), which is based on the common ob-servation that almost any formalized structure that is created tends to attempt to perpetuate itself. The tendency may be exaggerated in the public sector, but it also often pervades private-sector organizations, as several classic studies of voluntary organizations have demonstrated. Thus, to the extent that organiza-tions can become "virtual," as opposed to formalized, then a greater possibility of their being more adaptable to external change exists.

It is difficult to define a virtual organization. When the Gore Commission (National Performance Review) completed its formal work and was dissolving, it created what it called a virtual organization (B. Peters and Savoie 1994b). A group was designed to keep members of the NPR project in contact with one another on the Internet and to serve as an instrument for advocating the ideas of the report across the public sector. The development of technologies such as elec-tronic mail have made the creation of loose, informal organizations of this sort very easy. Other approaches include the creation of one-time, ad hoc organiza-tions that attempt to solve a specific question or the setting up of loose networks existing within and between other organizations, which are composed of like-minded individuals who retain their membership in their constituent organiza-tions.

These conceptions of virtual organizations are only slightly more formalized versions of the interorganizational, network thinking that is by now rather com-mon in organizational theory (Benson 1982; Hanf and Scharpf 1978). The basic logic is that any policy area, or almost any area of human endeavor, will be char-acterized by the existence of a host of organizations that interact to constitute a social institution, if not a formal institution (DiMaggio and Powell 1991). These networks will develop their own informal or formal rules and a set of norms that will guide actions. The members also tend to share a number of values and com-mitments. In short, under this definition, large numbers of virtual organizations are already in existence. The task for government may be to tap into this rich or-ganizational life and make use of it for policy advice, implementation, and coor-dination of programs.

One can think of the virtual organization as a means of managing govern-ment at the systemic level rather than at the organizational level. As analysts have pointed out for years, the organization is the basis of much of the behavior of the public sector (Seidman and Gilmour 1986; March and Olsen 1984). This ground-ing is in some ways a strength, providing identification for the members of the organizations (and for clients) and also linking programs with structures (Rose 1984). Yet it can also be a decided weakness in the system, resulting in rigidity and excessive identification with the organization.[12] The concept of the virtual orga-nization could be a means for overcoming the barriers to change that more formal organizations present, if ways can be found to circumvent the probable resistance to the idea.

Ranson and Stewart (1994, 140–42) discuss the problems of managing government at the systemic level. They point to the fragmentation and interorganizational dependence that exist in all contemporary governments and the importance of structuring systems so that the difficulties thus generated are ameliorated if not eliminated. Although they focus more on service delivery, especially at the local level, the same problems arise when policy is being formulated. Creating multiorganizational structures to cope with these problems will involve providing some overall direction to the institutional apparatus of government as a whole and, as Theodore Lowi (1972) has phrased it in a different context, will mean shaping the environment of behavior rather than the behavior itself. That is, it may be easier to create the circumstances in which the flow of information and influence makes certain types of decisions probable than it is to command decisionmakers to adopt those same decisions.

The fundamental question about virtual organizations becomes whether these public organizations will look and act any less permanent simply because they do not convene in a single place or are not really formalized structures. Will not their shared commitment to their policy goals and their continued association over time produce the same desire to maintain the institution's existence that is found in other forms of organization? Indeed, may not their very informality make them appear less "dangerous" than permanent structures and thus permit them to persist despite desires to trim down the size of the public sector?

MANAGEMENT

The manifest managerial implications of the temporary state are clear, but the latent implications are perhaps more interesting and important. On the former level the temporary approach stresses the ability of managers to adjust their labor forces to match changing demands. It can save a good deal of money for government and mitigate some of the public's perceptions of waste and empirebuilding. Moreover, this style of management may have some benefits for the personnel themselves, given the number of employment issues such as the impact on families of both parents working and the other stresses associated with the contemporary economy.

Flexible personnel management may permit governments to respond more quickly and effectively to crises or to rapidly increased demands for service. The potential service-delivery benefits tend to be discussed less than the cost-cutting benefits. If managers can add to their work forces without the fear of having longterm commitments to the employees, then coping with emergency and unanticipated needs is much easier. Even when it appears that the new level of demand may be permanent, maintaining flexibility is always a virtue for public managers.

Of course, in many settings this style of personnel management is already practiced, but an even greater loosening of the traditional system may produce real benefits.

One latent implication of this approach is some diminution of the commitment of employees to their public employers and with that a potential threat to public-service values and ethos. It now appears excessively idealistic to discuss the commitment of civil servants to their organizations and to the principles of public service. Yet there is substantial evidence that civil servants have been motivated by these values and that many would like to continue to be rather than by "just money" (Zussman and Jabes 1989). For many public employees, joining the public service was not the economic decision implied by the market approach but represented a commitment to achieve certain policy values through their careers in government (B. Peters 1994, 89–94).

Making more public-sector jobs temporary and part-time will almost certainly diminish the commitment of employees to their jobs and will tend to minimize their motivation for excellent performance. The flexible approach is therefore to a great extent antithetical to the ideas of the participatory state, given that temporary employees are unlikely to be interested in real involvement with the organization or capable of such participation (see Daley 1988). Thus, just when some of the management literature (public and private sector) is touting teams and employee involvement as the panaceas for all that ails organizations (Korsgaard, Schweiger, and Sapienza 1995; Berman 1995), workers are being told that their organizations have little or no real commitment to them as individuals, an extremely mixed set of messages to be sending to employees.

Further, temporary employment may make civil service values of probity, accountability, and responsibility even more difficult to enforce. Despite attempts to socialize temporary or part-time employees, they may not have any continuing interests in any one organization and little reason to invest their energy in complying with traditional public-service values. Their values are more likely to be the self-interested ones prevailing in the marketplace.[13] In short, one could argue that a good deal of conventional value may be sacrificed to gain some reductions in expenditures.

POLICYMAKING

The temporary state approach to questions of governance appears to have little to say directly about the role of the public service in making public policy. One can, however, explore its logical implications for an active policy role for the civil service. The implications appear to be potentially contradictory; some point toward an enhanced role for the civil service, and others seem to reaffirm the older wisdom of the elected classes' political dominance over policy, with civil servants in a subordinate position.

Emphasizing the fragility of government organizations diminishes the traditional sources of organizational power in a common culture and the commitment to existing policies. The old bureaucratic structures had both the advantage and disadvantage of stable personnel and stable policies. On the one hand, the permanent personnel provided a great deal of direction to policy and provided an experiential knowledge base for construction of any new policy initiatives. On the other, stability has been a barrier to innovations that would extend beyond the conventional wisdom about what is feasible in the policy area (Majone 1989, 69–94). The absence of such mortmain may permit political leaders to have a stronger role in altering policies than they might otherwise. A group of radical reformers, such as the Thatcherites or Reaganauts, would be pleased to have less organizational inheritance to counteract.

The pressures from this experimental approach, however, do not have the effect of making the life of political leaders easier. By removing the anchor of large, stable organizations, the elite of the civil service may be able to develop their own policy ideas more autonomously. To some extent the conception of the Senior Executive Service in the United States was that of a free-floating resource that could be used in a variety of managerial and policy-advice situations. Without large, permanent organizations to encumber them in the exercise of their own conceptions of good policy, these senior officials may in fact become creative forces in policymaking, clearly a development that most contemporary political officials would oppose.

In addition to its implicit advice about the role of the civil service in governing, the temporary state approach has some profound implications for policymaking. If indeed permanence is a problem, then impermanence may be a virtue and experimentation in policy becomes much more possible. Governments are often reluctant to take chances on policy, partly for political reasons; they do not want to be seen as wasting public money when they are not sure of the effects of their program.[14] Further, to have a program passed by the legislature often requires overselling, and admissions of uncertainty will almost inevitably assist the program's critics in causing its defeat. Thus, the dynamics of politics tend to push programs toward appearing to be permanent even if they are not.

To counter the ideas of permanence and the mortmain of existing policy understandings, several scholars have advocated a more experimental conceptualization of policy. In particular, Donald T. Campbell (1984) has long advocated the "experimenting society," in which government would quite explicitly try innovative policies, not always knowing if they will work. Rather than arguing that a program is the solution to a problem, an experimental approach would have the appropriate humility and honesty to say, "We don't really know if it will work or not, but we think it is important to try." Campbell's argument (1982) is that all policies (even well-established ones) are in essence theories about the capacity of government to alter behavior and outcomes and therefore deserve to be treated in an experimental manner rather than with any certainty.

In a similar vein Yehezkel Dror (1986; 1992) has advocated the concept of "policy gambling," in which policymakers must recognize quite explicitly that they are taking risks when they embark on any new venture.[15] Dror was speaking primarily in the context of foreign policy, but the same logic can be applied equally well for domestic policy changes. His point is that policymakers may make better decisions if they accept the uncomfortable fact that they really do not know a great deal about the context within which they make policy or even about the nature of their own policy "tools." Therefore, if they think about their policies as little more than gambles, whether against an actual adversary or simply against nature, then they will make better decisions than if they presume too much knowledge and too much control over outcomes. Thinking about policies as gambles may produce excessively conservative choices, or at least choices that have a "minimax" character, but governments also may be able to avoid massive and irreversible errors.[16]

Real-world politicians have been willing to adopt a more experimental approach to governing. President Franklin Roosevelt, for example, assuming office during the Great Depression, openly advocated trying a number of alternative approaches to the economic problems of the time in the hope that at least some of them would be successful. Perhaps more than any other president, he believed in flexible government, creating and destroying dozens of federal organizations while he was in office.[17] More recently, President Clinton has advocated that governments of the developed economies should engage in a variety of experiments to attempt to solve the continuing problems of unemployment and underemployment (1994). He said quite forthrightly that no government really knew the answers to these problems so that experimentation was perhaps the only way to find out what interventions could work. Linking scholarship and practice, Clinton's Secretary of Labor Robert Reich has argued for a progressive and experimental approach to government, especially in problems of employment policy (1983).

The continuing devolution of authority over policy in the United States, and to some degree in other countries, can be seen as a series of policy experiments. In some instances the call for social experimentation is quite explicit. In welfare reform, for example, policymakers do not really know how to alter the behavior of clients, and some states are already embarking on a series of experiments to produce behavioral change in program beneficiaries (Lampe 1995; J. Katz and Nixon 1994). The use of the states as the "laboratory of democracy" has produced a number of significant policy changes in the past, including trials of programs that eventually evolved into social security at the federal level.[18] At the present time other significant experiments at the state level are under way in providing health care to all citizens (Leichter 1992), an effort that so far has proved to be impossible at the federal level.

Institutionalizing some form of flexible government (another oxymoron?) makes adopting an experimental approach more palatable to political leaders. If politicians or administrators can be certain that when they initiate a program it need not be a permanent fixture on the public landscape but can be terminated rather easily, then experimentation is more likely to occur. The history of creating and (infrequently) destroying public organizations might lead a politician to be skeptical about the real capacity to produce rapid change in the organizational universe. Even organizations designed to be temporary occasionally persist for a very long time.[19] Still, writing more explicit terminations into legislation, placing limits on budgetary authorizations, and using sunset provisions (Opheim, Curry, and Shields 1994) can be means for creating a more flexible organizational frame, and a more flexible frame of mind, within government.

Even if the explicitly experimental approach implied by the model of flexible government is not adopted, an emphasis on flexible employment arrangements may generate some de facto experimentation. If a number of employees with limited training make decisions about cases and have little or no connection with the collective memory of the organization, then there will almost certainly be substantial variance in their decisions. In some ways the variance may be a positive outcome, if the differences in outcomes can be monitored and if the error is primarily in a direction preferred by the organization, that is, staff members might be instructed that if in doubt, to err on the side of granting benefits to the client or on the side of saving money for the government. This more random pattern of decisions, however, will almost certainly lead to the need for greater hierarchical supervision. Thus, workers would experience some loss of autonomy throughout the organization so that managing participatively may be difficult.

The budget process is an important part of policymaking, and ideas about flexible government have some potential implications for the allocation of public funds. The concept of flexibility would help to overcome what some budget analysts regard as the principal barrier to rational allocation of public funds, namely incrementalism (Hayes 1992). A number of attempts at budget reform, such as Planning, Programming Budgeting Systems (PPBS) and Zero Base Budgeting (ZBB) in the United States (Draper and Pitsvada 1981), Public Expenditure Survey (PESC), Programme Analysis and Review (PAR), and their successors in the United Kingdom (Thain and Wright 1992a; 1992b), envelope budgeting in Canada (Savoie 1990, 63–67), and Rationalization des Choixs budgetaires (RCB) in France, were justified partly by their capacity to reduce or eliminate commitments to existing organizations in favor of a more comprehensive evaluation of spending priorities.

Other analysts have argued that incrementalism is in fact a rational way of making spending decisions (Lindblom 1965; see Rubin 1990). They point out that the magnitude of contemporary public budgets is such that it is almost impossible for decisionmakers to consider priorities comprehensively. Therefore, the shortcuts provided by the marginal analysis in incrementalism are an aid to rational allocation of public funds. Having to recast the budgetary bargain anew each year or having to consider thoroughly a number of program terminations and reallocations may reduce the overall efficiency of the budget process. Central financial organizations are faced with the necessity of finding some sort of workable balance between permanence and flexibility, between incrementalism and synopticism, that will permit government to allocate funds efficiently without creating excessive disruption of services or imposing too heavy an analytic burden. Wildavsky (1978) has argued that the traditional budgeting system is just that sort of compromise; it does not work particularly well, but neither does it perform poorly.

Other changes in contemporary public budgeting also appear to enhance flexibility within government but at the loss of some degree of central financial control. I will discuss these budget reforms at greater length (102–3), but the shift to bulk budgeting and to allowing organizations to retain "profits" for future use deserves some mention here. As one component of the new managerialism in the public sector, government organizations are being granted the right to retain any unspent funds from one budget year to use in subsequent years. This budgetary flexibility, while making the time horizon of the public manager more like that of the private manager, also reduces the control of central agencies, and hence the public, on the actions of these organizations.

THE PUBLIC INTEREST

Of the four models, the flexible approach contains the least clearly articulated concept of the public interest. One obvious component is that lower costs for government are beneficial for society. If employing more temporary workers will reduce the costs of government and less permanent organizations prevent wasteful expenditure on dinosaur programs, then arguably the public benefits through lower taxes, even if particular clients of government services are potentially disadvantaged from the efforts of less knowledgeable and committed public-sector employees. This basic premise about the public interest is like that of the market model, although the causes for excess cost and the logic of remedying the problem are different.

A second implicit concept is that the public will be better off with a more innovative and less ossified government. One standard complaint about government is that the organizations within it represent special interests outside the public sector. These organizations fight for their programmatic turf on behalf of their clients and attempt to preserve themselves whether or not there is any real justification for their continued existence.[20] The conventional wisdom presents a somewhat exaggerated interpretation of the reality of the permanence of government organizations (B. Peters and Hogwood 1988), but there is still some truth in it. If change could become as much a part of existence in the public sector as is permanence, then there will be some chance of greater creativity and, perhaps again, some opportunities for saving the public money.

There is, of course, a reverse argument to be made in defense of permanent

structures, which is that the weakest segments of society experience the most difficulties in having their interests embodied in organizations. Thus, if the existence
of organizations is regularly brought into question, then it is just those organizations representing the most disadvantaged that are most likely to be terminated.[21]
For example, amid the organizations and programs in the federal government,
the ones most commonly threatened with dissolution are those serving the poor.
The Republicans' Contract with America attempted to eliminate a number of
programs of this sort, and even President Clinton, a Democrat, sought to cut back
or even terminate several such programs.

Even if the organizations serving the most disadvantaged members of society are not terminated, any broad-scale attempt to create greater organizational
flexibility is likely to generate uncertainty among the clients. Although some
politicians assume that uncertainty is a positive incentive for both employees and
clients, too much of it can result in dysfunctional behavior. One of the virtues of
bureaucrats, as opposed to politicians, is that they can adopt a somewhat longer
perspective on policy and do not have to think about the next election. If bureaucrats had to spend their time thinking about the next budget and what that might
bring, they might engage in the same short-term thinking that characterizes politicians, and they in turn would produce policies that could be suboptimal in the
long term.

Another argument for the virtues of permanence, or at least against the virtues of impermanence, is that evaluations of programs are at best inadequate, especially in the short term. Therefore, any attempt to make judgments about programs and to terminate those that are unsuccessful may shut down programs for
the wrong reasons. The evaluation literature is filled with examples of programs
with "sleeper effects" (Salamon 1979; Rossi and Freeman 1989, 350–71). The
benefits of these programs did not become apparent until after they had been
terminated.[22] The loss resulting from too-rapid termination was not only the time
and money that had been invested in the program but also the potential benefits
that might have been generated. Providing programs ample time to prove their
worth, therefore, appears a logical strategy, although analysts do not yet have any
agreed-upon means of deciding just how much time is ample.

Another implication of flexible government for the public interest is that although policy coherence generally is a good thing, it is difficult to determine a
priori the substantive dimensions of coordination and coherence that will be
most important at any particular time. For example, at one time an economics
ministry may require extensive coordination with social service organizations
in government, such as unemployment or education, but at another time foreign
trade issues could make coordination with the foreign ministry crucial. At still
other times agriculture and forestry may be the most important concerns for coordination. Thus, any formalized structure designed for coordination may solve
an immediate problem but may actually misdirect policymakers' attention when
the next issue arises and hamper solving that problem. The obvious answer is

flexibility, but achieving it in a world of government more accustomed to permanent organizations is difficult.

Given this fluidity of external influences on policy, therefore, the public interest is best served not only by the individual service-delivery organizations being more flexible but also by having a control superstructure oversee those delivery organizations. The superstructure usually will be in the form of central agencies that themselves are now under pressure to become more supple and agile in meeting changing external demands and pressures. The problem here is that central agencies tend to be the least reformed parts of the public sector and probably also the most resistant to any change (Seldon 1990; Savoie 1995b). The central agencies may persist in implementing the coordinative structures and ideas that have served them well in the past, despite the vast changes that have since occurred within the public sector.

Finally, the concept of flexibility tends to bring into question the fundamental point that governing is often about absolute rights rather than about more flexible programs and policies. Although efficiency is important, the protection of the basic rights of citizens is even more important for a functioning democracy. Flexibility and the defense of rights may well be incompatible, even when those rights are economic and programmatic, such as entitlements to social benefits. Thus designers of policy and administrative regimens must be careful to match those systems with the policies being administered and the clients being served.

The old stereotype of government organizations as permanent and inflexible is not altogether true, but neither is it totally false. There is no market to force government organizations out of business or to assist them in midcourse corrections that might enable them to make their programs more effective. Therefore, some critics of the existing arrangements in government have argued that the presumption of permanence should be shifted to a presumption of impermanence. The danger in this, as with so many reforms, is the possibility of creating excessive impermanence as the cure for excessive permanence. The real answer is to find the appropriate balance between the power to force organizations out of business and the ability to sustain organizations. Identifying and then achieving a balance of stability and movement is difficult in any set of organizations, however, not least among those in the public sector.

The dangers of impermanence appear more pronounced for employees than they do for organizations. I would argue that almost any organizational framework, peopled by individuals with a strong commitment to the public service and to achieving policy goals, might work effectively. Yet even the best structural arrangement inhabited by employees with little or no commitment to public service would find it extremely difficult to perform its tasks efficiently and in the public interest. It is problematic to expect individuals who have only minimal commitment to public service values to perform their jobs in the public interest, even if using temporary employees does save some money. Reformers must be cognizant of important values that transcend simple economic efficiency before they begin to manipulate public-sector organizations and the individuals working within them.

Although the actual programs motivated by each set of ideas may be effected at the same time, the flexible model of reform and the participation model appear fundamentally at odds with one another. The difference is especially true for their treatment of personnel management. The participation model requires strong commitment from public employees, and perhaps even from clients, but the flexible approach appears to treat employees rather shabbily. Flexible government assumes (much like many significantly older conceptions of management) that employees are almost interchangeable parts in the vast machine of government and that they can be replaced almost at will. Moreover, the flexible approach assumes that organizational values and the civil service ethos are of little importance and indeed may be an impediment to good government instead of a potential source of it.

The flexible model appears compatible with the market model, however, as does the participation model with deregulation (see 64–66). Therefore, as with so many other issues encountered in administrative reform, a fundamental trade-off of values is implied here. Flexibility and responsiveness can be bought at the price of substantially less organizational memory and less commitment from employees. The selection of one set of values over the other may then become a contingency question. That is, under what circumstances should the clever manager or political leader opt for one or the other of these approaches (or for the other two models) as the principal guide to reform? Most of the discussion of reform in government and in the academic literature has tended toward the simple one-size-fits-all approach to change, but that is almost certainly an oversimplification of the complex dynamics of the public sector and the efforts to make it work better.

5
Deregulated Government

The fourth option for reformers is to unleash the potential power and creativity lying within the public sector by "deregulating government" (J. Wilson 1989; Barzelay 1992; DiIulio 1994). This term (like the others we have discussed) has been used in several different contexts and with various meanings. In this context deregulation is not concerned with economic policy but with the internal management of government itself. Thus deregulating government could be seen as almost the complete antithesis of the politics of the 1980s, which attempted to reduce the activity of government and severely control the actions that remained. The politicians of the 1980s apparently had a special dislike and distrust of the public bureaucracy and sought to curtail its powers over policy. One basic assumption of deregulation is, however, that if some constraints on action are eliminated, government could perform its functions more efficiently. Moreover, government might even be able to undertake new and creative activities to improve the collective welfare of the society if some of its shackles were removed. This is the Nike theory of governing: "Just do it."

Constance Horner has clearly expressed this perspective on reform through deregulating the public sector:

> Deregulation of the public sector is as important as deregulation of the private sector, and for precisely the same reason: to liberate workers' entrepreneurial energies. We need a lean, resolute civil service able to decide and to act, rather than wait and see (1994, 87).

It should be remembered that Horner was a high-ranking official in the Reagan administration and might not be expected to advocate such an apparently activist position for government. The implications of the deregulatory approach, however, can be to free the energies contained within the public sector to produce higher levels of government activity. Presumably, with the removal of the constraints of internal red tape, that activity would be more creative, more effective, and more efficient. Further, conservatives sometimes assume that any activity created through deregulation will focus on programs they would approve rather than on social and regulatory programs that are generous to the poor and restrictive on industry.

From a second perspective, deregulating government may simply be another version of the market model and its managerialism. In the marketized version of deregulation, the principle purpose of removing internal controls is to advance the power of public managers to manage. So long as managers are constrained by the public sector's apparatus of personnel rules, budgeting rules, and the like, the true possibilities of enhanced efficiency through managerialism can never be achieved. Therefore deregulation and the market model can be seen as complementary approaches to reforming government. In particular, removing internal constraints over personnel management, purchasing, and similar functions will enable public-sector managers to act much like their private-sector counterparts and presumably make the public sector more efficient.

In a third conceptualization, the deregulatory version of reform also contains a number of the elements of the participatory model. Just as proponents of the latter argued in favor of involving workers more completely in the decisions of organizations, advocates of deregulation believe that discretion is superior to rules and regulations for producing effective public action (J. Stein 1995; Howard 1994). James Q. Wilson, one of the intellectual fathers of the deregulatory approach, has observed: "Most people do not like to work in environments in which every action is second guessed, every initiative is viewed with suspicion and every controversial decision is denounced as malfeasance" (1989, 369). The difference between the two models is that deregulation is linked almost entirely to enhancing efficiency rather than to values such as self-actualization and participation itself.

In the three conceptions of and justifications for deregulation, the enemy is essentially the same: a public sector that has become increasingly bureaucratized (in the pejorative sense) and constrained by its own rules and red tape. Deregulation advocates argue that the internal regulation of government prevents it from achieving its purposes as efficiently or as effectively as it might. Because of the distrust that politicians often have of the public bureaucracy, and because of the even greater distrust that their constituents have of it, control after control has been piled on public-sector managers. As a natural consequence, the managers believe that they do not have sufficient latitude to do their jobs as effectively as they could.

In most instances it is not the bureaucracy itself that brings about excessive internal regulation. Rather, it results from perceptions of the bureaucracy and its dysfunctions held by the public and their elected representatives. Members of the bureaucracy themselves are often as frustrated by the internal regulations imposed on them as are its clients. These administrators are rarely capable of convincing their political masters that the controls being imposed upon them are actually counterproductive. Indeed, imposing rules and controls on the bureaucracy is rarely bad electoral politics, and any politician who is too cozy with the civil service becomes suspect in the contemporary antigovernment political climate.

The rule-bound nature of public administration slows action and reduces flexibility in a number of areas. The civil service system itself has become a labyrinth of rules designed to protect public employees from abuse, to ensure more equitable hiring, and to prevent patronage and political exploitation of government positions. Other rules, such as preferential treatment for veterans in the United States, may prevent government from hiring the best candidates in favor of achieving other goals and serving other constituencies (U.S. GAO 1995b). In addition to achieving those laudable goals, civil service rules were supposed to enable managers to hire, reward, promote, and terminate employees. Many public managers find the rules a hindrance, and experiments with alternative methods of management appear to produce better outcomes (Feller et al. 1995).

The rules surrounding procurement and purchasing developed during the postwar era were even more restrictive than the personnel rules, requiring elaborate bidding procedures for even small purchases and preventing government from making purchases in ways that ultimately would have saved public money.[1] A history of corruption and preferential contracting may have justified those purchasing rules initially, but they may have outlived their usefulness. Budgeting rules designed to save money also imposed restrictions on agencies, for example, requiring them to return money to the general fund if it were not spent at the end of the budget year. These budget rules arguably cost the public money in the long run by promoting unwise spending and by limiting the initiative of public managers.[2]

There are cross-national differences in the extent to which rule-bound bureaucracy apparently presents problems for people in government. The complaint has been most prevalent in the Anglo-American countries, perhaps for good reason (but see Reichard 1994; Gibert and Thoenig 1992). Partly because of the comparatively low regard in which citizens of these countries have tended to hold their public services (Goodsell 1995, 49–75; B. Peters 1995b, chapter 2), there has been a tendency for their legislatures and central agencies to heap rules on top of regulations in order to control the public sector. The legislature has been a particular problem for public administration in the United States. Congressional "micromanagement" of individual programs (Gilmour and Halley 1994; J. Wilson 1994b), as well as of the public sector as a whole, has limited the flexibility and adaptability of federal programs.

On the other hand, countries operating within the Germanic and Napoleonic traditions (B. Peters and Loughlin 1995) tend to be burdened by much less specific sets of rules controlling actions in public organizations; general statutes seem to be sufficient in those legalistic regimes. Further, the public tends to hold their public services in higher regard in continental systems than in the Anglo-American world. As a consequence, the rules that have been imposed on these governments are less burdensome and result in less inefficiency than in the Anglo-American countries.[3] Therefore, the major action in deregulating has been in the United States and other Anglo-American countries, although some of the ideas have spread to other countries, including Scandinavia, which is usually not hostile to state involvement in society (Olsen 1991).

Advocacy of the deregulatory approach is ongoing, and a substantial amount of movement in that direction has already occurred. In some cases, as with the Glassco Commission in Canada, advocacy of deregulation began decades ago (Canada 1962). More recently, in the United States the federal Office of Personnel Management (OPM) with great fanfare has thrown out the 10,000-plus pages of personnel regulations amassed over the decades. OPM is now attempting to operate a highly decentralized and flexible personnel system in place of the more rule-driven system (see Perry 1993) and to devolve a good deal of personnel policy to individual agencies (Feller et al. 1995). Several other countries also have been in the process of deregulating their personnel systems (OECD 1990).

A number of countries have discarded many of their purchasing rules and are permitting departments to purchase most materials and services on their own, albeit subject to auditing and other ex post facto scrutinies (Kelman 1994; Haves 1993). Budgeting also has become much more deregulated, with central finance agencies in Australia, New Zealand, and Sweden willing to grant departments "bulk budgets" or "global budgets" and the latitude to make decisions on how to use money within wide boundaries; the departments are then held accountable for their actions (Schick 1988). Such leeway provides managers a great deal of latitude for action but raises a number of important questions about accountability.

Perhaps not surprisingly, many government organizations have found the newly deregulated world somewhat threatening. Internal regulations and procedures provided some certainty and predictability of action for both employees and clients. The individual civil servant did not have to take too much personal responsibility but could depend upon hierarchy, rules, and regulations for guidance. Avoidance of responsibility is the stereotypical behavior pattern of public employees and could easily become pathological and self-protective (Crozier 1964). Thus it is not surprising that some organizations have sought to reestablish the old, comfortable regime. Soon after the Office of Personnel Management had abolished its old personnel rules, many agencies within the federal government adopted the same set of rules as their own. Predictably, as new needs and issues arise these agencies will each add to its own stock of personnel rules, in different ways, with the consequence that the federal government may in effect become even more negatively influenced by rules than before deregulation simply because no common and understood set of rules exists that can guide action across the service.

In the United Kingdom some incompatibility apparently is emerging between the dominant market-based approach to reform and attempts at deregulation of the public sector. Although the Treasury has been arguing that it is decentralizing and deregulating itself, many aspects of its financial management and government purchasing have become even more rule bound (HMSO 1995). This expansion of regulation is being carried out with the good intention of saving public money. The purpose of deregulating is also to save money and to permit government to move more quickly, and even creatively, in procuring goods and services. The United Kingdom's experience, however, appears to be the paradoxical case of deregulatory intent being accomplished through highly regulatory mechanisms.

LEVELS OF GOVERNMENT

Central governments have had some success in deregulating themselves, but the performance of subnational governments in ridding themselves of excessive rules has been even more impressive (Light 1994). Much of the now-famous Osborne and Gaebler book on reinvention (1992) can be seen as descriptions of state and local governments in the United States deregulating themselves, albeit discussed under the rubric of reinvention. Even with the reforms already undertaken at the subnational level, there is advocacy of greater deregulation. The Winter Commission (Ehrenhalt 1993), for example, proposed significant deregulation of state governments, including changes in personnel, purchasing, and budgeting rules.

In addition to deregulation of the internal management of state and local governments, the intergovernmental system of the United States has become increasingly deregulated. One of the few components of the Republican Contract with America that could be passed during the first year was the pledge to end unfunded mandates from the federal government. That is, many federal laws had imposed certain requirements on state and local governments, such as compliance with clean drinking-water standards, but had not provided them with the money to meet those standards. The mandates that imposed substantial costs on subnational governments are now being eliminated; further, the federal government is permitting the states to experiment more with welfare reforms (Pear 1995).

Local governments in many other countries such as Canada have been engaging in the same processes of change, reinvention, and deregulation (Borins 1995a). And although the unitary governments of Scandinavia have always permitted a good deal of autonomy for their local governments (communes), the "free commune" experiments of the 1980s and 1990s are allowing them much more freedom in making local policy and in implementing national policies (Baldersheim 1993; Stromberg 1990). At the other end of the historical spectrum of local government autonomy, France now is providing much greater latitude for its local governments also (Loughlin and Mazey 1995).

One interesting case of lack of movement toward more deregulated management for local government is the United Kingdom, where local authorities remain under tight central control, despite the major administrative reforms occurring in much of the rest of British government (Elcock 1994). Indeed, central government controls, especially financial controls, have been tightened over the past fifteen years of Conservative rule (R. Rhodes 1992). Certainly there have been some managerial changes in local government (*Public Money and Management* 1994) but not to the extent that might have been expected given the pace of change elsewhere within the British public sector. Further, much of the change that has occurred in local government has been imposed through that central control instead of being adopted from below. In a sense, deregulation has come about through regulation in this one case.

The observed differences among levels of government are predictable. It is in most instances substantially easier for local governments to deregulate themselves than it is for central governments to eliminate the procedures that structure their activities. Local governments are generally of a more manageable size than any central government so that managerial control can be exercised without the need for impersonal rules. Moreover, the tasks that local governments perform (streets, sanitation, and so on) tend to be more readily measurable than those of central governments; thus exercising managerial control should be easier. A danger arises, in fact, in assuming that the experience of lower-level governments is readily transferable to central governments (Savoie 1995a). Even within the same country, the differences in tasks and managerial styles among levels of government may make the transfer of ideas difficult; hence, the enthusiasm with which Washington, D.C., greeted the Sunningdale experience may have been misplaced.

DEREGULATION AND ERROR

A general point to be made about deregulation of the public sector is that if this model is selected by governments, then a certain amount of error will have to be accepted. Human beings, even when highly motivated, ethical, and highly skilled, will make mistakes, some of which will be embarrassing for government. The likelihood that such mistakes will be exposed to public view is now greater than ever before, given the activity level of the media and the apparent public glee whenever any failures in the public sector are brought to their attention. Errors are almost inevitable in any administrative system, especially ones as large and complex as those of contemporary governments. Therefore, what should administrative and political leaders do when those errors occur?

One natural reaction for politicians faced with obvious and publicized errors in their departments is to retreat from the brave new world of deregulation and attempt to reassert ex ante controls. This reaction may be especially common in Westminster systems with their traditional conceptions of ministerial account-ability, even if those concepts now seem to be honored more in the breach than in the observance (Sutherland 1991; Marshall 1989). This political reaction to error reflects, to some degree, the history of the huge collection of internal regulations that existed before attempts at deregulation, and it would be easy to see a circular process of deregulation followed by reregulation emerging (see W. Muller and Wright 1994). Though it is difficult for them to deny the demands of their con-stituents for greater ex ante controls over bureaucracies, political leaders will have to exert some real leadership to maintain the gains (if the leaders conceptu-alize deregulation as that) that have been achieved.

A second point is that policies may have to be designed to minimize certain types of error while permitting other types more readily (Linder and Peters 1995; Ingram and Schneider 1991). For example, given the current political climate in many countries, it may be more palatable to design programs in which the a priori decision is to deny social welfare benefits to applicants rather than to grant them. This strategy may well be morally repugnant to many people, but the political fallout will probably be less than that resulting from programs in which numer-ous examples of ineligible applicants receive benefits. Other types of programs such as veterans' benefits, albeit similar in many ways, may best be designed with the opposite assumptions about desirable errors, given that their potential clients enjoy a higher status in society. Thus with careful initial design of programs, in-ternal deregulation may be maintained, despite relatively high rates of errors in judgment by the public bureaucracy in making decisions about individual eligi-bility.

STRUCTURE

The structural implications of the deregulation model are rather sparse. Al-though its advocates would not say so directly, structures apparently are much less important in their thinking than are the rules and procedures used to control public organizations and the people within them. It may also be that in their con-cerns about the ability of governments to act effectively, they find that traditional hierarchical structure is less of an anathema than it is in other, more modern con-ceptions of organizations. The premise that bureaucratic structures are almost inherently undesirable has become the conventional wisdom in public organiza-tions, but proponents of the deregulation model argue that they are indeed ac-ceptable, and even desirable, in certain situations.

Hierarchy is more important, and a more positive value, in the deregulatory model than in other models of reform for several reasons. First, most other mechanisms for internal control of personnel will have been removed through deregulating. Second, part of the reason for deregulating (like some aspects of the market model) is to unleash the creative energies of managers. Managers need to be able to produce concerted action within their organizations, and hierarchy would be the most practical way to do so. Therefore, unlike the participatory model that seeks to gain action through involving the lower orders within organizations, this approach places somewhat greater emphasis on the role of leadership.

Another possible structural implication of this model is that the control agencies developed by political leaders at the center of government are less desirable than they generally have assumed. The administrative history of many countries, perhaps especially the Anglo-American democracies, can be written in terms of changes in central agencies and their relationships to line departments (Heclo and Wildavsky 1974; C. Campbell and Szablowski 1979; Savoie 1995b). Governments have invested a great deal of effort attempting to find ways for central agencies to control spending, personnel, and purchasing, presuming that centralizing these decisions would produce more efficient government, eliminate redundancy, and prevent waste. Advocates of deregulation, however, tend to argue that the controls created waste instead of minimizing it, if for no other reason than that they require a large staff to manage them.

In the deregulated model deemphasizing centralized control structures would permit the individual organizations to develop and implement more of their own goals (C. Campbell and Szablowski 1979). Despite frequent protestations to the contrary, central agencies do exercise substantive policy control as well as managerial oversight, even in the devices that they may propose to use when deregulating their relationships with line departments. For example, an emphasis on mechanisms requiring quantification of outputs by departments gives the advantage to programs with clear and unambiguous indicators over programs with "softer" outcomes.[4]

A highly regulatory system from central agencies should be able to fulfill one of the goals of managerialism by allowing the political leaders enhanced control over policy. Domination by central agencies, however, clearly lessens the capacity of managers to manage and thus weakens one of the other managerialist goals. Internal regulations by central agencies can be used for a variety of purposes, with their actual impact being determined by the intentions of the superbureaucrats and the direction provided to them by their political masters.

The proposed reforms of the British Treasury represent a considerable attempt to deregulate a major central agency and to change its habits of imposing control. The White Paper on the Treasury, "Continuity and Change" (HMSO 1994a), seeks to initiate a new era of deregulated management within government. Although some of the initial changes have been structural (such as delayering at the top of the organization), there is also a felt need for changing the culture of control that exists within the Treasury (Norman 1994). Indeed, it is argued that the changes appearing in the White Paper represent only the beginning of the process of making the Treasury into a more user-friendly organization. The long decades of Treasury power over the details of personnel and expenditure may make the new image a difficult one for many civil servants to accept.

Although some central agencies will become less central under deregulation, if they do not wither away altogether, other organizations will have to become more central to governing. If one assumes the desirability of maintaining responsible democratic regimes, then some means of holding organizations accountable are necessary. Central agencies to some degree have managed evaluations by imposing their vision—and presumably that of the political leaders of the system—on policies before they are implemented or even while they are being formulated. This method is less permissible in a deregulated government, and therefore evaluation and controls after the policy is effected become the crucial means of enforcing accountability. Thus, if governments are able to pare down their central control agencies, they must in turn beef up their central evaluation agencies.

This shift also implies that the latter agencies will have to continue in the direction that they have already begun to go, i.e., becoming increasingly policy analytic rather than merely accountancy organizations (Rist 1990; A. Gray, Jenkins, and Segsworth 1993). Further, the trend will undoubtedly place pursuit of the deregulated model more directly at odds with the market model, at least as it has been practiced. One ironic feature of many of the administrative reforms that have been implemented over the past several decades is that with all the talk of efficiency and effectiveness there has been some tendency to dismantle the analytic capacities of government (Aberbach and Rockman 1989). For example, the Government Performance and Results Act in the United States (1992) stresses results but lacks adequate resources and methods to measure them (Kimm 1995). There is little institutionalized way of knowing whether government is indeed now more efficient than it was in the past.

Many of the market reformers, assuming that they were correct in their general interpretations of the problems and the solutions for what ailed government, have implemented their reforms with little or no formalized means for evaluating them. Further, to the extent that evaluation "shops" remained open in government, they were at the center and not within the agencies (Aberbach and Rockman 1989; but see Mayne 1994), partly because the market reformers did not trust the results they might get from agency-level evaluators who obviously would have had a vested interest in the outcomes.[5] Thus, if deregulation is to be successful it will have to re-create the analytic capacity that has been lost. The need for such a capacity to some extent will also apply in central agencies, such as the General Accounting Office or the National Audit Office, and in decentralized evaluation activities.

Other structural implications of the deregulatory model are not too dissimilar from those derived from the market model. If bureaucratic organizations are not really undesirable in the context of a deregulated model, then the active, entrepreneurial agencies being developed as a result of the market model, for example, Next Steps in Britain, might be even better. Not only would internal controls over "proper management" be weakened or eliminated, but the exposure to more real or potential competition might create even more effective deregulated organizations. The fundamental point is to encourage government organizations and their managers to use all available skills and energy to achieve their goals.

Unlike the participatory model, however, the deregulatory model appears to be much more compatible with hierarchy, or at least with strong leadership from the center in organizations. That being the case, the control that is exercised through hierarchy will mean that flatter organizations with middle-management levels removed may not be particularly congenial to deregulation. The organization may operate in a more fluid environment, but the individual employees within the organization may remain under control from above. Further, the logic behind this approach appears to be that of deregulating managerial activities in the pursuit of predetermined goals instead of employee participation in setting those goals. Thus, although individual civil servants may be freer to perform their tasks, they may not have any more real control over the policies they administer than they would have had within the conventional models of administration.

MANAGEMENT

The managerial implications of the deregulation model could go in two quite opposite directions, largely because management is apparently not one of its central concerns. On the one hand, advocates of deregulation argue that traditional forms of structure and management may not be as bad as some contemporary critics claim. This being the case, hierarchical management would be acceptable and even desirable. That style of management permits policy entrepreneurs who presumably are in positions at the top to generate action throughout the organization. This process, in turn, would depend to some degree on a common organizational culture within the organization that supports the policy direction advocated from above.

Deregulated government will place a heavy burden on managerial leadership within public organizations to reach its goals, but it is not the simple managerialism advocated in the market model (Behn 1991). In this conception, public managers must be not only the entrepreneurs required in the market model but they also must have some qualities of the democratic leaders visualized in the participatory model. Further, they must be moral leaders and create a climate of honesty, commitment to the public service, and accountability within their organizations if so many of the ex ante controls are to be removed successfully (see pp. 105-7. This is a large set of responsibilities, especially given the lack of respect from the public, and even from politicians, with which they are commonly confronted in the very societies that are stressing deregulation.

On the other hand, the alternative managerial implication would suggest a process similar to that advocated in the participatory state model. If the creative powers of government are indeed to be unleashed, then that goal may be reached most easily by involving all levels of the organizations, not just senior managers. Indeed the constraints of rules and regulations within government have been more stifling for lower-level employees than for the senior positions. If those rules are eliminated and their jobs can be done in a less constrained manner, then the employees should generate a burst of energy and commitment, or so the argument goes.

Thus, if government wants to be effective and creative it will require the commitment of all its available resources, most importantly its employees. This logic matches that of the participatory model and is in sharp contrast to the flexible state model, which does not assign any real importance to involving public employees in the performance of their agency. As with the participatory model, the assumption in the deregulatory approach is that individual public employees do want to do their jobs as well as possible. Further, it is assumed that if employees are allowed greater freedom, they will use it for the benefit of the organization and its clients.

The deregulatory approach generally is quite compatible with the market approach, but in some important managerial issues the two appear to clash. As managerialism has come to be practiced in many governments, it has begun to impose more procedures and internal management practices rather than fewer, all in the name of good management. In the United Kingdom, for example, attempts to improve the internal management practices of the National Health Service have produced claims, at least in Labour party campaign materials, that service providers have been replaced with accountants. Similarly, imposing resource accounting across the public sector (HMSO 1994b) may require a huge amount of accounting work and internal controls, under the rubric of improving management and enhancing performance (Kemp 1994). The merging procedures and controls, based on output (results) rather than input (budgets), actually may structure behavior more directly than did the old ex ante regulations, given that individual careers become more contingent on adequate performance on the new indicators.

Management and managerial tools in government have become something of a "cargo cult" for reformers (Hood 1991; Pollitt 1990). Their prevailing assumption appears to be that the simple copying of devices that are used in the private sector will almost certainly make the public sector more efficient. The deregulators, however, might see many of the same barriers to action in the private sector as they identify in the public. Further, mechanisms such as resource accounting may make more sense in the private sector because of more clearly identifiable costs and revenues than they would in the public sector. The deregulators, therefore, would argue that imposing different rules, especially where inappropriate, is really no better than keeping the old rules.[6]

Moreover, the deregulatory reforms can succeed only within the context of a dominant civil service ethos. The value system of the civil service—providing faithful service to any political master, fiscal probity, fairness, and so on—is just the system that would make a process with fewer ex ante controls on civil servants a viable alternative to the status quo. The new public management, conversely, tends to denigrate this culture and to laud (implicitly and sometimes explicitly) people who have rejected this value system and who are more committed to an individual, entrepreneurial value system. It may therefore be self-defeating, or dangerous, to attempt to implement some of these reforms simultaneously.

POLICYMAKING

The implications for policymaking are somewhat clearer than the other implications of the deregulatory model. Indeed, this model is primarily concerned with the procedures by which decisions are made and laws implemented. In the traditional view, which to some extent is reinforced by the new managerialism, policymaking is the prerogative of political leaders (Wright and Peters, 1996). The deregulatory model would assign a somewhat stronger role to the bureaucracy in making policy, the logic being that these organizations tend to be major repositories of ideas and expertise and hence should be allowed to make more decisions. To the extent that this logic also implies that the lower echelons of the organization, because of their expertise and close contacts with the environment, should have somewhat more influence, then the implications are similar to those of the participatory model.

This characterization of the deregulatory model should not be taken to mean that its advocates argue that policymaking powers should be entirely abrogated by political institutions in favor of the public bureaucracy. Rather, it means that policymaking is likely to be better on substantive grounds—if not in terms of democratic theory—if an active role is permitted for the bureaucracy. The positive role of the civil service may be especially evident for developing societies in which a large proportion of the available expertise is located in the public bureaucracy (B. Peters 1995a). The broad policy criteria used by the bureaucracy to guide decisions must be made to serve the goals of political leaders, but successful policies are unlikely to be adopted without an active role for career public servants.

Budgeting

One of the important dimensions of deregulation of government has been budgeting and the allocation of public money. Most efforts at budgetary reform in Western democracies have been attempts to balance competing values of "rationality" and political control over expenditures (Savoie 1990). Reforms such as program budgeting (PPBS in the United States and RCB in France), the Public Expenditure Survey in the United Kingdom, and "reconsideration" in the Netherlands (Van Nispen 1994) tended to place a larger burden on analysis and less on raw political power to guide the spending decisions governments make. Although analytical in character, these efforts were implemented, however, in the context of a top-down regulatory style in which the central financial organization—Treasury, Treasury Board, Office of Management and Budget, and so on—would make the final determinations about how much to spend and how best to use the money available.

Indeed, most of the budgetary reforms undertaken in the 1970s and 1980s tended to diminish the discretion available to agency officials in determining their own budgets. Even under the more analytic schemes used earlier the agency could negotiate on the basis of the outcomes of policy analysis, but the decisions were still made at the top. Other mechanisms such as cash limits in the United Kingdom (Thain and Wright 1992a; 1992b), Gramm-Rudman-Hollings and the Budget Enforcement Act in the United States (Kettl 1992), the "main alternative" in Sweden (Ericksson 1983), and even the envelope-budgeting system in Canada tended to diminish the capacity of managers to make financial decisions on their own. The common strategy was to replace judgment with formulas (Hanuschek 1987) and to use those formulas to drive down public spending.

The rather crude first round of reform under the market-oriented, antistate approach is now being replaced with a more deregulated style of financial management. The basic idea of the more contemporary approaches has been to permit managers to make decisions, albeit still within relatively firm overall program parameters. Further, by going toward multiyear budgeting and capital budgeting, the emerging financial system permits a manager to make longer-term decisions than would be possible under traditional budgetary systems. These long-term decisions may themselves, however, become a form of internal control as spending commitments made in one year constrain flexibility in subsequent years.

Coordination

Coordination appears to be an increasingly significant factor in policymaking for industrialized democracies. The increased impacts of the external socioeconomic environment and the need to generate better coordinated responses to an international political economy that is itself often incoherent in the pressures it places on domestic policymaking (Savoie 1995c) demand more consistent government responses. Further, political demands for cost-containment and efficiency mean that redundancy and overlap are even less acceptable than they have been in traditional public administration.

As with the market approach, deregulation appears to make coordination and policy coherence more problematic. Deregulation may make policy within each organization more coherent and integrated, given that presumably greater authority will be granted to policy entrepreneurs and managers to shape those policies and implement them throughout the organization. But the problem is that this internal coherence may well exacerbate the tendency of individual organizations to work in isolation from one another and to pursue their own goals and organizational self-interest at the expense of the greater collective good. Managers would have little or nothing to gain in a deregulated environment by investing money and effort in pursuing goals that did not directly benefit their organizations.

From the perspective of coordination the worst of all possible worlds may be the simultaneous acceptance of the structural ideas of the market model and the policymaking ideas of the deregulated model. Market reformers tend to break government down into a large number of smaller organizations, each with a single purpose or a limited range of purposes, such as Next Steps in the United Kingdom. The market model tends to assume some entrepreneurial freedom for these organizations, albeit acting within the context of signals sent from the marketplace to guide policymaking. The evaluative standards in the deregulated model are less clear, although there certainly is an idea of ex post performance evaluation. If the leaders of the decentralized organizations are granted substantial latitude, weak evaluation mechanisms, and few ex ante controls, there may be severe problems in making government work as an integrated set of organizations.

THE PUBLIC INTEREST

The deregulatory model by its very nature would substitute alternative forms of control for the rules and regulations that are usually employed as the means for producing accountability in the public sector. These differences are related to the distinction that William Gormley (1989) refers to as "muscles and prayers." He points out that most mechanisms for enforcing accountability depend upon "muscles," or direct controls, and argues instead for catalytic controls that would encourage members of the public sector—elective or nonelective—to act in ways that would enhance accountability. Although written well before the bulk of the deregulatory literature was conceived, Gormley's argument clearly points to means for having an accountable public sector without excessive ex ante controls. The approach is appealing, but it may be difficult for governments to overcome the temptation to use their muscles when confronted with apparent malfeasance.

The deregulatory model assumes that the public interest can be served through a more activist, and perhaps a less accountable, government. The latter characterization is perhaps unfortunate since more differences over the best forms of accountability exist than over the need for some form of it (Day and Klein 1987). The assumption behind most attempts to control government through structural and procedural devices is that without them the public bureaucracy will either behave abusively toward the public or (somewhat contradictorily) will do almost nothing.

The participatory model, on the one hand, increasingly emphasizes the role of the public and its participation as the best means of controlling the public sector, with grievance procedures being crucial to this model's success. The deregulatory model, on the other hand, assumes that the civil service is composed largely of dedicated and talented individuals who want to do as well as possible in serving the public. The view here is that if the putative controllers will get out of the way, albeit with a number of ex post facto controls remaining, then the system will probably function well. The debate between participation and deregulation is in many ways simply a restatement of the familiar Friedrich/Finer debate over accountability (Gruber 1987). It is a debate over whether formal rules are really capable of preventing the dishonest civil servant from engaging in corrupt activities or the inept civil servant from making mistakes. Are not the only real defenses against those problems more ethical and competent public employees rather than formal barriers?

The most important difference here is between ex ante and ex post controls over the public service. The traditional, regulated public sector depended heavily upon ex ante controls, although there certainly were a number of ex post controls, such as auditing, as well. Personnel, purchasing, and other sets of rules were designed to stop public employees from acting illegally or unethically and to provide a basis for punishment if the rules were violated. The problem was that following the rules almost became an end in itself rather than the means to other, more purposive ends.[7] Moreover, the detection of any loopholes or ambiguities in the rules as employees attempted to make the organizations function often was met with the imposition of even more rules, and with them greater rigidity.

To the extent that the current spate of reforms in the public sector is concerned with evaluation and control of program performance, the mechanisms imposed are almost entirely ex post. Indeed, there has been a substantial growth and development of central monitoring organizations in most industrialized democracies. Organizations such as the Auditor and Comptroller General in the United Kingdom, the Auditor General in Canada, Riksrevisionsverket in Sweden, and similar bodies in other countries have expanded their activities to include more extensive efficiency and effectiveness in auditing (Power 1994). In the United States the Inspectors General are charged with monitoring internal conduct and exposing administrative malfeasance (Light 1993) and have added another avenue of redress for clients and employees.

These auditing and oversight organizations can be described under the general term of counterbureaucracies (Gormley 1993). They are designed to control other organizations, ranging from central agencies responsible for overseeing public finance to monitoring administrative performance. In each case counterbureaucracies represent another form of control over bureaucracy although most tend to be ex post. The democratic pressures associated with enhanced participation, however, do tend to push for some enhanced ex ante controls in areas such as economic regulations and public spending.

Again one finds a fundamental contradiction underlying several approaches to reform. Many of the efforts to impose market reforms appear to require greater monitoring of programs, employees, and their behavior, a tendency seen most clearly in the monitoring of the economic and social regulations issued by public organizations. The market model requires that these regulations meet market standards, that is, that they create more economic benefits than costs for society. This approach demonstrates a great deal of ex ante regulation over the actions of bureaucracy. Although both models tout efficiency, their conceptions of it are different in this context.

The greater dependence on ex post controls over the public sector as a result of deregulation could impose a number of significant burdens on public servants (Wehrle-Einhorn 1994). In particular, deregulation would force public employees to make decisions without the guidance they would have under the traditional system. Those rules may have stifled some workers' creativity, but one person's creativity might be another's malfeasance; similarly, one person's red tape might be another's procedural due process (Kaufman 1977). It is not clear that in systems of democratic accountability the public wants civil servants to be extremely creative. Even without extensive deregulation, the appropriate limits for their actions and discretion have not been specified fully. Until they are detailed in more operational terms then perhaps the ex ante controls are desirable.

In using the deregulated model without ex ante controls, civil servants would almost certainly be held accountable for the decisions that were made; their increased freedom would translate into more personal responsibility. This result may then produce exactly the opposite reaction of that intended by the reformers. Although the advocates of reform may assume that civil servants want to take responsibility and work in a deregulated environment, that may not in fact be true for many of them, especially for those in the lower ranks.[8] Often they prefer the anonymity and protection afforded by large, bureaucratic structures to personal exposure and personal liability, no matter how empowering the changes might be. The net result of deregulation, therefore, may be to produce buck-passing and other familiar bureaucratic pathologies instead of leaner and more effective organizations.

No matter how it is phrased, the adoption of a deregulated model of governance will do some violence to traditional ideas, such as ministerial accountability (Marshall 1989). If decisional competence is devolved to lower echelons within an organization, then the capacity to hold ministers accountable for all actions within their organizations becomes even more of a fiction than it has always been. Indeed, in a deregulated (or even a market) model, such lack of direct involvement from the top in policy becomes a virtue rather than a vice, a change that clearly will require a fundamental rethinking of accountability.

Government and Society

The deregulatory model makes a statement about the role of government in society quite different from the role assigned to it by most successful politicians during the 1980s. The assumption here is that the public interest would be better served by a more active and interventionist public sector and that collective action is part of the solution, not part of the problem, for contemporary societies. Deregulation is far from a knee-jerk reaction in favor of big government; it represents a recognition that many of the most important problems facing society can only be solved collectively. Further, it recognizes that this solution in turn requires a major role for the public bureaucracy and that its involvement can be effective only if it is capable of swift and efficient action.

Proponents of the deregulatory model, however, apparently have not figured out how to mesh a deregulated civil service with empowered clients and with political leaders who want things done their own way. Most of the rules that govern administrative practice resulted from politicians' demands for greater control over the way bureaucracies worked. Some of the rules were to protect the public from excessive discretion, others were to protect the public purse from "fraud, waste and abuse," and still others were designed to ensure that elected officials controlled policy. These are laudable goals, and it remains unclear how a more deregulated government can guarantee the public interest if some of these external controls are removed.

Goals Beyond Efficiency

Some of the other implications of deregulating government for the public interest are more subtle but are nonetheless real. In the United States, for example, the Office of Personnel Management abolished SF-171, the form that had been used for several decades in the process of hiring new employees. It was discarded as being "excessively bureaucratic," the argument being that deregulating the recruitment process should make it more user-friendly for people unfamiliar with federal government practices (see Agresta 1994). The actual effect of deregulating personnel selection, however, may be quite the opposite: finding employment now may be more difficult for people unfamiliar with how government functions.

The old bureaucratic form, despite its embodiment of internal regulation, created a relatively level playing field for individuals seeking jobs in the federal government. With the abolition of the standardized form, experienced insiders may have a pronounced advantage over outsiders seeking employment. The latter may not be aware of facts that personnel managers within the system need to know about applicants and of particular information that might help the prospective employee appear competent. This disadvantage may be especially significant for minority candidates. These potential employees often lack the resources to use specialized employment agencies, or they may lack the informal networks to advise them about how to write the most effective résumé. The net effect of this particular deregulation thus may be to institutionalize the old-boys' network in the Washington community rather than to weaken it, which was one of the intentions of the reformers. One should not overplay the significance of this one change in internal controls, but it is indicative of the potential effects of a variety of deregulatory reforms.

The deregulatory approach also may give an advantage to certain groups within society at large, and the changes most likely will have the same negative redistributive consequences in society as they did in the bureaucracy itself.[9] If general purchasing rules such as open bidding are altered, or virtually eliminated, for example, then the provisions that have favored groups such as minorities and women may also be eliminated. Claims about the effects of minority set-aside programs and similar regulations in the United States vary (Mills 1994), but their general effect has been to encourage the formation of minority enterprises and to provide minorities with some means of making a start in the world of business.

Moreover, the search for efficiency within the public sector may deny government the capacity to use its powers to promote other worthy public goals. Environmental improvements, for example, can be pursued through the internal regulations attached to public programs and through the provisions imposed when awarding government contracts. The real question for governance, therefore, may not be so much whether rules within the public sector are good or bad per se but whether those rules allow the pursuit of the most appropriate goals. Rules that promote efficiency, such as competitive tendering (38–40), are now considered appropriate within the public sector, but rules that promote other goals, such as ethnic and gender equality, are now less valued.

The ability of government to purchase goods, hire people, and dispense grants provides it with a huge set of levers to achieve public ends, and indeed it may be inefficient to abrogate that range of possibilities, not only in a strictly economic sense but also in a political sense. There certainly has been substantial political furor raised over the issue of affirmative action (LaNoue 1993; Orlans and O'Neill 1992). Despite that, however, the use of rules associated with purchasing, hiring, and so forth may be less obtrusive instruments for reaching certain policy goals than would be other, more direct, approaches. Therefore any politician interested in achieving these goals would be well advised to pursue them through the internal regulations of the public sector rather than through a more visible and intrusive means.[10]

The deregulatory model of reform may be seen as containing some elements of the other three models, but it also contains some important contradictions to each of the others. Despite its being "marketed" by some academics as a relatively distinct approach to change, is deregulation of the public sector really so distinctive, or is it merely a restatement of some bits and pieces of the other models, dressed up in language that is appealing, especially for civil servants? If it is not distinctive, is anything gained by presenting this model as a unique manner of changing government?

If for no other reason, the deregulatory approach is distinctive because it emphasizes a unique set of problems within the public bureaucracy. While the market model tends to emphasize the negative consequences of monopoly, the participatory model hierarchy, and the flexible model organizational permanence, the deregulatory approach stresses internal regulations within public organizations as the principal source of dysfunctions so often observed in the public sector. Many, if not most, of the numerous "bureaupathologies" identified within the public sector (Caiden 1990, 127) can be laid at the doorstep of internal regulations.

The reformers of the past have tended to pile new rules on top of old ones as the preferred means of producing a better public sector (March and Simon 1957). Whenever anything went wrong in administering a program, the common reaction was to develop a new set of rules and procedures that would prevent the same problem from occurring in the future. Inevitably, new problems would arise that would require even more rules, and each set of internal regulations would create negative, unanticipated results that were solved by yet other rules. The argument of the deregulators is that internal rules for controlling the public sector are not the solution to the problems of governance; they are the fundamental problem.

Given that the diagnoses of the four models are different, the prescriptions offered for successful reform must also be different. In particular, the deregulatory approach, as that name implies, tends to focus most of its attention on changes in procedures within the public sector rather than on structures or the nature of the personnel who occupy administrative positions in government. The underlying assumption is that if the internal regulatory bonds that constrain its actions are loosened, then the bureaucracy will have the capacity and the willingness to make government function better. Advocates argue that this assumption is especially true for rules that cut across entire administrative systems, such as for civil service codes, but that it is also to some degree true of all internal controls within public organizations. The observation that rules that are developed within a single organization tend to be privileged is based upon the assumption that the rules were selected to meet the particular needs of that one entity instead of being designed to serve some central purpose.

Reformers, no matter how committed to their goals, should not expect government to become fully deregulated. Such a complete transformation is not going to happen, given the legitimate demands of the public for accountability and the real need of managers for some mechanisms for measuring and evaluating performance of their subordinates. The real questions, then, are how far can deregulation be extended, and what are the consequences of going down this road of change? There also may be important cross-national differences in how far deregulation can be extended. In Anglo-American countries, for example, the continuing distrust of and skepticism about the public bureaucracy may make such changes in the public sector difficult. Yet these are just the countries that may need the changes the most. In contrast, the Germanic systems may find this change relatively easy, given the limited amount of specific regulation imposed on the public sector and the capacity of the general code to handle most issues. Ironically, these are the countries that can profit least from such changes.

Deregulatory reforms must be considered in light of numerous other reforms that are being implemented in the same countries. Although these different types of reforms are sometimes advocated by the same people and appear similar to other types, at least on the surface, the changes proposed actually may be contradictory and antithetical. Wise reformers therefore must understand how their preferred administrative reforms correspond to the others being implemented and how one set of changes might be made to fit even better with the others. Moreover, they must find the political means to have these reforms accepted in the manner they desire. These are not easy tasks.

6
Can We Go Home Again?

The four alternative plans for moving government away from the traditional model of public administration have now been examined. Recommendations from some of the models are already being implemented widely; others are only in their nascent stages. Each case is implicitly or explicitly compared with the traditional model of administration and its clear separation of roles between administration and politics, a hierarchical management style and pyramidal structures, (largely) permanent organizations and career civil servants, and accountability through political means.[1] In each instance some or all of the old system is found to be deficient, and the reforms being proposed are intended to create a governing system that will function better. The political and analytic problem is that there are quite different definitions of what "better" might mean in this context.

For a capsule of the arguments already advanced emphasizing the multiplicity of government ills and possible solutions, see Table 6.1. Most if not all of the "dependent variables" for the reformers are the same. Many reformers want to address the same perceived shortcomings of government, for example, the remoteness of command and control regulation and the failures of program coordination. However, their strategies for addressing those perceived failings not only are quite different, but they also are often directly contradictory. Thus, selecting one option or the other should logically preclude simultaneous selection of other types of remedies.

Many of the problems that continue to arise in the application of one or another of these models are by no means novel. Coordination, for example, in almost all the cases is identified as a major problem. But it has been a problem for government ever since differentiated bureaucratic structures began to be developed. Some of the reforms being undertaken, most notably the creation of agencies to deliver programs, may exacerbate the inevitable coordination problems, yet they would still exist if governments were to return to an old-fashioned Weberian, ministerial bureaucracy.

111

Table 6.1. Answers to Basic Questions

	Market	Participation	Flexibility	Deregulation
Coordination	Invisible hand	Bottom up	Changing organizations	Managers' self-interest
Error detection/ correction	Market signals	Political signals	Do not institutionalize errors	Accept more error
Civil service systems	Replace with market mechanisms	Reduce hierarchy	Use temporary employment	Eliminate regulations
Accountability	Through market	Through consumer complaints	No clear recommendations	Through ex post controls

Similarly, the four models raise new issues about accountability and the public interest, but that concept has been a dominant, if not the dominant, concern for the designers of democratic political systems from their inception (Day and Klein 1987). These reforms, however, have not yet come close to solving the problems of evaluating public programs or of measuring and evaluating the performance of public officials. Indeed, many of the reforms being implemented place an increasing demand on evaluative systems that are, at best, imperfect reflections of how the public sector is performing (Cave, Kogan, and Smith 1990). In short, the problems are not new, even if the solutions do at times appear to be innovative or at least are marketed politically as such.

Nor are the reforms themselves particularly novel, either. Many of the same ideas for change have been lurking in government for decades, if not for centuries, and they keep reappearing, albeit with different names and slightly different twists. Take, for example, the idea of greater worker participation in public organizations, a concept that has been common in organizational and management theory since at least the 1940s. Likewise, the idea of empowering clients to participate more fully in making decisions about their own programs harks back at least to the days of urban programs such as Model Cities in the United States and the requirements for "maximum feasible participation" (Langton 1978; but see Moynihan 1969). The idea of enhanced organizational flexibility currently appears more viable, given contemporary information technology, but there have been attempts since at least the era of the New Deal to facilitate the creation and dissolution of organizations and to move people in and out of government positions more readily.

In pointing out that these ideas for change are not new I am not being excessively critical. Indeed, relatively few entirely new ideas about organizations and management are available for prospective analysts. Just as the problems appear ageless, so too do the solutions. As Simon (1947) has indicated, the solutions for organizational problems tend to come in opposing pairs, and almost inevitably reformers will argue that organizations have gone too far toward one end of the spectrum and will propose the opposite end as the solution (see also B. Peters 1996). When organizations become overly centralized, the obvious answer is to decentralize until the lack of control produced by that arrangement produces demands for a return to centralization; then the cycle starts again.

The standards by which success and failure of reforms would be judged are also not terribly new. Public-sector managers, with a few exceptions, have always wanted to produce policy outcomes efficiently and effectively, despite the denigration of traditional bureaucratic methods voiced by advocates of reform programs. Likewise, most reform efforts in democratic countries have valued the procedures by which policies are made as well as the substance of those policies. Reformers (while simultaneously enhancing procedural protections) also have wanted to reduce the infamous red tape and bureaucratization of public programs (Kaufman 1977; Crozier 1964). Perhaps most surprising in the midst of all this administrative change is that little systematic evaluation of reforms has been undertaken, especially of programs that allegedly are oriented toward improving the bottom line of the public sector (*FDA News* 1995). Generally, analysts really do not know what has been happening as governments invest huge amounts of time and energy to change themselves (but see Carter and Greer 1993).

Another especially surprising factor about the advocates of reform is their collective faith in manipulating formal structures and procedures. This (apparently naive) structuralism and proceduralism is in marked contrast to other components of the management and organizational literature that stress the need to transform the culture of an organization if there is to be successful long-term change in its functioning (B. Peters and Waterman 1982; Brooks and Bate 1994). An implicit target for many contemporary reforms is the traditional civil service culture or ethos, which is perceived (often incorrectly) to be excessively cautious, secretive, negative, or all three. There appears, however, to have been little attempt to replace that old culture with another culture or ethos, except perhaps to laud the entrepreneurial ideal (see Dunsire 1995, 25–33). This absence of an alternative ethos for the public service may be a great mistake for government (Kernaghan 1994). An alternative ethos is necessary because many of the reforms may be successful or palatable only if there is a value framework that supports them and that protects the public from the potential excesses of unrestrained managerialism in government.

THE IMPORTANCE OF CONTEXT

Before beginning a more thorough examination of the similarities and differences found among the four models, the importance of other dimensions for comparing administration and reform should be considered (B. Peters 1988). The context within which reform is being implemented is crucially important for understanding the ideas themselves and their relative success or failure in practice. One must therefore examine the impact of context on administrative change within two dimensions: time and the national setting.

Time

The four models for reforming bureaucracy are products of their age. A tautology, perhaps, but postmodernists might tend to deprive them of their context. The reforms represent at least two of the more important, and contradictory, contemporary patterns of thinking about government and public affairs. On the one hand, the market has become a shibboleth for anyone attempting to change government. Market-based economies and their brand of open competition were said to have demonstrated their superiority with the fall of the former Soviet bloc.[2] This alleged victory of the market has meant that its solutions have gained increased legitimacy as a means of solving all manner of social and economic problems and are applied almost without question.

On the other hand, the contemporary Zeitgeist appears in the participatory model, in all its varied forms. Just as for some analysts the market is the solution for all the world's ills, for other analysts the people would be capable of solving their own problems if large institutions—especially those of the public sector—would only get out of their way. Further, participation is seen to have value in and of itself so that any mechanism that fosters participation in organizations or between the mass public and government is automatically thought to be beneficial. Just as the marketeers are somewhat overly ambitious in their claims about the successes of competition (Self 1993), so too are the participators excessively romantic about the capacity of the average person to understand and solve the complex and multifaceted problems facing contemporary societies and their governments.

For both of these Zeitgeists, scarcity is a pervasive fact of life that conditions their behavior. Scarcity has always been a central component in economic thinking but has become more prominent in the thought on political economy since the middle 1970s (Rose and Peters 1978). This is partly a function of real insecurities about economic performance and partly a result of increased popular resistance to taxation (Botella 1994). The term "scarcity" here means that any thinking about how to make government function better must have as one of its principal components mechanisms for saving money and reducing the size of the public sector. For the marketeers this idea is central; the participators assume that the people should be allowed to decide on the balance between taxation and public expenditure.[3]

Neither approach advocates reforms based upon rationality and analysis (see Deleon 1994). Techniques such as program budgeting and management by objectives that were popular during the 1960s depended upon the application of highly rationalistic models of costs and benefits to the public sector, the end being to get the most "bang for the buck" for each unit of resource expended.[4] The Zeitgeist then was rationality and the belief that government could be made to work better if only the right analytic techniques were applied and their answers adopted into law. The governing style for the 1980s and 1990s, however, was more ideological. The proponents of the four models—especially of market reforms[5] and participation—advocate their brand of reform and do not talk about the application of analytic techniques to prove that their proposals will work. The proof is assumed to be self-evident; furthermore, the reforms are right simply because they are right.

The National Setting

The second important context for comparison is country. Most comparative politics use country as the unit of analysis, and in general this focus produces interesting and useful results. In this book the principal focus of analysis has been ideas, and country has been secondary. There are, however, significant differences among countries that merit some discussion. The ideas of reform have served as a relatively common stimulus to which the countries have responded, and the responses provide valuable insights into their administrative and political systems. Most of the examples of reforms provided here are derived from the Anglo-American parts of the world, but similar changes are being implemented in other developed and less-developed countries. This observation then leads to two relevant questions: Why are the Anglo-American countries the center of the reform universe? How do the reforms fare when they are taken from that context and placed into different political and administrative environments?

Of the two questions it is somewhat easier to answer the first one. The Anglo-American countries have been the home to much of the advocacy of free enterprise and the market while continental Europe has opted for a more restrained form of the mixed-economy welfare state even when conservative political parties are in power. Government (at least in the United States and Canada) has been more subject to influence from private-management consultants and other purveyors of reform ideas (A. Gray and Jenkins 1995, 85; O. White and Wolf 1995). Many of the reform techniques, such as Total Quality Management and strategic planning, have been imported directly from the private sector into government (Walters 1992c). Even when government is more closed to outsiders as it is in the United Kingdom, Conservative governments have become willing to use talent, Lord Rayner from Marks and Spencer, for example, from the private sector.[6]

Moreover, it can be argued that governments in the Anglo-American democracies required more assistance from several of the types of reform being advocated than did some other countries. The need for the reforms labeled deregulation may be especially apparent. Because of the public's pervasive distrust of government and the lack of integration of its bureaucracy into civil society, the tendency has been for rules to be laid on top of rules as a means of ensuring control over the system. Whereas some legalistic administrative systems, such as Germany's, can survive with a relatively compact administrative code, government in the United States (as perhaps the extreme example) developed thousands of pages of detailed personnel, budgeting, accounting, and procurement regulations. If government is to become more efficient, then perhaps there is a genuine need to clear away some of the underbrush of control and to permit the managers to get on with the business of managing.

Finally, because of the lack of a distinctive role assigned to the civil service constitutionally or in political theory (as would be found in most of continental Europe), the application of private-sector management techniques to the civil service is not a particularly radical action. To the extent that civil servants do have an elite position in society in the Anglo-American systems, it is because they have almost seized it instead of settling into it as a part of the state tradition. Therefore, treating them as one might treat employees in a bank or a shoe store has not been the insult that it might have been in Germany, France, or Scandinavia.

Nevertheless, these reforms have spread to countries where they might not be expected to be readily accepted. The market-based idea of pay for performance has been implemented successfully in Norway and Sweden where, all else being equal, one might have thought it to be anathema (Sjolund 1994a; Laegreid 1994). Other changes such as decentralization are also proceeding without excessive opposition (Pierre 1995b). Some of the ideas about creating agencies and decentralizing government have been adopted in the Netherlands, which has had a highly centralized government for a number of years (Kickert 1994). Even France, with its long history of administrative centralization, has begun to decentralize and deconcentrate government (de Montricher 1994), with the aim of increasing efficiency, participation, and service to the customer (Rouban 1991).

In many ways the countries in the Germanic tradition have been the least interested in reform. This reaction is especially true if reform implies embarking on an announced program of change and placing a good deal of political and administrative emphasis on altering the manner in which government is conducted. Certainly public administration in Germany has changed over the past several decades, as in the emphasis on *Burgernahe*. There has been much less adherence to fad and fashion than in other countries, however. This is partly because the administrative system has worked, even with the additional load of assimilating former East Germany (Derlien 1993; Goetz 1993). Further, the cooperative federal nature of German administration requires extensive bargaining among central and *Land* governments and therefore tends toward incremental solutions instead of the comprehensive answers advocated in most other countries.

COMMON PROBLEMS AND UNCOMMON SOLUTIONS

Several problems arise in relation to each of the proposed models of reform. Some of these are the endless searches for the philosopher's stone of providing perfectly coordinated and error-free government, problems that also plague other large, complex organizations. That timeless characteristic, however, should not disqualify them from serious consideration and from some analysis of the possible contributions of each model. There are three common problems identified in the discussions of the individual models: coordination, error detection and correction, and the fate of the civil service.

Coordination

Each of the four models offers a different view about the pursuit of coordination and coherence in the public sector. Among them they address at least in part the three principle strands of thought within social science about coordination: markets, hierarchies, and networks (see Maidment and Thompson 1993). Uniting the four is the common perception of the importance of this administrative value and the extent to which it is becoming even more difficult to achieve. Many of the reforms already implemented have helped create a greater need for coordinative structures and action while at the same time reducing to some extent the capacity of governments to coordinate effectively. In an increasingly complex and interdependent world, government appears to be squandering its capacity to present an integrated and coherent set of policies at the time that capacity is most needed.

For the market model the problem of coordination is not a separate managerial problem or at least is not recognized as a sufficiently significant one to warrant deviation from the basic model of decentralization and entrepreneurship. The market is lauded by true believers because it is a coordination device. The virtue of the free market is its ability to coordinate the independent decisions of purchasers and sellers to produce prices that clear the market. The assumption therefore is that the same logic could apply to the public sector if only activities there were sufficiently marketized. Thus, the creation of agencies and quasi-governmental bodies to carry out public functions should in principle be sufficiently controllable to be sustainable (Modeen and Rosas 1988), given the other associated virtues.

The implicit argument contained in the market approach to reform is that there should be enough efficiency gains from the application of market principles to justify any efficiency losses from reduced policy coordination. There is little evidence of the relative costs and benefits of those two possible outcomes, but market assumptions certainly would push in that direction. Thus, the application of the market model apparently will still leave a definite role for central agencies as instruments for imposing some common goals and directions on government. The basic model of the free market, for example, assumes that sellers and buyers do have common interests—exchange and profit—but for agencies with competitive purposes that exchange is not so easy to foster. These central bodies will continue to have a role in deciding just how government is to be cut up into agencies and then in attempting to knit their policies back together again.

The participatory model tends to visualize coordination as being driven from the bottom up rather than from the top down. In this view the best way to understand coordination is perhaps to think about it as being centered on the clients of programs rather than on the organizations that deliver the services and their bureaucratic relationships with one another. This view requires a population of clients who can articulate their demands effectively as well as a collection of organizations that is concerned with delivering more holistic services to them. The participatory approach to coordination may not entirely obviate the role of the central agencies, either. In some cases central agencies, such as the Office of Prime Minister and Cabinet in Australia, have organized themselves around client groups and the conventional functional policy areas in order to enhance coordination.

In its concern with coordination the flexible state model comes into its own. One of the central foci of this approach to governing is providing means for putting organizations together on a short-term basis in order to solve problems of coordination and coherence. The creation of virtual organizations and the generation of short-term task-force structures is one important way of integrating programs and generating comprehensive responses to the problems facing governments and their citizens. The flexible state approach is to some degree the apotheosis of network coordination, although it lacks some of the long-term interactions that some scholars associate with networks.

There is some question, however, as to whether the flexible perspective on governing is adequately prepared to cope with the persistent and continuing coordination problems arising in the public sector. The coordination question is not going to go away in a month or a year or ever, and therefore some coordination devices must remain for as long as there are programs to coordinate. Yet, flexibility may be necessary simply because the coordination questions change frequently, depending upon which political issues are at the top of the agenda. The organizations that need bringing together today may be very different from the ones that had to be coordinated yesterday, and making a coordinative device permanent may be as counterproductive as locking in any other organizational solution to policy problems.

Finally, proponents of deregulation argue that rules requiring coordination will not do the job adequately. The problem is that apparently there is little guidance coming from this approach to substitute for rules. If a major part of the ethos of the deregulatory model is to encourage individual managers to pursue their own organizational goals, then expecting them to invest in coordination with other equally aggressive and ambitious managers may be too much to ask. This approach to coordination, like that of the market approach, therefore must rely on an invisible hand. Thus the managers would recognize that they could reach their own goals more cheaply and effectively in the aggregate if they invested more in coordination.

The recognition of the collective interest of managers in promoting coordination would create a classic collective-action problem. Although all managers could benefit, each manager or organization or both would have little incentive to make the investment that would produce this collective benefit (Olson 1965). Entrepreneurs would be required who believe that they could gain enough from organizing the collective effort to justify the investment of time and other resources (Frohlich, Oppenheimer, and Young 1971). Managers whose own agencies were particularly affected by coordination problems or who somehow believe that they could advance their careers by being the organizers of the collective effort could play this role.

Coordination is a central and increasingly important problem for government. In some cases structural reforms have tended to exacerbate it, and there has not yet been a clear solution to this persistent difficulty. Much of the development of contemporary administrative structure and management seems to have progressed with little or no attention to putting the system back together again. The civil service ethos of the traditional system and top-down command generated more coordination than is sometimes perceived, but these concepts now have been lost in the pursuit of other values.

Error Detection and Correction

A second common problem addressed by the four models, albeit sotto voce at times, is error detection and correction. Organizations in government or in the private sector will inevitably make errors; too many decisions and too many people are involved to get it right every time. Moreover, many contemporary ideas about public-sector management stress the importance of risk-taking in environments that traditionally have been more conservative and risk-averse. If the new entrepreneurial wind is to blow through the public sector, then people must be willing to take some chances and to fail.

The idea of risk-taking in government runs counter to most political cultures and to bureaucratic traditions. The public sector is often expected to be error free, at least in the public's mind (Savoie 1994b; 1995a), partly because the taxpayers expect government to be responsible with their money. Further, the public sector is often concerned with the rights of citizens, not just with simple economic transactions. For these and other reasons, public-sector administrators and elected representatives find the admission of mistakes unpalatable and attempt to find ways to minimize or deny them. Most of the traditional methods for ensuring accountability are organized to expose errors and tend to be much less effective in finding ways to prevent them in the future.

Some of the errors occur in the formulation of policy responses to problems, others in the allocation of resources within the organization, and yet others in the implementation of programs. The public and many politicians tend to assume that problems arise in implementation and blame the bureaucracy, but many problems actually have their roots in an earlier part of the process. Since errors are inevitable, the real question is how to detect, minimize, and then correct them.

Dealing with error is particularly important for public-sector organizations, given the rather low opinion in which they are held by much of the population and the pressures from politicians to publicize and punish those responsible for errors.

Each of the four models provides its own distinctive perspective on the problem of detecting and eliminating errors in the public sector (see also Rose 1987a). As with so many other issues, the answer provided by the market model is the clearest and simplest but also perhaps the least effective. The assumption is that the market will take care of the problem, perhaps a somewhat hyperbolic statement but not too much so. If a market functions effectively, then the leadership of any organization in that market will know when an error has been made. That information will come through falling profits, loss of market share, or expressions of dissatisfaction by consumers. One of the presumed virtues of the market, in fact, is the numerous signals that it provides to its participants.

For organizations within the public sector operating within a market framework, or what passes for one, the information flow apparently is not as good as that assumed by the conventional models of the firm in neoclassical economics. In the first place, most of these public-sector organizations still function with a virtual monopoly on their service. The Passport Agency in Britain may be called an agency and may be separated from the Home Office, but there is no other place that a citizen can go to get a permit to travel abroad.[7] In these settings surrogate indicators—target service figures and benchmarks, for example—take the place of the usual market indicators. Targets apparently do not provide useful information for managers, partly because they often are manipulated by those very managers (Dopson 1993).

In the second place, many of the so-called markets within which public-sector organizations function are highly contrived so that adequate signals could hardly be said to be generated from the convoluted interactions of purchasers and providers. The quasi market developed within the National Health Service, for example, apparently does not generate enough information about costs or quality to guide doctors or hospitals that may be making errors to correct them (Birchall, Pollitt, and Putnam 1995). Further, there may simply be no realistic alternative to the particular purchaser or provider for a participant, unless the patient is trundled the length and breadth of the British Isles.

Consumerism in the market does provide some opportunities for error detection and correction, but even that device may have severe limitations. Most of the consumer standards used in government are generated by government itself and hence may be only those hurdles that organizations are confident they can jump. There may be less opportunity, albeit an increasing one, for citizens to define the performance standards that they would like to see established for each service. Moreover, many of the services that may be most prone to error may be the very ones for which consumer feedback is likely to be the most muted. Social service agencies, the best example, have relatively powerless clients who typically are quite reluctant to complain about poor services or abuses of discretion for fear they will lose their benefits (but see Goodsell 1981b).

The participatory model places its faith in the willingness of citizens to become active participants in the political and administrative processes. As a consequence, this model faces many of the same problems as those identified for the consumer in the market model. That is, the very people who may have the most to gain from participation may be the same people who are least likely actually to participate in the policy process. Given its democratic ethos, however, implementors of a democratic model may be more proactive and actually seek out participation rather than simply wait for the ideas and complaints to come into public organizations. That initiative can be supplemented by politicians who may have something to gain, even while in power, from promoting citizens' involvement and even citizens' complaints (Chubb 1992).

The participatory model does have the virtue, however, of seeking to involve the public at all stages of the policy process, not just in ex post complaints and feedback about the way in which a policy was executed. This active stance may allow errors to be corrected before they occur, although the decisionmakers will have to be open to innovative ideas that may be advanced, which is often not the case. Administrators' range of vision about policies tends to be constrained by their professional and organizational allegiances so that only a limited number of proposals can be fitted into the acceptable set. The scope of acceptable ideas may be somewhat greater for the instruments used to implement the program, but even then organizations tend to have commitments to tools as well as to policies (Linder and Peters 1993).

The flexible state model depends upon its very flexibility to generate the means for error correction. Its advocates would argue that errors are inevitable and that the only significant problems occur when those errors become institutionalized as a part of a permanent solution to a policy problem. If the idea of impermanence can be made paramount in the minds of institutional designers, then there is a consequent ongoing opportunity for continuous error correction and program improvement. Similarly, bringing people into government from outside organizations can be conceptualized as a part of the process of error correction. If the employees of government have become excessively set in their ways, then bringing in outsiders to challenge assumptions may be crucial to forcing new ways of thinking and correcting firmly institutionalized errors.

Finally, proponents of the deregulatory model have their own views on error correction. First, simply getting rid of the large number of unnecessary and counterproductive regulations within the public sector is a step toward ameliorating errors in and of itself. This assumption would be contested, however, by more traditional administrators who would see deregulation as eliminating rules intended to prevent errors by constraining the latitude of civil servants. Thus, the deregulatory approach appears to need some other means of identifying and addressing errors even though it seems more willing to accept error than other approaches to governing. It is insufficient in a democratic society simply to accept more errors in exchange for greater ease in doing business and for a government that responds more quickly.

Despite the presumed benefits of deregulation, therefore, this approach would have to apply some of the logic of the market and the participatory models. Its proponents, however, might not be as willing to allow decisions, and the definitions of error, to be determined primarily by citizen feedback. The operating assumption appears to be that if some of the ex ante controls are removed, then there will be more latitude for decisionmakers to function. In the deregulated vision, the decisionmakers should be able to implement their decisions without having to look over their shoulders too much, either at the public or at politicians. The slogan of much of the managerial reform in government has been "let the managers manage," but there are few clear statements of the criteria for any restraints that should be imposed upon their actions.

Lest this discussion of error correction appear to be too negative, I should point out that another managerial task, one that is discussed less frequently, is the detection of outstanding performance. Most administrative effort is directed toward correcting the negative anomalies of government, and most analytic time is spent on identifying irregularities (Pierre and Peters 1996). If the reform efforts do indeed merit the time and trouble invested, then there should be some exceptional outcomes to report and to emulate (T. Miller 1984). Government reform need not be about just preventing problems; it should also recognize when the experiments (and reforms are always experiments) do indeed bear fruit (D. Campbell 1988).

The increasing concern with applying performance measures in public administration is one means of addressing the search for exceptional performance. Although it is in many ways a welcome change in public management, the effort is not without its problems. There is some sense that these measures are more oriented toward the negative than the positive and are perhaps used more to punish than to reward. This may be entirely perceptual, but given that the measures are being applied at a time in which the public sector is reducing employment by a significant amount, it is not surprising that some people feel threatened by them.

The Civil Service

Each of the four approaches to reform must cope with a third problem: the civil service. The system was developed over decades to solve some important political and managerial problems, weaknesses that included political favoritism in recruitment, inadequately trained professional staff, and a lack of regular career paths for capable personnel. Generally, civil service laws and systems were extremely successful in meeting these objectives. Indeed, to their critics, these personnel systems were far too successful, having become overly institutionalized to the point that public managers could not adequately control their own staffs. Each of the four models sees the civil service as in need of reform, but from a distinctive perspective and as presenting somewhat different problems that require particular solutions.

For proponents of the market model the civil service is not conceived of as a service but as a group of self-aggrandizing individuals using public office and public money for their own purposes. The principal problem from the market perspective is that bureaucratic agencies and their permanent employees have established monopoly powers over particular domains within the public sector. Those monopolies have enabled each agency to extract excess money from the budget for its own purposes instead of using available funds to provide genuine public services. Thus, to these critics the civil service is a principal villain, if not the principal villain, in the story of how government grew too big (according to their own standards).

To rectify the problems, the civil service needs to be changed fundamentally, according to the market advocates. Primarily, they believe that the civil service needs to be disaggregated so that the traditional model of a career, integrated personnel system would be eliminated. Likewise, its reward system, in which all individuals in the same rank are paid the same, would be eliminated in favor of a more personalized regimen. Then the closed personnel system would be opened up to encourage or even to require more movement between the public and private sectors. This open-door approach is meant to ensure that the values and experiences of the public service would not be significantly different from the private sector.

For advocates of the participatory model, the civil service is not nearly so much a villain as it is for those of the market model. The former see the traditional civil service as a hierarchical system of ranks and grades and the participatory model as attempting to create greater equality within organizations. The civil service, of course, tends to be closed to outside applicants. But the market model is less concerned with inculcating market values into the system than it is with injecting those values into nonofficial groups in society, perhaps most importantly the clients of public programs. Still, the civil service, by granting tenure and permanence to its members, may in fact create an environment allowing for more participation and frankness than political appointees who were dependent upon the whims of their political masters would have.

Advocates of greater flexibility in governing view the civil service as a significant impediment to good governance. Almost by definition the civil service confers permanent employment upon its members. Thus, a personnel system organized around the civil service would make flexible personnel management and the use of more temporary employees difficult. Personnel management of that sort would not be impossible, and indeed most public personnel systems already are increasingly dependent upon temporary and part-time employees. Still, there are impediments to creating the type of flexibility envisioned by some of the more extreme versions of flexible government. Nevertheless, the career protection afforded by civil service systems may facilitate institutionalizing greater change in public organizations themselves. In most instances career civil servants do not have to worry about their jobs and therefore should be more willing to conceive of the rapid creations and terminations of organizations advocated by flexible government.

The deregulatory approach to reform appears to have some implications for the civil service similar to those of the market approach. They are derived, however, from rather different first principles. Both approaches seemingly would dismantle much of the legal and regulatory structure for personnel management in the public sector. The logic behind this dismantling for the market advocates is that it would allow for the imposition of greater discipline on public employees, making them more efficient and more in line with market principles. For the deregulators, the principal purpose of removing the personnel regulations is to release the creativity and energy of public employees so that government can be effective.

The similarity of the market and the deregulatory approaches, however, may be more apparent than real. The marketeers generally want to dismantle the civil service and the ethos that has supported it. They tend to regard the civil service as part of the cause of the isolation of public employees from the real world, that is, the market. The deregulators, on the other hand, in some way require a professional, career civil service for their reforms to be manageable. In order to be able to remove the ex ante controls over personnel, purchasing, and budgeting there must be an ingrained commitment to public service values and personal probity. That type of civil service is unlikely to be found in a public sector dominated by market principles.

The civil service system as it has been developed over decades is unlikely to disappear easily. The reforms that have been proposed would modify the existing system more or less extensively, but probably only the extreme version of the market approach would fully dismantle it. There will surely always be a need for a core of public employees who have gained substantial experience in making and administering policy. They must serve as the repository of values and organizational memory for the governing system. Indeed, if the plans for introducing greater flexibility into government are implemented, and increasing numbers of managers are recruited from outside the career system, then the career employees who remain in office will become that much more important.

MATCHING PROBLEMS AND SOLUTIONS

As well as perceiving numerous shared problems in government, the four approaches to reform are united in providing almost ideological conceptions of government and governing. In at least two of the models—the market and the participatory—the prescriptions for reform are indeed linked closely with these broader intellectual and ideological conceptions (Self 1993; Dryzek 1990; J. Wilson 1989). The other two models, however, tend to advocate one perspective or the other as an overall solution to governing problems rather than as a particular solution to a particular problem. The true believers in each camp seem to think that their particular remedy is the cure for all the ills of the public sector and to see the particular deficiency they recognize in government as pervasive.

I am arguing for the need for a more highly differentiated and contingent view of the problems and prospects for governing. There is some validity to all the positions advanced about the public sector, including the traditional notions that serve as the backdrop for the attempts at reform. The questions, then, are when and where is each reform's perspective of the greatest utility and how can we choose in advance. The history of contingency theories in the public sector has not been a very happy one, with most of the attempts to develop such approaches to problems and solutions failing (Greenwood, Hinings, and Ranson 1975a; 1975b; but see Dunsire and Hood 1989). Still, the contending approaches to reform call out for analytic attempts to relate them more closely to specific problems and situations (Pollitt 1995).

Matching the market model with particular situations, for example, would be perhaps the easiest part of the analysis. The public sector already provides a number of services that in principle are marketable (Rose et al. 1985). It is certainly true that a number of public corporations are making products—steel, airplanes, gasoline—or providing services—transportation, banking—that are marketed in many countries. Other services that are often considered as appropriately being in the public sector—education, pensions, health care—are in principle marketable, and some countries do provide them, in whole or in part, through the private sector. It seems logical, therefore, to think that there are a number of policy areas here for which the market model might provide a reasonable form of structuring for public services.

The marketization of services, however, may be limited by a conception of entitlement to the service. For example, although pensions may be readily marketable in principle, they may not be once government has begun to provide them through social insurance. Once citizens perceive that they have paid their premiums for the insurance (their payroll taxes), they believe that they have the right to collect that pension under the terms that have been operative for decades. Other programs, such as housing, that lack this contributory and entitlement characteristic may be converted into market programs much more readily.

The market model is also limited by being inappropriate for policy areas where efficiency is not really an immediate concern. Take, for example, preparing for unusual events and natural disasters. Organizations such as the Federal Emergency Management Agency (FEMA) in the United States prepare for eventualities such as earthquakes and hurricanes that are unpredictable and that may not occur for years. Some areas where planning of this sort goes on may never suffer a significant disaster. Proponents of the market approach to governance might argue that the preparation and stockpiling of resources is inefficient. Government might be better off in the long run (in economic terms) not to plan at all for these events but simply to cope with them when and if they do occur. Moreover, given organizations such as the Red Cross, the private sector might be able to handle the problems. Although FEMA clearly could be more efficient than it sometimes is, the answer of neglecting preparation is clearly not acceptable.

Certain types of programs and policies appear to require a more participatory mode of service delivery than do others. There has been some change in this direction in all policy areas across time, as most contemporary societies become more participatory (Berman 1995). Still, there are differences in the extent of participation being demanded. For example, education policy has almost always been an area that citizens, and especially parents, believe needs to be more open to their input. More recently issues of land-use planning and environmental issues, through the Not in My Back Yard (NIMBY) and Not Over There Either (NOTE) phenomena, have generated a great deal of public involvement in policies. These issues have also demonstrated some of the potential difficulties with encouraging participation, given the tendency for mobilized citizens to block any proposed solution, no matter how pressing the problem, such as the disposal of nuclear wastes.

The match between flexible organizational solutions and particular policies is somewhat less clear, but some points can still be made. Although it may be difficult to determine them in advance, some problems and policies will require greater linkage with other policies. Although on average the need for coordination appears to be increasing across all policy areas, policies such as drug enforcement and programs dealing with specific target populations—the elderly, youth, women, aboriginal peoples, immigrants—still require greater coordinative activity and greater flexibility. Likewise, it is relatively easy to identify programs that need seasonal employment, but it may be less clear which programs may be well run with seasonal employees (recreation, road repairs) and which may suffer if there is excessive seasonal and temporary employment (tax policy).

The deregulatory model in some ways applies across the entire range of the public sector. The argument is a general one: if there are fewer internal rules, government will function better.[8] Still, it is also clear that governments in the countries being discussed will almost certainly require some internal rules for purposes of accountability and democratic control, if not also for addressing some basic management requirements. The question then becomes which rules are appropriate or inappropriate for which organizations. One of the clearest targets for deregulatory reforms has been central agencies and their tendency to second-guess the line departments that actually deliver public services. Yet the central agencies are the actors charged with coordinating the program of the government of the day and with pursuing other goals (cost reduction, affirmative action) through their central positions in the policy process. How can those tasks be performed without using some internal regulatory devices?

The best way to think about imposing the deregulatory model may be to focus less on differences among organizations and more on differences among the rules themselves. In the first place, a number of rules in government are redundant. These rules are sometimes imposed on outside organizations and individuals, but occasionally they are imposed internally as well. Clearly, a deregulatory strategy should attempt to reduce redundant and contradictory rules. As a second step, the deregulators might want to attack rules that establish strict prohibitions or confining mandates and leave in place rules that set standards and goals for behavior. Deregulators indeed seem much more concerned about ex ante prohibitions than they do about ex post evaluations and even punishments.

Finally, one should ask if certain policy areas are more suited to deregulation than are others. The question is actually easier to answer the other way round: What policy areas are less suitable to deregulation? I would argue that the policy areas concerned with basic rights of citizens—criminal justice, civil rights, and so on—should be less subject to deregulation than policy areas concerned with simple economic benefits (or costs) of citizenship. The distinction between rights and economics is not always easy to maintain. The difficulty is clear in regard to many social and economic programs that are now defined as "entitlements" or "the new property" (C. Reich 1973; but see Epstein 1990) and in the crucial role that some programs play in maintaining the lives of some citizens. Still, there are marked differences between being denied free access to a park and being faced with capital punishment.

Weaknesses of the Approaches

In addition to identifying the particular applicability of one or another of the models of reform, I should also point to their relative weaknesses. Success may result from careful matching of approaches to problems. Yet it may be easier to prevent disasters by understanding what can go wrong, or what is likely to go wrong, and where the sources of failure reside for each model. For all the models the principal danger arises from overstepping the bounds and assuming that a mechanism that will work well for some policies and issues will work for all. Beyond that general problem there are some specific difficulties that arise from each model. The most fundamental weakness of the market model, for example, is that it assumes patterns of behavior that simply may not be present in the real world.

Empirical Implications

The contingencies for selecting one or another of the models of reform have been explored primarily from a normative perspective—what government should do.

One can also think of these contingencies as empirical predictions of success and failure, perhaps even empirical predictions about the adoption of one form of administrative change or another. It appears that policy areas have been differentially affected by reforms, with some—health care in the United Kingdom and land use in Canada as but two examples—being especially prone to them, albeit of different types. What qualities do these policies have that tended to place them at the center of controversies over government management and over which goals should be pursued through collective activity?

EXPLORING CONTRADICTIONS

One feature of the emerging patterns of governance that led to my writing this book was the sense that academics and practitioners alike were advocating a series of ideas about reform and that the ideas were being adopted willy-nilly. Further, they were being adopted without careful examination of the contradictions inherent in the disparate approaches. The problem was not a shortage of ideas about how to make government work better; the problem was too many ideas and not enough systematic thinking about which ones were applicable to particular situations and whether the ideas were compatible with one another. Government reformers were like candidates in a New York City election who go through the city eating pizza in an Italian neighborhood, pirogies in a Polish neighborhood, blintzes in a Jewish neighborhood, and enchiladas in a Hispanic neighborhood. Each of these is itself a tasty dish, but at the end of the day the politician is quite dyspeptic.

Some of the apparent problems with sorting out contradictions arise when different schools of reformers use the same terms but mean quite different things. People have a right to use the terminology they choose, but when the same term is used to imply different ways of solving a problem, then confusion results. Take, for example, the terms "consumerism" and "choice," which are central concepts in both the market and the participatory models. In both cases the terms imply an enhanced role for the citizen in the policy process, but they would achieve that goal through very different means (see Ranson and Stewart 1994, 74–76). Choice, for example, can mean either the right to make an individual choice in a quasi market providing a service or the right to participate in a political process that will make collective choices.

Many of the contradictions go well beyond semantics and involve fundamental differences about what is wrong with government and what should be done to fix it. When the discussion is carried on at the level of identifying problems and broad categories of interventions, the incompatibility of different ideas is obvious. Market advocates and participation advocates tend to begin with very different perceptions of the world and its problems, and their mutual lack of confidence in the other can become apparent rapidly. The contradictions are also probably

irrelevant because the theoretical discussions have little real impact on government until the ideas are converted into programs and mechanisms for making
policies work better.

When these more philosophical ideas are converted into specific proposals
for action, however, their roots are sometimes forgotten and the contradictions
are less obvious. Take, for example, a case in which reformers decide that the most
fundamental solution for their problem is empowerment of workers. That may
well be the case, and involving employees in their jobs and in their organizations
often produces real benefits for the workers and their organizations. Yet such a
reform would be incompatible with some of the ideas about flexibility on the job
and the creation of virtual organizations and virtual employees. Temporary employees would not be prepared to invest the time and energy required to participate effectively, not knowing just how long they would be a part of the organization. Further, treating employees as interchangeable parts of a machine is in
fundamental opposition to the organizational humanism of the participative
model (Donkin 1995). The example is not totally hypothetical; the human resource management report to the Gore Commission (National Performance Review 1993b) appears to contain all these ideas, and more.

HOW CAN WE INTERVENE?

Each of the four models has offered a diagnosis of the problem, and each has
had a solution. Yet each model appears to lack a clear strategy for intervention.
Changing an institutional structure as large as the public bureaucracy is a difficult chore; even changing one organization within it has been enough to defeat
some experienced and skilled practitioners (Szanton 1981). Therefore, success for
any (or potentially all) of these models requires careful attention to the strategy
and tactics of change.

Interestingly, to the extent that these models do have prescriptions about
how to intervene, they tend to favor (or actually assume) the use of political
power to force, or to encourage, the transformation. Although this strategy might
be expected in the market model, given its close connections with political leaders who had few compunctions about using political power, it is surprising in the
other three. Indeed, it seems to run exactly counter to the philosophy of the participative and the deregulatory models. The assumption appears to be that organizations must be forced to be participative and flexible, even if the pressing is
done by other organizations, such as central agencies, which are not noted for
their flexibility.

Another aspect of the strategies for intervention that appears somewhat surprising is the emphasis placed on formal structure and procedure. In each of the
four models it was easier to uncover the recommendations about structure and
formal rules within the organization than about any other aspect of the proposed

changes. What appeared to be lacking was an emphasis on organizational culture and on changing the way in which employees, managers, and clients thought about the organization. Although the strategy of changing organizational culture seems loose and inchoate, changing it may be at once extremely difficult and extremely rewarding, as has been argued in some of the private-sector literature (T. Peters and Waterman 1982).

The concept of "institutional negotiation" provides another way of looking at strategies for generating change in organizations (Zifcak 1994, 186–88). This view is similar to Allison's concept of bureaucratic politics (1971), although it would occur more within government instead of being directed toward some external policy goal. The fundamental idea is that any attempt to produce organizational change, especially when conducted systemwide as many of these programs are, will upset long-standing institutional arrangements and power configurations. Somebody is going to win and somebody is going to lose, and the probable losers will attempt to forestall the changes, using any legal mechanisms at their disposal (and perhaps a few more).

In reality most major administrative changes produce the political battles described so politely as "institutional negotiations." A more appropriate strategy for achieving enduring change, however, might not be imposition (especially imposition by a political or central-agency actor who is unlikely to lose) but more genuine bargaining and negotiation. This approach would appear to be a natural outflow of thinking about enhancing participation in organizations. Creating such a bargaining arena is difficult, especially given that many of the participants will be distrustful of at least some other participants—usually the central financial and management agencies. Still, if such a bargaining arrangement can be reached, then any outcomes are likely to be more enduring than those imposed upon unwilling victims.[9]

Zifcak (1994) discusses changing the "appreciative system" of an organization, or of the organizational environment of government, as a means of generating change. This approach is very much like producing cultural change but may go even further. The fundamental point is that organizations often operate the way they do because of their own self-images (Morgan 1986). Therefore, to produce meaningful change may require changing that self-image and with it the pattern of behavior. This view is similar to Schon and Rein's ideas (1994) of altering perceptual "frames" in order to produce meaningful policy change. They argue that individuals and organizations tend to become locked into one frame or another and therefore can not visualize alternative ways of doing things, much less implement them.

To generate this type of fundamental appreciative change, however, may require significant challenges to the existing ways of doing business in the public sector. Most administrative systems are locked into long-standing traditions and modes of thought that prevent their considering alternative conceptualizations. Developments in the environment of the public sector over the past several decades, however, have constituted sufficient shocks for many administrative systems to make them at least consider change. The loss of secure and seemingly endless tax funding for programs along with political assaults from leaders such as Reagan, Thatcher, and Mulroney have made the lives of public administrators much less comfortable than they had been. For other countries such as Germany, however, the stimuli for reform have been much less overt, and there may be no pressing reason to consider significant reform. In fact, the major change in German government and administration, reunification with the eastern *Länder*, has to some extent strengthened the dominant model of administration instead of weakening it (Konig 1993).

To the extent that reform initiatives are occurring through altering the appreciative systems of public organizations, conflict within those organizations almost certainly is being created. Conflict during times of organizational change is to be expected, but the measure that may differentiate change within the context of altering appreciative systems is the extent to which the issues raised will be based upon first principles. Different segments of an administrative structure within the public sector may have extremely different fundamental beliefs about the role of government, the most effective ways to manage organizations, and the role of the civil service in providing governance. Attempting to reconcile these disparate internal views and still make an organization function will be a continuing challenge for public managers in the foreseeable future, and probably forever.

Even if the participants in government wanted to, could they ever return to the comfortable system, now largely lost, of running the state? To some degree the emphasis on management, on the greater political reliability of civil servants, on the empowerment of staff and clients, and on flexibility drives the political system toward an alteration of the tacit social contract that had existed among the participants in governance. No longer are politicians willing to cede some control over policy to their civil servants in exchange for the expertise and skills of the permanent staff. Likewise, civil servants do not appear to be willing to accept job security in exchange for relatively low pay, loss of real influence over policy, and a diminution of their professional standing (whether real or only perceived on their part).

Both sides of this contract can gain some advantages from the changes in their relationship, although the advantages appear to go primarily to politicians and secondarily to previously disadvantaged tiers within public organizations. Similarly, the principal disadvantages of reform appear to accrue to the senior civil service. Politically, then, returning to the status quo ante may be virtually impossible. The one group most disadvantaged by the changes also may have the least legitimacy with relevant groups other than itself. It lacks connections with the public either electorally or as the direct provider of services, so that generating any movement to restore the (self-perceived) rightful place of the senior bureaucrat is unlikely to stir many hearts among the public. Nevertheless, governance may be better served by some attention to the experience and expertise that these senior career leaders in the public sector can provide.

If there is to be a return to the bureaucratic Garden of Eden, then a strong restatement of the desirability of that move will be required. Given that the public service is not the most popular element of government in most political systems, there is probably not a natural constituency for such a move. Therefore, political activity is required to produce the movement. This can be justified in part through the traditional values of neutrality and competence in the civil service and the need to stress values such as public service instead of thinking of government as providing services like any other business. The waning of market ideology in a number of other Western countries may initiate public discourse on ideas of public service in a way not possible recently.[10]

The role of public administration in governance is perhaps the most significant aspect of a reassertion of the function of the public service. Still, one must contrast the role of the civil service as expressed through the ideology of the traditional model of governance to the reality of that role within the model in practice. The existence of a powerful and entrenched civil service essentially created the conditions for a strong policy role for that bureaucracy. Although the market model in particular would appear to give somewhat enhanced power to the civil service, any redistribution of power would be in the role of manager rather than as policymaker and adviser. Indeed, the practice of the market model has been to attempt to centralize power in the political leadership and to limit the autonomy of the presumably entrepreneurial actors created by the reforms.

The traditional model of the public service and its role in government, however, is more than merely a rationalization for civil servants to make policy. It is also a statement of basic values about matters such as probity, accountability, and responsibility, values about which the present alternatives, and the market model in particular, have little to say. The concept of a permanent and professional civil service providing policy advice as well as management is seen by advocates of the traditional model as almost a sine qua non for good government. Traditionalists see the civil service as embodying the mechanisms for providing citizens (and politicians) both the best advice and the best service. Although critics perceive the permanence of the bureaucracy as a severe problem, its advocates see it as the source of stability, reliability, and predictability. Organizational permanence is also seen as the best means of ensuring that government can be held accountable for its actions.

The discussion has focused on these four models as distinct alternatives for organizing the entire public sector, but another way to consider them is to think of the possible desirable matches between particular governmental tasks and the alternative forms of organizing and managing (J. Wilson 1989). It may well be that for the provision of certain marketable services the market model is adequate and desirable, but that same model would be totally inappropriate for many social services, for example, education. Likewise, the participatory model would be well suited for urban planning or environmental issues but would produce difficulties for many criminal justice programs. The flexible model probably would work well for complex issues such as the drug problem and also for transient concerns such as disaster relief. Although attempts at complex contingency theories for public administration appear to have generated relatively little benefit, one should still think about ways of making the punishment fit the crime.

My purpose is not so much to force choices among the alternative models of governance but to make the implications of the choices that now face governments more evident. To the extent that these models have been implemented in the real world (particularly the market model) they have been put forward for ideological reasons as much as from any thorough and impartial consideration of their relative merits. Each of the four alternatives does have its merits, but each also will impose some costs on society and on actors involved in government. Any choice of paradigms for government and administration is unlikely to be Pareto optimal, but the benefits and sacrifices should be clear in making judgments about governance.

Perhaps most fundamentally, analysts and citizens alike should ask which components of the old system, once abandoned, are worth saving. Clearly some critics would say absolutely nothing should be salvaged and would be quite willing to throw it all out and start anew. It should be obvious by now that I am less sure of the vices of the old system or confident in the virtues of the alternative replacements. The old system did place a high value on accountability and on service to the public as a whole, if not always to each individual client or customer. Those values are crucial for any public organization and should not be dismissed without adequate reflection. Through this book I hope to stimulate more of that necessary reflection.

Notes

1. CHANGING STATES, GOVERNANCE, AND THE PUBLIC SERVICE

1. We should separate imperialism *within* government—organizations fighting for control of problems and budgets—from more overt imperialism—government searching for problems to solve. The former is much more common than the latter.

2. There may now be a substitute consensus developing around the market (Grice 1995).

3. Nixon did, of course, attempt to curb some of the power of the existing bureaucracy and can hardly be considered a benign figure in American politics, but it is also too easy to ignore some of his domestic policy achievements.

4. For an excellent discussion of the (no longer?) conventional wisdom, see K. Walsh and Stewart (1992) for the United Kingdom and Stillman (1991) for the United States.

5. The implementation of merit ideals has been far from perfect in many of these settings, but the principles do tend to be enshrined in law.

6. It should be remembered, however, that at least for Wilson and the other Progressives, public administration was superior to politics: administration could be studied and reformed scientifically; politics was more an art (see Doig 1983).

7. The Republican Contract with America is pledged to reduce the volume and intrusiveness of rulemaking activity, but that may be difficult to do in any modern government.

8. Indeed, the most radical use of the variety of market-based reforms available to government was implemented by the Labour government of New Zealand (Scott, Bushnell, and Sallee 1990). More recently, the Social Democratic government in Sweden has undertaken a number of market-oriented changes in governance, and Tony Blair, leader of the Labour party in Britain, now accepts many of the administrative changes imposed during the Thatcher years.

9. Even some Conservatives now argue that the same excesses have occurred during the privatization of public utilities in the United Kingdom, as directors have awarded themselves massive salary increments with little or no control (Riddell 1995). The tales of scandals in privatized firms in Italy are also legion.

10. This autonomous role is not unfamiliar in the United States but is extremely unusual and threatening in Westminster systems. The Ponting affair in Britain and the Al-Mashat case in Canada are important examples of the significance of this change in the Westminster norms of governing (Chapman 1993; Sutherland 1991).

11. This pattern is already used rather widely in several European systems (see, for example, Fournier [1987] and his discussion of coordination within French government). In other settings—task forces, projets de mission, Projektgruppen, and a variety of other organizations—devices are used to coordinate and manage cross-cutting issues (Timsit 1988).

12. When there have been such attempts, the record appears to indicate that they have closed down generally as intended. Even if they did not, the real culprit would appear to be the legislatures that continued to fund them.

13. This is similar to the Tiebout model of local taxation and expenditure in public finance (see Tiebout 1956).

14. This reaction has been true even in Britain and Canada, which have histories of more deferential political cultures (see Taggart 1995).

15. This is to a great extent a function of the shifts of employment in Western countries from manufacturing to service, a shift linked with the globalization driving other aspects of these changes.

2. MARKET MODELS

1. For good reviews, see Wright (1994).

2. In these cases the market model is generally not adopted autonomously but is imposed by granting agencies, such as the World Bank and the International Monetary Fund, seeking to ensure that their money is used effectively.

3. This is not to say that some members of the administration, such as David Stockman, were not willing to press those ideas but only that at the top there was more of a vague ideology rather than a real set of intellectual principles (Stockman 1986, 9). Reagan appeared to practice the "politics of impulse" rather than the politics of ideas.

4. Some of these critiques pertain specifically to the model's application to the public sector, others to its applicability for private-sector organizations.

5. This group includes some analysts who would not normally be associated with the political right.

6. The self-interest of bureaucrats does not differentiate them from other individuals. The problem is the assumption, inherent in the traditional model, that members of the public service will necessarily act in the public interest.

7. This discussion runs counter to H. Simon's (1947) famous argument that administrators will be satisfiers rather than maximizers. That is, they will seek solutions that are "good enough" rather than those that are optimal.

8. Firms may, however, compete over quality rather than just price. No two products or services are exactly identical; thus the customer may choose according to price, quality, or other attributes.

9. In practice, governments have established redundant organizations and allowed them to compete. For example, Franklin Roosevelt's New Deal had a number of organizations performing approximately the same duties.

10. For the regulated, redundancy may enable them to play one agency off against the other. For example, both the Federal Trade Commission and the Antitrust Division of the Department of Justice enforce antitrust laws in the United States, with some leeway for firms to "choose" one over the other (see B. Peters 1996).

11. Britain has attempted to create some competition among its water and electricity companies, but even these are segmented regionally so that no effective competition exists.

12. This artificial creation, in the view of the New Public Management, could be used to enable civil servants to enhance their own position. Thus, this approach to the role of the market in public affairs is not entirely distinct from the first one discussed.

13. They usually want to export these techniques at a profit.

14. The United States also has a tradition of autonomous agencies within the cabinet departments, although that autonomy is derived as much from political realities as from institutional design (Seidman and Gilmour 1986).

15. Devolving services to lower levels of government is sometimes seen as a solution to many problems, but often may be simply substituting one hierarchy and one bureaucracy for another.

16. Apparently, large corporations in the private sector had an equal, or greater, propensity to reward middle managers with corporate welfare, and, like the public sector, are being forced to change (see Sampson 1995).

17. Pay in the public sector has tended to be somewhat more egalitarian than in the market, with lower echelons paid better than the going market rates and senior managers being paid substantially less than people with equal responsibilities in the private sector (S. Smith 1977; Sjölund 1989).

18. Actually, in the private sector there appears to be an inverse relationship between performance of businesses and the rewards of top managers, as noted in the *Economist,* "Failure-Related Pay," 2 September 1994, 22.

19. In the Department of Social Services in the United Kingdom, for example, overhead services such as information technology are devolved to a separate organization, which then charges other agencies for its services.

20. The United States has been a visible laggard in this regard but is considering modernization of its budgetary processes (see Paul L. Posner, Budget Structure: Providing an Investment Focus in the Federal Budget, Testimony to House Committee on Government Reform and Oversight, 29 June 1995).

21. In Canada the same types of reviews are being undertaken by the Chretien government, more at the initiation of the government itself than through the Treasury as in Britain. In the United States the Department of Defense has been engaging in a review of its spending from the bottom up.

22. Private-sector contractors appear to do well when bidding for routine functions such as janitorial services, managing food services, and so on, but they do much less well for more policy-focused activities or for delivering more complex services.

23. That entrepreneurship would probably be frowned upon if the creativity cost more money. Further, this is risky behavior that may ultimately cost money even when attempts are made to "make" or save money. The risk element of the market model is sometimes ignored when its proponents advocate moving to marketlike provision of services.

24. Those of us who deal regularly with airlines and Blue Cross–Blue Shield may consider being treated like the customer of a private concern to be a threat.

25. It is interesting, however, that some of the countries most satisfied with their educa-

tional systems are virtual state monopolies, e.g., France and Japan. Perhaps some other variable is to blame for the perceived poor performance of American and British education.

3. THE PARTICIPATORY STATE

1. Following the Conservative party defeats in spring 1995, Prime Minister John Major made several tours around Britain to try to find out what the people wanted (Baggott 1995).

2. Perhaps the most important alternative description would be communitarianism, although that model appears to lack some of the direct participatory ethos that motivates this particular conceptualization.

3. This view is in sharp contrast to the conception of the public primarily as the consumers of public services, as in the market approach.

4. Jack Kemp as secretary of Housing and Urban Development in the United States is a prime example. He was a pioneer in efforts to debureaucratize housing projects and to permit tenant self-management. For a discussion of debureaucratization of housing projects, see Hula (1991).

5. Like advocates of the market approach, these scholars tend to assume that public and private organizations are the same. It should be pointed out that this group is basing their assumptions on human behavior in organizations rather than on a set of techniques.

6. TQM is market oriented in the sense that it is designed to increase productivity and improve products, but its logic is not that of monetary incentives.

7. Most Americans regard the title of this organization as an oxymoron.

8. The limited evidence available indicates that the situation is not as positive in the less developed systems (see Goodsell 1976).

9. Although somewhat beyond the scope of this book, the same paradox holds true for elected officials, at least in the United States. Voters hate Congress but love their individual congressman.

10. The term "contravention" actually comes from Simmel (see Gillin and Gillin 1948).

11. The Food and Drug Administration is required to use a formal rulemaking procedure, a public hearing in which evidence is taken from interested parties and then a formal ruling on a drug license is issued. The errors that are made tend to be in refusing to license potentially useful drugs rather than in licensing harmful ones.

12. As the street-level bureaucracy people would argue, however, determining how to do something is often determining what that something really is.

13. The United States allows more participation than do most other Anglo-American countries, including allowing broad participation even in court decisions through amici briefs (Caldeira and Wright 1990). And even the former East German regime used consultation as a means of legitimation, although certainly not of real policy formulation (Boyle 1994).

14. The leader of the Labour party in Britain went so far as to praise, albeit in guarded terms, the actions of the British Conservative party in creating organizations of this type.

15. Of course, within Europe there will also be differences. The Scandinavian countries are accustomed to opportunities to express grievances about government, but German and British citizens may be more reluctant to do so.

16. This language is usually reserved for the implementation process but can also be applied to the process more generally (see B. Peters 1994).

17. Market advocates argue that the market does provide the strongest control, the capacity for customers to take their business elsewhere. Monopolies in the public sector eliminate that restraint.

18. The language comes from the 1946 U.S. Administrative Procedure Act.

19. Cooptation is not meant to be a pejorative term here but only a description of the manner in which groups and individuals are made parts of a larger program. In these cases there is really a form of mutual cooptation.

20. This study was performed before the current spate of interest in empowering individuals and organizations. It is difficult to ascertain just what the differences might be after that cultural change.

21. In fairness, other scholars of coordination of organizations, such as Mary Parker Follett (1941) and Russell Hardin (1982), have also noted the extent to which zero-sum games emerge in interactions among organizations.

22. The fear of technocracy is a long-standing concern of scholars committed to participatory and democratic values in public policy (see, for example, Ellul 1980 and Meynaud 1969).

4. FLEXIBLE GOVERNMENT

1. Aberbach, Putnam, and Rockman (1981, 67-71) found that the large majority of public employees in the developed democracies they studied had spent almost none of their working lifetimes outside central government. This varied substantially by country, with almost no British civil servants working elsewhere but half of German civil servants having such experiences. In other countries, e.g., France and Japan, public managers frequently leave government for lucrative positions in the private sector, but there is little flow in the other direction.

2. One interesting manifestation of this trend is the demand for term limits for public officials in the United States. The idea appealed to politicians more when they were on the outside than it did after they were elected, and the initial proposals were defeated in the House of Representatives in March 1995.

3. Interestingly, some of the public-choice literature has been seeking means of designing organizations that will be conservative and that will preserve the same policies over time (McCubbins, Noll, and Weingast 1989).

4. This self-delusory activity is not confined to public-sector organizations. Some private-sector firms have persisted in losing their way even in the face of overwhelming evidence. These instances often result when organizations have performed well at one time but are then incapable of responding to change.

5. For Niskanen and his allies, permanence appears to have been assumed as a part of the argument, but the important dynamic forces were monopoly and the ability to mask the true costs of production from the sponsor.

6. One argument is that public spending will go up more rapidly than private-sector spending because of the lower returns to capital investment (Baumol 1967). The revolution in information technology, however, may have made that argument outmoded.

7. The assumption is probably more fallacious given that any policy that has survived

for some period of time must be doing something right. There are anecdotal examples to the contrary, but on average the evaluative mechanisms of government are not totally inadequate.

8. The possibility that private-sector employees and their organizations might understand government better does not appear to be a part of the thinking, although it is certainly an equal possibility.

9. Temporary employment has been most obvious at managerial levels (Mackenzie 1987) but is also true for other positions at all levels of government.

10. The usual models of "bounded rationality" may not be applicable since we are asking decisionmakers to think about fundamental shifts from the status quo rather than marginal adjustments.

11. State and local governments in the United States have already made more moves in this direction with sunset laws and other devices that force relatively frequent reconsideration of the existence of their organizations. The assumption is that unless an organization is reauthorized, it will go out of existence automatically, which reverses the usual presumption that unless an organization is actively terminated it will remain in existence.

12. It has been argued, for example, that budgetary reforms such as Planning, Programming Budgeting System (PPBS) failed because they threatened organizations (Wildavsky 1978). The perhaps excessive focus on organizations tended to undermine what could have been an important change in the budgetary system.

13. An increasing number of accountability issues in the public sector have to do with private-sector firms and individuals, not members of the public sector itself, using public money inappropriately.

14. It is not clear that governments ever can be sure of an outcome, but certainly the outcomes of some programs are more predictable than others.

15. Dror has discussed policymaking as "fuzzy gambling," derived from the ideas of fuzzy sets in mathematics. In this view, decisionmakers do not know the parameters of the risks that they are assuming. Given the lack of knowledge about probabilities in some important policy areas, e.g., nuclear regulation, the term is appropriate.

16. "Minimax" is a term drawn from game theory meaning that one optimal strategy for a player may be to "minimize maximum losses."

17. As something of a record, the Defense Public Works Division of the Federal Works Agency remained in existence only sixteen days before being absorbed into a larger organization (see B. Peters and Hogwood 1988).

18. The phrase is usually attributed to Justice Louis Brandeis. The exact quote: "It is one of the happiest incidents of the federal system that a single courageous state may, if its citizens choose, serve as a laboratory, and try novel experiments without risk to the rest of the country" (*New State Ice Co. v. Liebmann,* 285 U.S. 262, 311 [1932]).

19. A classic example is the Renegotiation Board, established to monitor excessive profits from defense contracts in the Korean War but was not terminated until 1979 (see Kaufman 1976; 1991).

20. Arguably, after some period of existence, organizational motivations become less concerned with their clients and more simply focused on self-preservation, regardless of the needs and wishes of the clients.

21. This argument is, of course, exactly the opposite principle of Rawls's (1972) "justice principle," in which the interests of the least advantaged should be considered paramount in determining policy.

22. The reverse problem is a program that has positive benefits in the short term, but those benefits decay over time to the point that the beneficiaries become no different from members of the population who had not been beneficiaries.

5. DEREGULATED GOVERNMENT

1. The abuses of military purchasing rules have been most notorious, e.g., $800 toilet seats, but some of the same restraints (and apparent silliness) also have applied in domestic policy sectors. The ash tray example that Vice-President Gore developed as a part of Reinventing Government in the United States pointed clearly to some of the dysfunctions of purchasing controls.

2. The budget game tends to be that managers do not want to underspend lest they be seen not to need the same amount of money (or more) in the next budget year. Therefore, the last weeks of the budget year often find somewhat ill-considered expenditure decisions being made just to get rid of the money.

3. Of course, citizens in any country will complain but perhaps not with the intensity recently encountered in Anglo-American systems.

4. We may question whether any such powerful indicators exist for public programs.

5. There was, of course, also a financial reason for cutting back on evaluators. If the goal was to reduce the size of government employment, cutting evaluators could achieve that end without directly affecting service delivery.

6. One possible counterargument would be that the new rules are conceptualized as aids to managerial decisionmaking rather than as ex ante controls.

7. This is, of course, the classic problem of "displacement of goals" in public organizations, or indeed in any highly structured organization.

8. This assumption is in many ways a reworking of the old Theory X and Theory Y arguments about human nature within organizations. Deregulating is not necessarily premised on a pessimistic view of human nature, but it is not based on the assumption that public employees are clamoring to be made more personally liable for their actions.

9. By negative redistribution I do not mean any normative claim but only that the more affluent will become even more so and the less affluent even less so.

10. This statement assumes that these goals are relatively unpopular. For some politicians, such as, those with strong ties to minorities and women, the goals may be very popular, and the politician may want to push to deliver these programs more visibly. The politician will, however, have a higher probability of having the programs implemented through the less obtrusive means.

6. CAN WE GO HOME AGAIN?

1. These attributes are more characteristic of administration in the Anglo-American democracies than in other countries, but these features do have some applicability in all industrialized democracies.

2. Henry Mintzberg (1979), however, makes the point that it was not the market that triumphed but balance between the market and political forms of allocation. Not even the United States could be said to have been a truly free market.

3. That exercise is doomed to be disappointing to the advocates of participation, given that the public tends always to choose lower taxes and higher expenditures.

4. In France, is it "frappe for the franc"?

5. Terms such as Thatcherism and Reaganism came to be applied to the reforms implemented during the 1980s, and some of the market reforms advocated by Republicans after the 1994 elections have a pervasive ideological, extrarational element.

6. Lord Rayner was brought in to manage a series of efficiency scrutinies. Most of the work was done by young civil servants but they were directed by him, the outsider (Warner 1984).

7. In fact, before the creation of the Passport Agency, British citizens could obtain short-term passes from their local post offices to travel to the Continent. That practice was eliminated as "inefficient" by the Passport Agency.

8. This is, of course, an overstatement, but like all hyperboles it is intended to make a point.

9. The idea of envelope budgeting in Canada shares some similarities with this idea. This system made an initial allocation of funds to a number of large "envelopes" and then charged the ministers within that broad policy area to negotiate among themselves over the allocation among the programs.

10. John Major's government is substantially less ideological than the Thatcher government before it, the Tories may soon lose in Canada, the right-leaning Schluter government has lost office in Denmark, and so on.

Bibliography

Aberbach, J. D., R. D. Putnam, and B. A. Rockman (1981). *Politicians and Bureaucrats in Western Democracies.* Cambridge: Harvard University Press.

Aberbach, J. D., and B. A. Rockman (1976). Clashing Beliefs Within the Executive Branch: The Nixon Administration Bureaucracy. *American Political Science Review* 70: 456–68.

—— (1988). Mandates or Mandarins? Control and Discretion in the Modern Administrative State. *Public Administration Review* 48: 607–12.

—— (1989). On the Rise, Transformation, and Decline of Analysis in U.S. Government. *Governance* 2: 293–314.

Adler, M., and S. Asquith (1981). *Discretion and Power.* London: Heinemann.

Adler, M., A. Patch, and J. Tweedie (1990). *Parental Choice and Educational Policy.* Edinburgh: University of Edinburgh Press.

Agresta, R. J. (1994). OPM Needs a Mission—Not a Funeral. *Government Executive* 26 (9): 70.

Alexander, E. R. (1992). A Transaction Cost Theory of Planning. *Journal of the American Planning Association* 58: 190–200.

Allard, C. K. (1990). *Command, Control and the Common Defense.* New Haven: Yale University Press.

Allison, G. T. (1971). *The Essence of Decision.* Boston: Little, Brown.

—— (1987). Public and Private Management: Are They Fundamentally Alike in All Unimportant Respects? In *Classics of Public Administration,* ed. J. M. Shafritz and A. C. Hyde. Homewood, IL: Dorsey.

Almond, G. A., and H. D. Lasswell (1934). Aggressive Behavior by Clients Toward Public Relief Administrators. *American Political Science Review* 28: 643–55.

Altfeld, M. F., and G. J. Miller (1984). Sources of Bureaucratic Influence: Expertise and Agenda Control. *Journal of Conflict Resolution* 28: 701–30.

Andersen, N. A. (1994). Danmark: Förvaltningspolitikkens utvikling. In *Förvaltningspolitik i Norden,* ed. P. Laegreid and O. K. Pedersen. Kobenhavn: Jurist-og Økonomforbundets Forlag.

Anheier, H. K., and W. Seibel (1990). *The Third Sector: Comparative Studies of Non-Profit Organizations.* Berlin: De Gruyter.

Argyris, C. (1964). *Integrating the Individual and the Organization.* New York: Wiley.

Ascher, K. (1987). *The Politics of Privatization: Contracting Out Public Services.* London: Macmillan.

Ashton, C. (1993). A Focus on Information Overload. *Managing Service Quality* (July): 33–36.

Atkinson, A. B., and J. E. Stiglitz (1980). *Lectures on Public Economics.* New York: McGraw-Hill.

Aucoin, P. (1990). Administrative Reform in Public Management: Paradigms, Principles, Paradoxes and Pendulums. *Governance* 3: 115–37.

Australia (1992). *Performance Assessment of Policy Work, Report of the Working Group.* Canberra: Australian Government.

Bachrach, P., and M. S. Baratz (1962). The Two Faces of Power. *American Political Science Review* 56: 947–52.

Bachrach, P., and A. Botwinick (1992). *Power and Empowerment: A Radical Theory of Participatory Democracy.* Philadelphia: Temple University Press.

Baggott, R. (1995). From Confrontation to Consultation Under John Major? *Parliamentary Affairs* 48: 485–502.

Baldersheim, H. (1993). Kommunal organisering: Motar sel, men ressursar avgjer? In *Organisering av Offentlig Sektor,* ed. P. Laegreid and J. P. Olsen. Bergen, Norway: Tano.

Ban, C., and P. W. Ingraham (1984). *Legislating Bureaucratic Change: The Civil Service Reform Act of 1978.* Albany: State University of New York Press.

Banks, J. S., and B. R. Weingast (1992). The Political Control of Bureaucracies Under Asymmetric Information. *American Journal of Political Science* 36: 509–24.

Barber, B. (1984). *Strong Democracy: Participatory Politics for a New Age.* Berkeley: University of California Press.

Barker, A. (1994). Enriching Democracy: Public Inquiry and the Policy Process. In *Developing Democracy: Comparative Research in Honour of J. F. P. Blondel,* ed. I. Budge and D. McKay. London: Sage.

Barker, A. P. and B. G. Peters (1993). *The Politics of Expert Advice.* Pittsburgh: University of Pittsburgh Press.

Barnes, M., and D. Prior (1995). Spoilt for Choice? How Consumerism Can Disempower Public Service Users. *Public Money and Management* 15 (3): 53–58.

Barzelay, M. (1992). *Breaking Through Bureaucracy.* Berkeley: University of California Press.

Baumol, W. J. (1967). The Macroeconomics of Unbalanced Growth. *American Economic Review* 57: 415–26.

Behn, R. D. (1991). *Leadership Counts: Lessons for Public Managers from the Massachusetts Welfare, Training and Employment Program.* Cambridge: Harvard University Press.

—— (1993a). Customer Service: Changing an Agency's Culture. *Governing* 6 (12): 76.

—— (1993b). Performance Measures: To Reward or to Motivate? *Governing* 6 (10): 84.

Bendor, J. S. (1985). *Parallel Systems: Redundancy in Government.* Berkeley: University of California Press.

—— (1990). Formal Models of Bureaucracy: A Review. In *Public Administration: The State of the Discipline,* ed. N. Lynn and A. Wildavsky. Chatham, NJ: Chatham House.

Bendor, J., S. Taylor, and R. Van Gaalen (1985). Bureaucratic Expertise and Legislative

Authority: A Model of Deception and Monitoring in Budgeting. *American Political Science Review* 79: 1041–60.

Benson, J. K. (1982). A Framework for Policy Analysis. In *Interorganizational Coordination,* ed. D. L. Rogers and D. A. Whetten. Ames: Iowa State University Press.

Berman, E. M. (1995). Empowering Employees in State Agencies. *International Journal of Public Administration* 18: 833–50.

Beyme, K. von (1993). Regime Transition and Recruitment of Elites in Eastern Europe. *Governance* 6: 409–25.

Bipartisan Commission of Entitlement and Tax Reform (August 1994). *Interim Report to the President.* Washington, DC: Government Printing Office.

Birchall, J., C. Pollitt, and K. Putman (1995). Freedom to Manage: The Experience of the NHS Trusts, Grant-Maintained Schools and Voluntary Transfers of Public Housing. Paper presented at UK Political Studies Association, York, 18–20 April.

Black, J. (1993). The Prison Service and Executive Agency Status—HM Prisons PLC? *International Journal of Public Sector Management* 6: 27–41.

Blau, P. M. (1960). Orientation Toward Clients in a Public Welfare Agency. *Administrative Science Quarterly* 5: 341–61.

Bleeker, S. E. (1994). The Virtual Organization. *Futurist* 28: 9–12.

Blondel, J. (1988). Ministerial Careers and the Nature of Parliamentary Government: The Cases of Austria and Belgium. *European Journal of Political Research* 16: 51–71.

Blumann, C., and A. van Soligne (1989). La commission, agent d'exécution du droit communitaire: La Comitologie. In *La commission au couer du système institutionel des Communautés Européenes,* ed. J-V. Louis and D. Waelbroeck. Brussels: Universite de Bruxelles, Institut d'etudes Europeenes.

Bodiguel, J.-L., and L. Rouban (1991). *Le fonctionnaire detrône?* Paris: Presses de la Fondation Nationale des Science Politiques.

Booker, C., and R. North (1994). *The Mad Officials: How Bureaucrats Are Strangling Britain.* London: Constable.

Borins, S. J. (1995a). Public Sector Innovation: The Implications of New Forms of Organization and Work. In *Governance in a Changing Society,* ed. B. Guy Peters and Donald J. Savoie. Montreal: McGill/Queens University Press.

——— (1995b). The New Public Management Is Here to Stay. *Canadian Public Administration* 38: 122–32.

Borjas, G. J. (1995). The Internationalization of the U.S. Labor Market and the Wage Structure. *Economic Policy Review* 1: 3–8.

Boston, J. (1991). The Theoretical Underpinnings of State Restructuring in New Zealand. In *Reshaping the State,* ed. J. Boston et al. Auckland, New Zealand: Oxford University Press.

——— (1992a). Assessing the Performance of Departmental Chief Executives: Perspectives from New Zealand. *Public Administration* 70: 405–28.

——— (1992b). The Problems of Policy Coordination: The New Zealand Experience. *Governance* 5: 88–103.

——— (1993). Financial Management Reform: Principles and Practice in New Zealand. *Public Policy and Administration* 8: 14–29.

Botella, J. (1994). How Much Is Too Much? An Overview of Fiscal Attitudes in Western Europe. Working paper 1194/54, Instituto Juan, Madrid. March.

Bothun, D., and J. C. Comer (1979). The Politics of Termination: Concepts and Processes. *Policy Studies Journal* 7: 540–53.

Bowen, D. E., and B. Schneider (1988). Services Maketing and Management: Implications for Organizational Behavior. *Research in Organizational Behavior* 10: 43–80.

Bowler, M. K. (1974). *The Nixon Guaranteed Income Proposal: Substance and Process in Policy Change.* Cambridge, MA: Ballinger.

Boyle, M. (1994). Building a Communicative Democracy: The Birth and Death of Citizen Politics in East Germany. *Media, Culture and Society* 16: 183–215.

Boyte, H. C., and F. Riessman (1986). *The New Populism: The Politics of Empowerment.* Philadelphia: Temple University Press.

Braibanti, R. J. D. (1966). *Asian Bureaucratic Systems Emergent from the British Imperial Tradition.* Durham, NC: Duke University Press.

Breton, A. (1974). *An Economic Theory of Representative Government.* Chicago: Aldine.

Brockman, J. (1992). Total Quality Management. *Public Money and Management* 12: 6–9.

Brooks, J., and P. Bate (1994). The Problems of Effecting Change Within the British Civil Service: A Cultural Perspective. *British Journal of Management* 5: 177–90.

Burkitt, B., and P. Whyman (1994). Public Sector Reform in Sweden: Competition or Participation? *Political Quarterly* 65: 275–84.

Burstein, C. (1995). Introducing Reengineering to Government. *Public Manager* 24: 52–54.

Butler, D., and A. Ranney (1994). *Referendums Around the World: The Growing Use of Direct Democracy.* Washington, DC: AEI Press.

Byrne, P. (1976). Parliamentary Control of Delegated Legislation. *Parliamentary Affairs* 29: 366–77.

Caiden, G. (1990). *Administrative Reform Comes of Age.* Berlin: Aldine de Gruyter.

Caldeira, G. A., and J. R. Wright (1990). Amici Curiae Before the Surpeme Court: Who Participates When and How Much? *Journal of Politics* 52: 782–806.

Calista, D. J. (1989). A Transaction-Cost Analysis of Implementation. In *Implementation Theory,* ed. D. Palumbo and D. Calista. Lexington, MA: Lexington Books.

Campbell, C. (1983). The Search for Coordination and Control: When and How Are Central Agencies the Answer? In *Organizing Government, Government Organizations,* C. Campbell and B. G. Peters. Pittsburgh: University of Pittsburgh Press.

—— (1993). Public Service and Democratic Accountability. In *Ethics in Public Service,* ed. R. A. Chapman. Edinburgh: University of Edinburgh Press.

Campbell, C., and J. Halligan (1992). *Political Leadership in an Age of Constraint: The Australian Experience.* Pittsburgh: University of Pittsburgh Press.

Campbell, C., and B. G. Peters (1988). The Politics/Administration Dichotomy: Death or Merely Change? *Governance* 1: 79–99.

Campbell, C., and G. Szablowski (1979). *The Superbureaucrats: Structure and Behaviour in Central Agencies.* Toronto: Macmillan of Canada.

Campbell, D. T. (1982). Experiments as Arguments. *Knowledge: Creation, Diffusion, Utilization* 3: 327–37.

—— (1988). The Experimenting Society. In *Methodology and Epistomology in the Social Sciences: Selected Essays,* D. T. Campbell. Chicago: University of Chicago Press.

Canada (1962). *The Royal Commission on Government Operations.* Glassco Report. Ottawa: Queen's Printer.

—— (1991). *Speech from the Throne to Open the Third Session, Thirty-fourth Parliament of Canada,* May 13.

Carter, N., P. Day, and R. Klein (1992). *How Organizations Measure Success.* London: Routledge.

Carter, N., and P. Greer (1993). Evaluating Agencies: Next Steps and Performance Indicators. *Public Administration* 71: 407–16.

Cate, F. A., and D. A. Fields (1994). The Right to Privacy and the Public's Right to Know: The "Central Purpose" of the Freedom of Information Act. *Administrative Law Review* 46: 41–74.

Cave, M., M. Kogan, and R. Smith (1990). *Output and Performance Measurement in Government: The State of the Art.* London: Jessica Kingsley.

Chapman, R. A. (1993). Reasons of State and the Public Interest: A British Variant of the Problem of Dirty Hands. In *Ethics in Public Service,* ed. R. Chapman. Edinburgh: University of Edinburgh Press.

Chisholm, D. (1989). *Coordination Without Hierarchy.* Berkeley: University of California Press.

Christensen, T. (1994). Utviklingen av direktoratene—aktorer, tenking og organisasjonsformer. In *Forvaltningskunskap,* ed. T. Christensen and M. Egeberg. 2d ed. Oslo: Tano.

Chubb, B. (1992). *The Government and Politics of Ireland.* 3d ed. London: Longman.

Chubb, J. E., and T. Moe (1990). *Politics, Markets and America's Schools.* Washington, DC: Brookings Institution.

Clark, I. D. (1991). Special Operating Agencies. *Optimum* 22 (2): 13–18.

Clark, P. B., and J. Q. Wilson (1961). Incentive Systems: A Theory of Organizations. *Administrative Science Quarterly* 6: 129–66.

Clarke, M., and J. Stewart (1992). *Empowerment: A Theme for the 1990s.* Luton, UK: Local Government Management Board.

Clinton, W. J. (1994). Remarks at the Group of Seven Jobs Conference in Detroit. *Weekly Compilation of Presidential Documents* 30 (11): 508–18.

Coase, R. H. (1960). The Problem of Social Cost. *Journal of Law and Economics* 3: 1–44.

Cohen, J., and J. Rogers (1994). Solidarity, Democracy, Association. *Politische Vierteiljahrschrift* Sonderheft 25: 136–59.

Commission on Social Justice (1994). *Social Justice: Strategies for National Renewal.* London: Vintage.

Common, R., N. Flynn, and E. Mellon (1992). *Managing Public Services: Competition and Decentralization.* Oxford: Butterworth Heinnemann.

Connolly, M., P. McKeown, and G. Milligan-Byrne (1994). Making the Public Sector User-Friendly? A Critical Analysis of the Citizens' Charter. *Parliamentary Affairs* 47: 23–37.

Cook, F. L., and E. J. Barrett (1992). *Support for the American Welfare State.* New York: Columbia University Press.

Cooper, P. (1995). Accountability and Administrative Reform: Toward Convergence and Beyond. In *Governance in a Changing Environment,* ed. D. Savoie and B. G. Peters. Montreal: McGill/Queens University Press.

Cox, R. H. (1992). After Corporatism: A Comparison of the Role of Medical Professionals and Social Workers in the Dutch Welfare State. *Comparative Political Studies* 24: 532–52.

Cronin, T. E. (1989). *Direct Democracy: The Politics of Initiative, Referendum and Recall.* Cambridge: Harvard University Press.

Crook, R. C. (1989). Patrimonialism, Administrative Effectiveness and Economic Development in Cote d'Ivoire. *African Affairs* 88: 205–28.

Crozier, M. (1964). *The Bureaucratic Phenomenon*. Chicago: University of Chicago Press.

Daley, D. (1988). Profile of the Uninvolved Worker: An Examination of Employee Attitudes Toward Management Practices. *International Journal of Public Administration* 11: 63–90.

Davies, A., and J. Willman (1992). *What Next? Agencies, Departments and the Civil Service*. London: Institute for Public Policy Research.

Day, P., and R. Klein (1987). *Accountabilities*. London: Tavistock.

Deleon, P. (1994). Reinventing the Policy Sciences: Three Steps Back to the Future. *Policy Sciences* 27: 77–95.

Deming, W. E. (1988). *Out of the Crisis: Quality, Productivity and Competitive Positions*. Cambridge: Cambridge University Press.

Department of Finance (1987). *FMIP and Program Budgeting: A Study of Implementation in Selected Agencies*. Canberra: AGPs.

Department of Health (October 1994). *A Framework for Local Community Care Charters in England*. London: Department of Health.

Derlien, H.-U. (1991). Horizontal and Vertical Coordination of German EC-Policy. *Hallinnon Tutkimus* 27: 3–10.

——— (1993). German Unification and Bureaucratic Transformation. *International Political Science Review* 14: 319–34.

——— (1994). Germany. In *Rewards at the Top*, ed. C. Hood and B. G. Peters. London: Sage.

——— (1995). Germany. In *Learning from Experience: Lessons of Administrative Reform*, ed. J. Olsen and B. G. Peters. Pittsburgh: University of Pittsburgh Press.

Derlien, H.-U., and G. Szablowski (1993). *Regime Transitions, Elites and Bureaucrats in Eastern Europe*. Oxford: Blackwell.

Dexter, L. A. (1990). Intra-Agency Politics: Conflict and Contravention in Administrative Entities. *Journal of Theoretical Politics* 2: 151–72.

Dicken, P. (1992). *Global Shift: The Internationalization of Economic Activity*. London: Chapman.

DiIulio, J. J. (1994). *Deregulating the Public Service: Can Government Be Improved?* Washington, DC: Brookings Institution.

DiMaggio, P. J., and W. W. Powell (1991). Introduction. In *The New Institutionalism in Organizational Analysis*, P. J. DiMaggio and W. W. Powell. Chicago: University of Chicago Press.

Doern, G. B. (1993). The U.K. Citizens' Charter: Origins and Implementation in Three Agencies. *Policy and Politics* 21: 17–29.

Doig, J. (1983). "When I See a Murderous Fellow Sharpening a Knife Cleverly": The Wilsonian Dichotomy and the Public Administration Tradition. *Public Administration Review* 43: 292–304.

Donkin, R. (1995). Tales of the Office Nomad. *Financial Times*, 29 May.

Dopson, S. (1993). Are Agencies an Act of Faith? *Public Money and Management* 13 (2): 17–23.

Downs, A. (1960). Why the Government Budget Is Too Small in a Democracy. *World Politics* 12: 541–63.

——— (1967). *Inside Bureaucracy*. Boston: Little, Brown.

——— (1972). Up and Down with Ecology—The "Issue-Attention Cycle." *Public Interest* 28: 38–50.

Downs, G. W., and P. D. Larkey (1986). *The Search for Government Efficiency: From Hubris to Helplessness.* Philadelphia: Temple University Press.

Draper, F. D., and B. T. Pitsvada (1981). ZBB—Looking Back After Ten Years. *Public Administration Review* 41: 76–83.

Dror, Y. (1986). *Policymaking Under Adversity.* New Brunswick, NJ: Transaction.

―――― (1992). Future View: Fuzzy Gambles with History. *Futurist* 26 (4): 60.

Dryzek, J. S. (1990). *Discursive Democracy: Politics, Policy and Political Science.* Cambridge: Cambridge University Press.

Duncan, A., and D. Hobson (1995). *Saturn's Children.* London: Sinclair-Stevenson.

Dunleavy, P. (1985). Bureaucrats, Budgets and the Growth of the State. *British Journal of Political Science* 15: 299–328.

―――― (1991). *Democracy, Bureaucracy and Public Choice.* Brighton, UK: Harvester Wheatsheaf.

Dunn, W. N. (1988). Methods of the Second Type: Coping with the Wilderness of Conventional Policy Analysis. *Policy Studies Review* 7: 720–37.

Dunsire, A. (1995). Administrative Theory in the 1980s: A Viewpoint. *Public Administration* 73: 17–40.

Dunsire, A., and C. Hood (1989). *Cutback Management in Public Bureaucracies: Popular Theories and Observed Outcomes in Whitehall.* Cambridge: Cambridge University Press.

Dupuy, F., and J.-C. Thoenig (1985). *L'administration en miettes.* Paris: Fayard.

Durant, R. F., and L. A. Wilson (1993). Public Management, TQM, and Quality Improvement: Toward a Contingency Strategy. *American Review of Public Administration* 23: 215–45.

Dvorin, E. P. and R. H. Simmons (1972). *From Amoral to Humane Bureaucracy.* San Francisco: Canfield.

Economist (1995). E-lectioneering, 17 June.

Egeberg, M. (1995). Bureaucrats as Public Policy-Makers and Their Self Interests. *Journal of Theoretical Politics* 7: 157–67.

Ehrenhalt, A. (1993). The Value of Blue-Ribbon Advice. *Governing* 7 (August): 47–56.

Eisenberg, E. F., and P. W. Ingraham (1993). Analyzing the Pay for Performance Literature: Are There Common Lessons? *Public Productivity and Management Review* 17: 117–28.

Elcock, H. (1994). Editorial: Democracy and Management in Britain and the United States of America. *Public Policy and Administration* 9(3): 1–5.

Elder, S. (1992). Running a Town the 17th Century Way. *Governing* 5: 29–30.

Ellul, J. (1980). *The Technological System.* New York: Continuum.

Epstein, R. A. (1990). No New Property. *Brooklyn Law Review* 56: 747–86.

Ericksson, B. (1983). Sweden's Budget System in a Changing World. *Public Budgeting and Finance* 3: 64–80.

Etheredge, L. S. (1985). *Can Government Learn? American Foreign Policy and Central American Revolutions.* New York: Pergamon Press.

Etzioni, A. (1993). *The Spirit of Community.* New York: Crown Publishers.

FDA News (1995). "Competing for Quality" Gets Overdue Review. May, 1–2.

Feller, I., et al. (1995). Decentralization and Deregulation of the Federal Hiring Process. Paper presented at Trinity Symposium on Public Management Research, San Antonio, TX, July 1995.

Fiorina, M. P. (1989). *Congress: Keystone of the Washington Establishment*, 2d ed. New Haven: Yale University Press.

―― (1992). Coalition Governments, Divided Governments and Electoral Theory. *Governance* 4: 236–49.

Fischer, F. (1990). *Technocracy and the Politics of Expertise.* Newbury Park, CA: Sage.

Follett, M. P. (1940). *Dynamic Administration: The Collected Papers of Mary Parker Follett*, ed. H. C. Metcalf and L. Urwick. New York: Harper.

Foreman, C. (1988). *Signals from the Hill: Congressional Oversight and the Challenge of Social Regulation.* New Haven: Yale University Press.

Forsberg, E., and J. Calltorp (1993). Ekonomiska incitament förandrar sjukvarden. *Lakartidningen* 90: 2611–14.

Foster, C. D. (1992). *Privatization, Public Ownership and the Regulation of Natural Monopoly.* Oxford: Blackwell.

Fournier, J. (1987). *Le Travail Gouvernmental.* Paris: Presses Universitaires Françaises.

Frederickson, G. (1980). *New Public Administration.* University: University of Alabama Press.

Frenkel, M. (1994). The Communal Basis of Swiss Liberty. *Publius* 23: 61–70.

Friedman, M. (1962). *Capitalism and Freedom.* Chicago: University of Chicago Press.

Frohlich, N., J. A. Oppenheimer, and O. R. Young (1971). *Political Leadership and Collective Goods.* Princeton: Princeton University Press.

Garvey, G. (1993). *Facing the Bureaucracy: Living and Dying in a Public Agency.* San Francisco: Jossey-Bass.

General Services Administration (April 1993). *Agenda for Action.* Washington, DC

Germann, R. (1981). *Ausserparlamentarische Kommissionen: Die Milizverwaltung des Bundes.* Bern: Haupt.

Gibert, P., and J.-C. Thoenig (1992). La gestion publique entre l'apprentissage et l'amnesie. Communication presented at International Conference of *PMP,* Paris, February.

Gilbert, G. R. (1993). Employee Empowerment: Law and Practical Approaches. *Public Manager* 22 (3): 45–48.

Gillin, J. L., and J. P. Gillin (1948). *Cultural Sociology.* New York: Macmillan.

Gilmour, R. S., and A. A. Halley (1994). *Who Makes Public Policy? The Struggle Between Congress and the Executive.* Chatham, NJ: Chatham House.

Glynn, J., A. Gray, and B. Jenkins (1992). Auditing the Three Es: The Challenge of Effectiveness. *Public Policy and Administration* 7: 56–72.

Goetz, K. H. (1993). Rebuilding Public Administration in the New Länder: Transfer and Differentiation. *West European Politics* 16: 447–69.

Golembiewski, R. (1995). *Managing Diversity in Organizations.* Tuscaloosa: University of Alabama Press.

Goodin, R. E. (1982). Rational Politicians and Rational Bureaucrats in Washington and Whitehall. *Public Administration* 60: 23–41.

Goodman, J. B., and G. W. Loveman (1991). Does Privatization Serve the Public Interest? *Harvard Business Review* 69 (6): 26–38.

Goodnow, F. J. (1900). *Politics and Administration: A Study in Government.* New York: Macmillan.

Goodsell, C. T. (1976). Cross-Cultural Comparison of Behavior of Postal Clerks Toward Clients. *Administrative Science Quarterly* 21: 140.

—— (1981a). *The Public Encounter: Where State and Citizens Meet.* Bloomington: Indiana University Press.

—— (1981b). Looking Once Again at Human Service Bureaucracy. *Journal of Politics* 43: 763–78.

—— (1995). *The Case for Bureaucracy.* 3d ed. Chatham, NJ: Chatham House.

Gormley, W. T. (1989). *Taming the Bureaucracy: Muscles, Prayers and Other Strategies.* Princeton: Princeton University Press.

—— (1993). Counter-Bureaucracies in Theory and Practice. Paper presented at Annual Meeting of the American Political Science Association, Washington, DC, September.

Gray, A., and B. Jenkins (1995). From Public Administration to Public Management: Reassessing a Revolution. *Public Administration* 73: 75–100.

Gray, A., B. Jenkins, and B. Segsworth (1993). *Budgeting, Auditing and Evaluation: Functions and Integration in Seven Countries.* New Brunswick, NJ: Transaction.

Gray, A., and W. I. Jenkins (1991). The Management of Change in Whitehall: The Experience of FMI. *Public Administration* 69: 41–59.

Gray, B. (1985). Conditions Facilitating Interorganizational Coordination. *Human Relations* 38: 911–36.

Greenwood, R., C. R. Hinings, and S. Ranson (1975a). Contingency Theory and the Structure of Local Authorities, Part 1: Differentiation and Integration. *Public Administration* 53: 1–23

—— (1975b). Contingency Theory and the Structure of Local Authorities, Part II: Contingencies and Structure. *Public Administration* 53: 169–90.

Greer, P. (1994). *Transforming Central Government: The Next Steps Initiative.* Buckingham, UK: Open University Press.

Grice, A. (1995). The Man with an Eye on No. 10: Blair Salutes Enterprise Culture. *Sunday Times,* 23 April, 7.

Grindle, M. S., and J. W. Thomas (1991). *Public Choices and Policy Change: The Political Economy of Reform in Developing Countries.* Baltimore: Johns Hopkins University Press.

Gruber, J. (1987). *Controlling Bureaucracies: Dilemmas in Democratic Governance.* Berkeley: University of California Press.

Gulick, L. (1933). Politics, Administration and the "New Deal." *Annals of the American Academy of Political and Social Science* 169 (September): 45–78.

Gurwitt, R. (1992). A Government That Runs on Citizen Power. *Governing* 6 (3): 48–54.

Gustafsson, B. (1979). *Post-Industrial Society.* London: Croom Helm.

HMSO (1988). *Improving Management in Government: The Next Steps.* London: HMSO.

—— (1991). *Competing for Quality.* London: CM. 1730.

—— (1993). *Career Planning and Succession Planning.* London: HMSO.

—— (1994a). *The Civil Service: Continuity and Change.* London: HMSO, CM. 2627.

—— (1994b). *Better Accounting for the Taxpayer's Money: Resource Accounting and Budgeting in Government.* London: HMSO, CM. 2626.

—— (1995). *Setting New Standards: A Strategy for Government Procurement.* London: HMSO.

Habermas, J. (1984). *The Theory of Communicative Action I: Lifeworld and System.* Boston: Beacon.

Hancock, M. D., J. Logue, and B. Schiller (1991). *Managing Modern Capitalism: Industrial*

Renewal and Workplace Democracy in the United States and Western Europe. New York: Greenwood Press.

Handler, J. (1986). Dependent People, the State and the Modern/Postmodern Search for the Dialogic Community. *UCLA Law Review* 35: 999–1113.

Hanf, K., and F. W. Scharpf (1978). *Interorganizational Policy Making: Limits to Coordination and Central Control.* Beverly Hills, CA: Sage.

Hanushek, E. A. (1987). Formula Budgeting: The Economics and Analytics of Fiscal Policy Under Rules. *Journal of Public Policy Analysis and Management* 6: 3–19.

Hardin, R. (1982). *Collective Action.* Baltimore: Resources for the Future.

Harmon, M. M. (1995). *Responsibility as Paradox: A Critique of Rational Discourse on Government.* Thousand Oaks, CA: Sage.

Harrigan, P. (1994). Consumer Voices in Australian Drugs Approval. *Lancet* 344 (13 August): 464.

Harrison, S., N. Small, and M. Baker (1994). The Wrong Kind of Chaos? The Early Days of an NHS Trust. *Public Money and Management* 14 (1): 39–46.

Harter, P. (1982). Negotiating Regulations: A Cure for the Malaise. *Georgetown Law Journal* 71: 17–31.

Haves, J. R. (1993). Should Bureaucrats Make Decisions? *Forbes* 152: 247.

Hayek, F. A. von (1968). *The Constitution of Liberty.* London: Macmillan.

Hayes, M. (1992). *Incrementalism and Public Policy.* New York: Longman.

Heclo, H., and A. Wildavsky (1974). *The Private Government of Public Money.* Berkeley: University of California Press.

Henkel, M. (1991). The New Evaluative State. *Public Administration* 69: 122–36.

Hennessy, P. (1989). *Whitehall.* London: Secker & Warburg.

Hesse, J. J. (1993). From Transformation to Modernization: Administrative Change in Central and Eastern Europe. *Public Administration* 71: 219–57.

Hirst, P. (1994). *Associative Democracy: New Forms of Economic and Social Governance.* Cambridge, UK: Polity.

Hogwood, B. W. (1993). Restructuring Central Government: The "Next Steps" Initiative. In *Managing Public Organizations,* ed. K. A. Eliassen and J. Kooiman. 2d ed. London: Sage.

—— (1995). The "Growth" of Quangos: Evidence and Explanations. *Parliamentary Affairs* 48: 207–25.

Hogwood, B. W., and B. G. Peters (1983). *Policy Dynamics.* Brighton, UK: Harvester.

Hood, C. (1989). The Tools of Government. Chatham, NJ: Chatham House.

—— (1990). De–Sir Humphreying the Westminster Model of Bureaucracy. *Governance* 3: 205–14.

—— (1991). A Public Management for All Seasons? *Public Administration* 69: 3–19.

—— (1995). "Deprivileging" the UK Civil Service in the 1980s: Dream or Reality. In *Bureaucracy in the Modern State,* ed. J. Pierre. Cheltenham: Edward Elgar.

Hood C., and B. G. Peters (1994). *The Rewards of High Public Office.* London: Sage.

Hood, C., and G. F. Schuppert (1989). *Delivering Public Services in Western Europe.* London: Sage.

Hood, C., B. G. Peters, and H. Wollmann (1995). Public Management Reform: Putting the Consumer in the Driver's Seat. Unpublished paper, London School of Economics.

Horner, C. (1994). Deregulating the Federal Service: Is the Time Right? In *Deregulating the Public Service,* ed. J. J. DiIulio. Washington, DC: Brookings Institution.

Howard, P. K. (1994). *The Death of Common Sense.* New York: Random House.

Hula, R. C. (1990). *Market-based Public Policy.* New York: St. Martin's.

—— (1991). Alternative Management Strategies in Public Housing. In *Privatization and Its Alternatives,* ed. W. T. Gormley. Madison: University of Wisconsin Press.

Hult, K. M. (1987). *Agency Merger and Bureaucratic Redesign.* Pittsburgh: University of Pittsburgh Press.

Hupe, P. (1993). The Politics of Implementation: Individual, Organisational and Political Co-Production in Social Services Delivery. In *New Agendas in the Study of the Policy Process,* ed. M. Hill. London: Harvester/Wheatsheaf.

Inglehart, R. (1990). *Culture Shift in Advanced Industrial Societies.* Princeton: Princeton University Press.

Inglehart, R., and Abramson, P. R. (1994). Economic Security and Value Change. *American Political Science Review* 88: 336–54.

Ingraham, P. W. (1987). Building Bridges or Burning Them? The President, the Appointees and the Bureaucracy. *Public Administration Review* 47: 425–35.

—— (1993). Of Pigs and Pokes and Policy Diffusion: Another Look at Pay for Performance. *Public Administration Review* 53: 348–56.

—— (1995a). *The Foundation of Merit: Public Service in American Democracy.* Baltimore: Johns Hopkins University Press.

—— (1995b). Quality Management in Public Organizations: Prospects and Dilemmas. In *Governance in a Changing Environment,* ed. B. G. Peters and D. J. Savoie. Montreal: McGill/Queens University Press.

Ingram, H., and A. Schneider (1991). Target Populations and Policy Design. *Administration and Society* 23: 333–56.

International Political Science Review (1993). Public Administration and Political Change (Special Issue) 14 (4).

Jaques, E. (1990). In Praise of Hierarchy. *Harvard Business Review* 68: 127–33.

Jenkins, S. (1995). Milk and Water Communities. *The Times* (London), 25 March, 14.

Jennings, E. T., and D. Krane (1994). Coordination and Welfare Reform: The Quest for the Philosopher's Stone. *Public Administration Review* 54: 341–48.

Jerome-Forget, M., J. White, and J. M. Wiener (1995). *Health Care Reform Through Internal Markets.* Montreal: Institute for Research on Public Policy.

Johnson, R. N., and G. D. Liebcap (1994). *The Federal Civil Service System and the Problem of Bureaucracy.* Chicago: University of Chicago Press.

Jonsson, S., S. Rubenowitz, and J. Westerståhl (1995). *Decentraliserad Kommun: Exemplet Göteborg.* Göteborg, Sweden: SNS.

Jordan, A. G. (1990). Political Community Realism versus "New Institutionalism" Ambiguity. *Political Studies* 38: 470–84.

—— (1994). *The British Administrative System: Principles versus Practice.* London: Routledge.

Kato, J. (1994). *The Problem of Bureaucratic Rationality: Tax Politics in Japan.* Princeton: Princeton University Press.

Katz, D., B. A. Gutek, R. L. Kahn, and E. Barton (1975). *Bureaucratic Encounters.* Ann Arbor: Institute for Social Research, University of Michigan.

Katz, E., and B. Danet (1973). *Bureaucracy and the Public.* New York: Basic Books.

Katz, J. L., and S. J. Nixon (1994). Food Stamp Experiments Spark Welfare Debate. *Congressional Quarterly Weekly Report* 52: 2261–63.

Kaufman, H. (1956). Emerging Doctrines of Public Administration. *American Political Science Review* 50: 1059–73.

—— (1976). *Are Government Organizations Immortal?* Washington, D.C.: Brookings Institution.

—— (1977). *Red Tape: Its Origins, Uses and Abuses.* Washington, D.C.: Brookings Institution.

—— (1978). Reflections on Administrative Reorganization. In *Setting National Priorities: The 1978 Budget,* ed. J. A. Pechman. Washington, D.C.: Brookings Institution.

—— (1991). *Time, Chance, and Organizations.* 2d ed. Chatham, NJ: Chatham House.

Kavanagh, D., and P. Morris (1994). *Consensus Politics: From Atlee to Major.* Oxford: Blackwell.

Kazin, M. (1995). *The Populist Persuasion: An American History.* New York: Basic Books.

Kearns, K. (1996). *Accountability in Public and Non-Profit Management.* San Francisco: Jossey-Bass.

Keating, M., and M. Holmes (1990). Australia's Budgetary and Financial Management Reforms. *Governance* 3: 168–85.

Kelman, S. (1985). The Grace Commission: How Much Waste in Government? *Public Interest* 78 (Winter): 62–82.

—— (1992). Adversary and Cooperationist Institutions for Conflict Resolution in Public Policymaking. *Journal of Public Policy Analysis and Management* 11: 178–206.

—— (1994). Deregulating Federal Procurement: Nothing to Fear but Discretion Itself? In *Deregulating the Public Service: Can Government Be Improved?* ed. J. J. DiIulio. Washington, DC: Brookings Institution.

Kemp, P. (1994). The Civil Service White Paper: A Job Half Finished. *Public Administration* 72: 591–98.

Kenis, P., and V. Schneider (1991). Policy Networks and Policy Analysis: Scrutinizing a New Analytical Toolbox. In *Policy Networks: Empirical Evidence and Theoretical Considerations,* ed. B. Marin and R. Mayntz. Boulder, CO: Westview.

Kernaghan, K. (1991). Career Public Service 2000: Road to Renewal or Impractical Vision? *Canadian Public Administration* 34: 551–72.

—— (1992). Empowerment and Public Administration: Revolutionary Advance or Passing Fancy? *Canadian Public Administration* 35: 194–214.

—— (1994). The Emerging Public Service Culture: Values, Ethics and Reforms. *Canadian Public Administration* 37: 614–30.

Kerwin, C. M. (1994). *Rulemaking: How Government Agencies Write Law and Make Policy.* Washington, DC: CQ Press.

Kettl, D. F. (1988). *Government by Proxy: (Mis?)Managing Federal Programs.* Washington, DC: CQ Press.

—— (1992). *Deficit Politics: Public Budgeting in Its Institutional and Historical Context.* New York: Macmillan.

—— (1993). *Sharing Power: Public Governance and Private Markets.* Washington, DC: Brookings Institution.

Kettl, D. F., and J. J. DiIulio, Jr. (1995). *Inside the Reinvention Machine: Appraising Governmental Reform.* Washington, DC: Brookings Institution.

Kickert, W. J. M. (1994). Administrative Reform in British, Dutch and Danish Civil Service. Paper presented at ECPR Workshop on Administrative Reform, Madrid, April.

——— (1996). Public Governance in the Netherlands: An Alternative to Anglo-American Managerialism. *Administration and Society* (forthcoming).

Kiel, L. D. (1989). Nonequilibrium Theory and Its Implications for Public Administration. *Public Administration Review* 49: 544–51.

Kimm, V. J. (1995). GPRA: Early Implementation Lessons. *Public Manager* 24 (Spring): 11–14.

King, D. S. (1987). *The New Right: Politics, Markets and Citizenship.* London: Macmillan.

——— (1995). *Actively Seeking Work? The Politics of Unemployment and Welfare Policy in the United States and Great Britain.* Chicago: University of Chicago Press.

Kobach, K. W. (1993). *The Referendum: Direct Democracy in Switzerland.* Aldershot, UK: Dartmouth.

Koehn, P. H. (1990). *Public Policy and Administration in Africa: Lessons from Nigeria.* Boulder, CO: Westview Press.

König, K. (1993). Administrative Transformation in Eastern Germany. *Public Administration* 71: 135–49.

Kooiman, J. (1993). Governance and Governability: Using Complexity, Dynamics and Diversity. In *Modern Governance,* ed. J. Kooiman. London: Sage.

Korsgaard, M. A., D. M. Schweiger, and H. J. Sapienza (1995). Building Commitment, Attachment and Trust in Strategic Decision-making Teams. *Academy of Management Journal* 38: 60–84.

Koven, S. G. (1992a). Co-production of Law Enforcement Services: Benefits and Implications. *Urban Affairs Quarterly* 27: 457–69.

——— (1992b). Base Closings and the Politics-Administration Dichotomy. *Public Administration Review* 52: 526–31.

Laegreid, P. (1994). Norway. In *Rewards at the Top,* ed. C. Hood and B. Peters. London: Sage.

Lamont, B. T., R. J. Williams, and J. J. Hoffman (1994). Performance During "M-form" Reorganization and Recovery Time. *Academy of Management Journal* 37: 153–66.

Lampe, D. (1995). Welfare Reform: Congress Debates, States Move. *National Civic Review* 84: 60–61.

Lan, Z., and D. H. Rosenbloom (1992). Public Administration in Transition? *Public Administration Review* 52: 535–37.

Landau, M. (1969). Redundancy, Rationality and the Problem of Duplication and Overlap. *Public Administration Review* 29: 346–58.

Lane, J.-E. (1993). *The Public Sector: Concepts, Models and Approaches.* London: Sage.

Langton, S. (1978). *Citizen Participation in America.* Lexington, MA: Lexington Books.

LaNoue, G. R. (1993). Social Science and Minority "Set Asides." *Public Interest* 110 (Winter): 49–62.

Larsson, T. (1986). *Regeringen och dess kansli.* Stockholm: Studentlitteratur.

Laughlin, R., and J. Broadbent (1994). The Managerial Reform of Health and Education: Value for Money or a Devaluing Process? *Political Quarterly* 65: 152–67.

Laux, J. A., and M. A. Malot (1988). *State Capitalism: Public Enterprise in Canada.* Ithaca, NY: Cornell University Press.

LeGrand, J. (1989). Markets, Welfare and Equality. In *Market Socialism,* ed. S. Estrin and J. LeGrand. Oxford: Clarendon Press.

——— (1991a). *Equity and Choice.* London: HarperCollins.

——— (1991b). The Theory of Government Failure. *British Journal of Political Science* 21: 423–42.

Leichter, H. (1992). *Health Policy Reform in America: Innovations from the States.* Armonk, NY: M. E. Sharpe.

LeLoup, L. T., and P. T. Taylor (1994). The Policy Constraints of Deficit Reduction. *Public Budgeting and Finance* 14: 3-25.

Lemco, J. (1995). Canada: The Year of the Volatile Vote. *Current History* 94 (590): 118-22.

Leonard, M. (1988). *The 1988 Education Act: A Tactical Guide for Schools.* Oxford: Blackwell.

Levacic, R. (1994). Evaluating the Performance of Quasi-Markets in Education. In *Quasi-Markets in the Welfare State,* ed. W. Bartlett et al. Bristol, UK: School of Advanced Urban Studies.

Levine, C. H., and P. L. Posner (1981). The Centralizing Effects of Austerity on the Intergovernmental System. *Political Science Quarterly* 96: 67-86.

Lewis, N. (1994). Citizenship and Choice: An Overview. *Public Money and Management* 14 (October-November): 9-16.

Lewis, N., and P. Birkinshaw (1993). *When Citizens Complain: Reforming Justice and Administration.* (Buckingham, UK: Open University Press.

Light, P. C. (1993). *Monitoring Government: Inspectors General and the Search for Accountability.* Washington, DC: Brookings Institution.

—— (1994). Creating Government that Encourages Innovation. In *New Paradigms for Government,* ed. P. W. Ingraham and B. S. Romzek. San Francisco: Jossey-Bass.

—— (1995). *Thickening Government: Federal Hierarchy and the Diffusion of Accountability.* Washington, DC: Brookings Institution.

Likert, R. (1961). *New Patterns of Management.* New York: McGraw-Hill.

Lindblom, C. (1965). *The Intelligence of Democracy: Decision-Making Through Mutual Adjustment.* New York: Free Press.

Linden, R. M. (1994). *Seamless Government: A Practical Guide to Re-Engineering the Public Sector.* San Francisco: Jossey-Bass.

Linder, S. H., and B. G. Peters (1987). A Design Perspective on Policy Implementation: The Fallacy of Misplaced Precision. *Policy Studies Review* 6: 459-75.

—— (1989). Instruments of Government: Perceptions and Contexts. *Journal of Public Policy* 9: 35-58.

—— (1993). Conceptual Frames Underlying the Choice of Policy Instruments. Paper, Conference on Policy Instruments, Erasmus University, Rotterdam, April.

—— (1995). A Design Perspective on the Structure of Public Organizations. In *The Structure of Public Institutions,* ed. David Weimer. Dordrecht, Netherlands: Kluwer.

Lindquist, E. (1994). Citizens, Experts and Budgets: Evaluating Ottawa's Emerging Budget Process. In *How Ottawa Spends, 1994-95,* ed. S. D. Phillips. Ottawa: Carleton University Press.

Lipsky, M. (1980). *Street-level Bureaucracy.* New York: Russell Sage Foundation.

Llewellyn, S. (1994). Applying Efficiency Concepts to Management in the Social Services. *Public Money and Management* 14 (2): 51-56.

Loughlin, J., and S. Mazey (1995). The End of the French Unitary State? Ten Years of Regionalization in France (1982-1992). *Regional Politics and Policy* 4, 3 (special issues).

Lovell, R. (1992). The Citizens' Charter: The Cultural Challenge. *Public Administration* 70: 395-404.

Lowi, T. J. (1972). Four Systems of Politics, Policy and Choice. *Public Administration Review* 32: 298–310.

Luhmann, N. (1990). *Political Theory in the Welfare State.* New York: De Gruyter.

Lundell, B. (1994). Sverige: institutionella ramar for förvaltningspolitiken. In *Förvaltningspolitiken i Norden,* ed. P. Laegreid and O. K. Pedersen. Copenhagen: Jurist og Økonomforbundets Forlag.

Macey, J. R. (1992). Organizational Design and Political Control of Regulatory Agencies. *Journal of Law, Economics and Organization* 8: 93–110.

Machinery of Government Committee (1918). *Report.* Cmnd. 9320. London: HMSO. Haldane Report.

Mackenzie, G. C. (1987). *The In and Outers.* Baltimore: Johns Hopkins University Press.

Maidment, R., and G. Thompson (1993). *Managing the United Kingdom: An Introduction to Its Political Economy and Public Policy.* London: Sage.

Majone, G. (1989). *Evidence, Argument and Persuasion in the Policy Process.* New Haven: Yale University Press.

Malpass, P. (1990). *Reshaping Housing Policy: Subsidies, Rents and Residualization.* London: Routledge.

Manring, N.J. (1994). ADR and Administrative Responsiveness: Challenges to Public Administration. *Public Administration Review* 54: 197–203.

Mansbridge, J. (1994). Public Spirit in Political Systems. In *Values and Public Policy,* ed. H. J. Aaron, T. E. Mann, and T. Taylor. Washington, DC: Brookings Institution.

March, J. G. (1991). Exploration and Exploitation in Organizational Learning. *Organizational Science* 2: 71–87.

March, J. G., and J. P. Olsen (1983). Organizing Political Life: What Administrative Reform Tells us About Governing. *American Political Science Review* 77: 281–97.

—— (1984). The New Institutionalism: Organizational Factors in Political Life. *American Political Science Review* 78: 734–49.

—— (1989). *Rediscovering Institutions.* New York: Free Press.

—— (1995). *Democratic Governance.* New York: Free Press.

March, J. G., and H. A. Simon (1957). *Organizations.* New York: John Wiley.

Marini, F. (1971). *Toward a New Public Administration.* Scranton, PA: Chandler.

Marshall, G. (1989). *Ministerial Responsibility.* Oxford: Oxford University Press.

Masa, F. (1990). *Gestion prive pour services publics.* Paris: Inter Editions.

Massey, A. (1993). *Managing the Public Sector.* Aldershot, UK: Edward Elgar.

Mastracco, A., and S. Comparato (1994). Project: Federal and State Coordination—A Survey of Administrative Law Schemes. *Administrative Law Review* 46: 385–573.

Mayne, J. (1994). Utilizing Evaluation in Organizations: The Balancing Act. In *Can Governments Learn?* ed. F. L. Leeuw, R. C. Rist, and R. C. Sonnischen. New Brunswick, NJ: Transaction Press.

Mayntz, R. (1993). Governing Failures and the Problem of Governability: Some Comments on a Theoretical Paradigm. In *Modern Governance,* ed. J. Kooiman. London: Sage.

Mayntz, R., and F. W. Scharpf (1975). *Policy-Making in the German Federal Bureaucracy.* Amsterdam: Elsevier.

McCubbins, M. D., R. G. Noll, and B. R. Weingast (1989). Structure and Process, Politics and Policy: Administrative Arrangements and the Political Control of Agencies. *Virginia Law Review* 75: 431–82.

McGarrity, T. (1991). *Reinventing Rationality: The Role of Regulatory Analysis in the Federal Bureaucracy.* Cambridge: Cambridge University Press.

McGuire, T. (1981). Budget Maximizing Government Agencies: An Empirical Test. *Public Choice* 36: 313–22.

McLean, I. (1987). *Public Choice: An Introduction.* Oxford: Basil Blackwell.

Meier, H. (1969). Bureaucracy and Policy Formation in Sweden. *Scandinavian Political Studies* 4: 103–16.

Mellett, H., and N. Marriott (1995). Depreciation Accounting in the Public Sector: Lessons from the NHS. *Public Money and Management* 15 (July): 39–43.

Meyer, F. (1985). *La politisation de l'administration publique.* Brussels: Institut Internationale d'administration publique.

Meynaud, J. (1969). *Technocracy.* New York: Free Press.

Michiletti, M. (1990). Toward Interest Inarticulation: A Major Consequence of Corporatism for Interest Organizations. *Scandinavian Political Studies* 13: 255–76.

Miller, G. J. (1992). *Managerial Dilemmas: The Political Economy of Hierarchy.* Cambridge: Cambridge University Press.

Miller, G. J., and T. M. Moe (1983). Bureaucrats, Legislators and the Size of Government. *American Political Science Review* 77: 297–322.

Miller, T. (1984). Conclusion: A Design Science Perspective. In *Public Sector Performance: A Conceptual Turning Point,* ed. T. Miller. Baltimore: Johns Hopkins University Press.

Miller, W. (1988). *Irrelevant Elections? The Quality of Local Democracy in Britain.* Oxford: Oxford University Press.

Millett, R. A. (1977). *"Examination of Widespread Citizen Participation" in Model Cities Programs.* San Francisco: R & E Research Associates.

Mills, N. (1994). *Debating Affirmative Action: Race, Gender, Ethnicity and the Politics of Inclusion.* New York: Delta.

Milward, H. B. (forthcoming). Symposium on the Hollow State: Capacity, Control and Performance in Interorganizational Settings. *Journal of Public Administration Research and Theory.*

Mintzburg, H. (1979). *The Structuring of Organizations.* Englewood Cliffs, NJ: Prentice-Hall.

Mishan, E. J. (1988). *Cost-benefit Analysis: An Informal Introduction.* 4th ed. London: Unwin-Hyman.

Modeen, T., and A. Rosas (1988). *Indirect Public Administration in Fourteen Countries.* Åbo, Finland: Åbo Akademi Press.

Moe, R. (1993). Let's Rediscover Government, Not Reinvent It. *Government Executive* 25: 46–48.

——— (1994). The Reinventing Government Exercise: Misinterpreting the Problem, Misjudging the Consequences. *Public Administration Review* 54: 111–22.

Moe, T. (1984). The New Economics of Organizations. *American Journal of Political Science* 28: 739–77.

——— (1989). The Politics of Bureaucratic Structure. In *Can the Government Govern?* ed. J. E. Chubb and P. E. Peterson. Washington, DC: Brookings Institution.

Mommsen, W. J. (1989). *The Political and Social Theory of Max Weber: Collected Essays.* Oxford: Polity Press.

de Montricher, N. (1994). *La deconcentration.* Paris: Centre National de Recherche Scientifique.

Morgan, G. (1986). *Images of Organizations.* London: Sage.

Mosher, F. (1979). *The GAO: The Quest for Accountability in American Government.* Boulder, CO: Westview.

Moynihan, D. P. (1969). *Maximum Feasible Misunderstanding: Community Action Programs in the War on Poverty.* New York: Free Press.

Mulgan, G. (1993). *Politics in an Antipolitical Age.* Oxford: Polity.

Mulhall, S., and A. Swift (1992). *Liberals and Communitarians.* Oxford: Oxford University Press.

Muller, P. (1985). Un schema d'analyse des politiques sectorielles. *Revue Française de science politique* 35: 165–88.

Muller, W. C., and V. Wright (1994). Reshaping the State in Western Europe: The Limits to Retreat. *West European Politics* 17: 1–11.

Muramatsu, M., and E. Krauss (1995). Japan's Administrative Reform: The Paradox of Success. In *Learning from Experience: Lessons from Administrative Reform,* J. P. Olsen and B. G. Peters. Oslo: Scandinavian University Press.

National Performance Review (March 1993a). *Creating a Government That Works Better and Costs Less.* The Gore Report. Washington, DC: Government Printing Office.

—— (September 1993b). *Reinventing Human Resource Management.* Washington, DC: Government Printing Office.

Niskanen, W. (1971). *Bureaucracy and Representative Government.* Chicago: Aldine/Atherton.

—— (1994). *Bureaucracy and Public Economics* Aldershot, UK: Edward Elgar.

Norman, P. (1994). Cultural Revolution in Whitehall. *Financial Times,* 18 July, 16.

Northcote, S., and Trevelyan, C. (1853). *Report on the Organization of the Permanent Civil Service.* Reprinted as Appendix B, Vol. 1, Committee on the Civil Service *Report* (The Fulton Report). London: HMSO, 1968.

Novick, D. (1965). *Program Budgeting, Program Analysis and the Federal Budget.* Cambridge: Harvard University Press.

Oates, W. E. (1995). Green Taxes: Can We Protect the Environment and Improve the Tax System at the Same Time? *Southern Economic Journal* 61: 914–22.

OECD (1987). *Administration as Service, Public as Client.* Paris: Organization for Economic Cooperation and Development.

—— (1990). *Flexible Personnel Management in the Public Service.* Paris: Organization for Economic Cooperation and Development.

—— (1993). *Internal Markets.* Paris: Organization for Economic Cooperation and Development, Market-Type Mechanisms, series no. 6.

Olsen, J. P. (1986). *Organized Democracy.* Oslo: Universitetsforlaget.

—— (1991). Modernization Programs in Perspective: An Institutional Perspective on Organizational Change. *Governance* 4: 125–49.

Olsen, J. P., and B. G. Peters (1995). *Learning from Experience: Lessons from Administrative Reform.* Pittsburgh: University of Pittsburgh Press.

Olson, M. (1965). *The Logic of Collective Action.* Cambridge: Harvard University Press.

Opheim, C., L. Curry, and P. M. Shields (1994). Sunset as Oversight. *American Review of Public Administration* 24: 253–68.

Orlans, H., and J. O'Neill (1992). Affirmative Action and the Clash of Experiential Realities. *Annals* 523 (September): 144–58.

Osborne, D., and T. Gaebler (1992). *Reinventing Government.* Reading, MA: Addison-Wesley.

Ostrom, E. (1986). An Agenda for the Study of Institutions. *Public Choice* 48: 3–25.

Oughton, J. (1994). Market Testing: The Future of the Civil Service. *Public Policy and Administration* 9 (2): 11–20.

Overman, E. S., and A. G. Cahill (1994). Information, Market Government, and Health Policy: A Study of Health Data Organizations in the States. *Journal of Public Policy Analysis and Management* 13: 435–53.

Painter, J. (1991). Compulsory Competitive Tendering in Local Government: The First Round. *Public Administration* 69: 191–210.

Painter, M. (1981). Central Agencies and the Coordinating Principle. *Australian Journal of Public Administration* 40: 265–80.

Pallot, J. (1991). Financial Management Reform. In *Reshaping the State: New Zealand's Bureaucratic Revolution,* ed. J. Boston, J. Martin, J. Pallot, and P. Walsh. Auckland, New Zealand: Oxford University Press.

Parris, H. (1969). *Constitutional Bureaucracy.* London: George Allen and Unwin.

Pateman, C. (1970). *Participation and Democratic Theory.* Cambridge: Cambridge University Press.

Peacock, A. T. (1983). Public X–Inefficiency: Informational and Institutional Constraints. In *Anatomy of Government Deficiencies,* ed. H. Hanusch. Berlin: Springer.

Peacock, A. T., and H. Willgerodt (1989). *Germany's Social Market Economy: Origins and Evolution.* Basingstoke, UK: Macmillan.

Pear, R. (1995). A Welfare Revolution Hits Home, but Quietly. *New York Times,* 13 August, A-7.

Pennock, J. R., and J. W. Chapman (1975). *Nomos XVI: Participation in Politics.* New York: Lieber-Atherton.

Perrow, C. (1984). *Normal Accidents: Living with High-risk Technologies.* New York: Basic Books.

Perry, J. (1993). Transforming Federal Civil Service. *Public Manager* 21 (Fall): 14–16.

—— (1994). Revitalizing Employee Ties with Public Organizations. In *New Paradigms for Government,* ed. P. W. Ingraham and B. S. Romzek. San Francisco: Jossey-Bass.

Perry, J., and H. G. Rainey (1988). The Public-Private Distinction in Organization Theory: A Critique and a Research Strategy. *Academy of Management Review* 13.

Peters, B. G. (1985). Administrative Change and the Grace Commission. In *The Unfinished Agenda for Civil Service Reform,* ed. C. H. Levine. Washington, DC: Brookings Institution.

—— (1988). *Comparing Public Bureaucracies: Problems of Theory and Method.* University: University of Alabama Press.

—— (1992). Public Policy and Public Bureaucracy. In *History and Context in Comparative Public Policy,* ed. D. Ashford. Pittsburgh: University of Pittsburgh Press.

—— (1994). Alternative Modellen des Policy-Prozesses: Die Sicht "von unten" und die Sicht "von oben." *Politische Vierteiljahrschrift* Sonderdruck 24: 289–303.

—— (1995a). The Politics of Bureaucratic Change in Transitional Governments. *International Social Science Journal,* 147: 122–36.

—— (1995b). *The Politics of Bureaucracy.* 4th ed. New York: Longman.

—— (1995c). *American Public Policy: Promise and Performance.* Chatham, NJ: Chatham House.

—— (1996). The Antiphons of Administrative Reform. Unpublished paper, Department of Political Science, University of Pittsburgh.

Peters, B. G., and B. W. Hogwood (1985). In Search of the Issue-Attention Cycle. *Journal of Politics* 47: 238–53.

——— (1988). Births, Deaths and Marriages: Organizational Change in the U.S. Federal Bureaucracy. *American Journal of Public Administration* 18: 119–33.

Peters, B. G., and J. Loughlin (1995). State Traditions and Administrative Reform. Paper, Department of Political Science, University of Pittsburgh.

Peters, B. G., and D. J. Savoie (1994a). Civil Service Reform: Misdiagnosing the Patient. *Public Administration Review* 54: 418–25.

——— (1994b). Reinventing Osborne and Gaebler: Lessons from the Gore Commission. *Canadian Public Administration* 37: 302–22.

Peters, B. G., and Wright, V. (1996). The Public Bureaucracy. In *The New Handbook of Political Science,* ed. R. E. Goodin and H. D. Klingemann. Oxford: Oxford University Press.

Peters, T. J., and R. H. Waterman (1982). *In Search of Excellence: Lessons from America's Best-Run Companies.* New York: Harper and Row.

Petersen, J. E. (1992). The Property Tax Revolt: Here We Go Again. *Governing* 5 (4): 4.

Petersson, O., and D. Söderlind (1994). *Förvaltningspolitik.* 2d ed. Stockholm: Almänna Forlag.

Petersson. O., A. Westholm, and G. Blomberg (1989). *Medborgarnas Makt.* Stockholm: Carlsson.

Pierce, N. R. (1992). Oregon's Rx for Mistrusted Government. *National Journal,* 29 February, 529.

Pierre, J. (1991). *Självstyrelse och omvarldsberoende.* Lund, Sweden: Studentlitteratur.

——— (1995a). The Marketization of the State. In *Governance in a Changing Environment,* ed. D. J. Savoie and B. G. Peters. Montreal: McGill/Queens University Press.

——— (1995b). Administrative Reform in Sweden: The Decline of Executive Capacity? Paper presented at conference on Modernization of Administration in Europe, Paris, June.

Pierre, J., and B. G. Peters (1996). Citizens vs. the New Public Manager: The Problem of Mutual Empowerment. Paper, University of Gothenberg, Sweden.

Piven, F. F., and R. A. Cloward (1993). *Regulating the Poor: The Function of Public Welfare.* 2d ed. New York: Vintage.

Plamondon, A. L. (1994). A Comparison of Official Secrets and Access to Information in Great Britain and the United States. *Communications and the Law* 16: 51–68.

Pliatzky, L. (1989). *The Treasury Under Mrs. Thatcher.* Oxford: Basil Blackwell.

Plowden, W. (1994). *Ministers and Mandarins.* London: Institute for Public Policy Research.

Pollitt, C. (1986). Beyond the Managerial Model: The Case for Broadening Performance Assessment in Government and the Public Services. *Financial Accountability and Management* 12: 115–20.

——— (1990). *Managerialism and the Public Service.* Oxford: Basil Blackwell.

——— (1995). Management Techniques for the Public Sector: Pulpit or Practice? In *Governance in a Changing Environment,* ed. B. G. Peters and D. J. Savoie. Montreal: McGill/Queens University Press.

Power, M. (1994). *The Audit Explosion.* London: Demos.

Pritzker, D., and D. Dalton (1990). *Negotiated Rulemaking Sourcebook.* Washington, DC: Administrative Conference of the United States.

Pross, A. P. (1992). *Group Politics and Public Policy.* 2d ed. Toronto: Oxford University Press.

Prottas, J. M. (1979). *People Processing: The Street Level Bureaucrat in Public Service Bureaucracy.* Lexington, MA: D. C. Heath.

Public Money and Management (1994). Reorganizing Local Government, 14, 1 (theme issue).

—— (1995). Fraud and Corruption in the Public Sector, 15, 1 (theme issue).

Racine, D. P. (1995). The Welfare State, Citizens and Immersed Civil Servants. *Administration and Society* 26: 434–63.

Ranade, W. (1995). The Theory and Practice of Managed Competition in the National Health Service. *Public Administration* 73: 241–62.

Ranson, S., and J. Stewart (1994). *Management in the Public Domain.* Basingstoke, UK: Macmillan.

Rawls, J. (1972). *A Theory of Justice.* Cambridge: Harvard University Press.

Reich, C. (1973). The New Property. *Yale Law Journal* 73: 733–64.

Reich, R. B. (1983). *The Next American Frontier.* New York: Times Books.

Reichard, C. (1994). *Umdenken im Rathaus: Neue Steureungsmodelle in der Deutsche Kommunalverwaltung.* Berlin Edition: Sigma.

Rhodes, R. A. W. (1992). Local Government Finance. In *Implementing Thatcherite Policies: Audit of an Era,* ed. D. Marsh and R. A. W. Rhodes. Buckingham, UK: Open University Press.

—— (1994). The Hollowing Out of the State. *Political Quarterly* 65: 138–51.

Rhodes, R. A. W., and D. Marsh (1992). New Directions in the Study of Policy Networks. *European Journal of Political Research* 21: 181–205.

Rhodes, T. (1995). U.S. Looks Longingly at Major's Citizens' Charter, *The Times* (London), 17 April.

Richards, S. (1992). Changing Patterns of Legitimation in Public Management. *Public Policy and Administration* 7: 15–28.

Richards, S., and J. Rodrigues. Strategies for Management in the Civil Service. *Public Money and Management* 13 (2): 33–38.

Richardson, J. J. (1984). Doing Less by Doing More: British Government 1979–1993. *West European Politics* 17: 178–97.

Riddell, P. (1995). When Ministers Must Decide, *The Times* (London) 29 May.

Riggs, Fred W. (1964). *Administration in Developing Countries.* Boston: Houghton-Mifflin.

Rist, R. C. (1990). *Program Evaluation and the Management of Government: Patterns and Prospects Across Eight Countries.* New Brunswick, NJ: Transaction.

Roberts, J. (1995). Food and Drug Administration Under Assault. *British Medical Journal* 310 (14 January): 82.

Robinson, R., and J. LeGrand (1994). *Evaluating the NHS Reforms.* London: Kings' Fund Institute.

Rochefort, D. A., and R. W. Cobb (1993). Problem Definition, Agenda Access and Policy Change. *Policy Studies Journal* 21: 56–71.

Roethlisberger, F. J., and W. J. Dickson (1941). *Management and the Worker.* Cambridge: Harvard University Press.

Rogers, D. L., and C. L. Mulford (1982). The Historical Development. In *Interorganizational Coordination,* ed. D. L. Rogers and D. A. Whetten. Ames: Iowa State University Press.

Romzek, B. S. (1990). Employee Investment and Commitment: The Ties That Bind. *Public Administration Review* 50: 374–82.

Romzek, B. S., and M. J. Dubnick (1994). Issues of Accountability in Flexible Personnel Systems. In *New Paradigms for Government*, ed. P. W. Ingraham and B. S. Romzek. San Francisco: Jossey-Bass.

Roniger, L., and A. Ghuneps-Ayata (1994). *Democracy, Clientelism and Civil Society*. Boulder, CO: Lynne Reinner.

Rose, R. (1974). *The Problem of Party Government*. London: Macmillan.

—— (1984). *Understanding Big Government: The Programme Approach*. Beverly Hills: Sage.

—— (1987a). Giving Direction to Permanent Officials: Signals from Electorates, the Market and from Self-expertise. In *Bureaucracy and Public Choice*, ed. J. E. Lane. London: Sage.

—— (1987b). *Ministers and Ministries: A Functional Analysis*. Oxford: Clarendon Press.

Rose, R., and B. G. Peters (1978). *Can Government Go Bankrupt?* New York: Basic Books.

Rose, R., et al. (1985). *Public Employment in Western Nations*. Cambridge: Cambridge University Press.

Rossi, P. H., and H. E. Freeman (1989). *Evaluation: A Systematic Approach*. 4th ed. Newbury Park, CA: Sage.

Rouban, L. (1991). Le client, l'usager et le fonctionnaire: quelle politique pour l'administration publique. *Revue française d'administration publique* 59: 435–44.

Rubin, I. (1990). *The Politics of Public Budgeting*. Chatham, NJ: Chatham House.

Sabatier, P. A. (1988). An Advocacy Coalition Model of Policy Change and the Role of Policy-Oriented Learning Therein. *Policy Sciences* 21: 129–68.

Salamon, L. M. (1979). The Time Dimension of Policy Evaluation: The Case of the New Deal Land Relief Programs. *Public Policy* 27: 129–84.

Sampson, A. (1995). *Company Man: The Rise and Fall of Corporate Life*. London: Harper-Collins.

Savoie, D. J. (1990). *The Politics of Public Spending in Canada*. Toronto: University of Toronto Press.

—— (1994a). *Reagan, Thatcher, Mulroney: In Search of a New Bureaucracy*. Pittsburgh: University of Pittsburgh Press.

—— (1994b). Truth About Government. *Ottawa Citizen*, 13 October, 15.

—— (1995a). What Is Wrong with the New Public Management? *Canadian Public Administration* 38: 112–21.

—— (1995b). *Central Agencies: Looking Backward*. Ottawa: Canadian Centre for Management Development.

—— (1995c). Globalization and Governance. In *Governance in a Changing Environment*, ed. B. G. Peters and D. J. Savoie. Montreal: McGill/Queens University Press.

Sawer, M. (1982). Political Manifestation of Australian Libertarianism. In *Australia and the New Right*, ed. M. Sawer. Sydney: George Allen and Unwin.

Scharpf, F. W. (1989). Decision Rules, Decision Styles and Policy Choices. *Journal of Theoretical Politics* 1: 149–76.

—— (1991). Die Handlungsfähigkeit des Staates am Ende des zwanzigsten Jahrhunderts. *Politische Vierteiljahrschrift* 4: 621–34.

Schick, A. (1978). The Road from ZBB. *Public Administration Review* 38: 177–81.

——— (1988). Micro-Budgetary Adaptations to Fiscal Stress in Industrialized Countries. *Public Administration Review* 48: 523–33.

——— (1990). *The Capacity to Budget.* Washington, DC: Urban Institute Press.

Schmitter, P. C. (1974). Still the Century of Corporatism? *Review of Politics* 36: 85–131.

——— (1989). Corporatism Is Dead: Long Live Corporatism. *Government and Opposition* 24: 54–73.

Schoenbrod, D. (1993). *Power Without Responsibility: How Congress Abuses the People Through Delegation.* New Haven: Yale University Press.

Schon, D., and M. Rein (1994). *Frame Reflection: Resolving Intractable Policy Issues.* New York: Basic Books.

Schorr, P. (1987). Public Service as a Calling: An Exploration of a Concept. *International Journal of Public Administration* 10: 465–94.

Schultze, C. L. (1977). *The Public Use of Private Interest.* Washington, DC: Brookings Institution.

Scott, G., P. Bushnell, and N. Sallee (1990). Reform of the Core Public Sector: The New Zealand Experience. *Governance* 3: 138–67.

Scott-Clark, C. (1995). Parents Decry School "choice" as a Failure. *Sunday Times* (London), 4 June, 8.

Sears, D. O., and J. Citrin (1985). *Tax Revolt: Something for Nothing in California.* 2d ed. Cambridge: Harvard University Press.

Seidman, H., and R. Gilmour (1986). *Politics, Power and Position: From the Positive to the Regulatory State.* New York: Oxford University Press.

Seldon, A. (1990). The Cabinet Office and Coordination, 1979–87. *Public Administration* 68: 103–21.

Self, P. (1993). *Government by the Market?* Boulder, CO: Westview.

Sharp, E. B. (1994). *The Dilemma of Drug Policy in the United States.* New York: Harper-Collins.

Shepsle, K. (1989). Studying Institutions: Some Lessons from the Rational Choice Approach. *Journal of Theoretical Politics* 1: 131–48.

——— (1992). Bureaucratic Drift: Coalitional Drift and Time Consistency: A Comment on Macey. *Journal of Law, Economics and Organization* 8: 111–18.

Silberman, B. S. (1993). *Cages of Reason: The Rise of the Rational State in France, Japan, the United States and Great Britain.* Chicago: University of Chicago Press.

Simon, H. (1947). *Administrative Behavior.* New York: Free Press.

——— (1973). The Structure of Ill-Structured Problems. *Artificial Intelligence* 4: 181–201.

Sjölund, M. (1989). *Statens Lönepolitik, 1977–88.* Stockholm: Almänna Forlaget.

——— (1994a). Sweden. In *Rewards at the Top,* C. Hood and B. G. Peters. London: Sage.

——— (1994b). Transition in Government Pay Policies. *International Journal of Public Administration* 17: 1907–35.

Skogstad, G. (1993). Policy Under Siege: Supply Management in Agricultural Marketing. *Canadian Public Administration* 36: 1–23.

Skowronek, S. (1982). *Building a New American State: The Expansion of National Administrative Capacity, 1877–1920.* Cambridge: Cambridge University Press.

Smart, H. (1991). *Criticism and Public Rationality: Professional Rigidity and the Search for Caring Government.* London: Routledge.

Smith, M. J., D. Marsh, and D. Richards (1993). Central Government Departments and the Policy Process. *Public Administration* 71: 567–94.

Smith, S. P. (1977). *Equal Pay in the Public Sector: Fact or Fantasy?* Princeton: Department of Economics.

Spicer, M. W. (1990). A Contractarian Approach to Public Administration. *Administration and Society* 22: 303–16.

Spragens, T. A. (1990). *Reason and Democracy.* Durham, NC: Duke University Press.

Spulbar, N. (1989). *Managing the American Economy: From Roosevelt to Reagan.* Bloomington: Indiana University Press.

Squires, P. (1990). *Anti-Social Policy: Welfare, Ideology and the Discipline State.* London: Harvester Wheatsheaf.

Ståhlberg, K. (1987). The Politicization of Public Administration: Notes on the Concepts, Causes and Consequences of Politicization. *International Review of Administrative Science* 53: 363–82.

State Services Commission (1994). *New Zealand's Reformed State Sector.* Wellington: State Services Commission.

Stein, E. W. (1995). Organizational Memory. *International Journal of Information Management* 15: 17–32.

Stein, J. (1995). Building a Better Bureaucrat. *Regulation* (3): 24–32.

Stillman, R. J. (1991). *Preface to Public Administration: A Search for Themes and Direction.* New York: St. Martin's.

Stockman, D. (1986). *The Triumph of Politics: How the Reagan Revolution Failed.* New York: Harper and Row.

Stromberg, L. (1990). Det svenska frikommunsforsoket. In *Frikommunsforsoket i Norden,* ed. K. Ståhlberg. Åbo, Finland: Åbo Akademi.

Sutherland, S. L. (1991). The Al-Mashat Affair: Administrative Responsibility in Parliamentary Institutions. *Canadian Public Administration* 34: 573–603.

Swiss, J. (1993). Adapting Total Quality Management (TQM) to Government. *Public Administration Review* 52: 356–62.

Szanton, P. (1981). *Federal Reorganization: What Have We Learned?* Chatham, NJ: Chatham House.

Taggart, P. (1995). New Populist Parties in Western Europe. *West European Politics* 18: 34–51.

Tarschys, D. (1981). Rational Decremental Budgeting. *Policy Sciences* 14: 49–58.

––––– (1986). From Expansion to Restraint. *Public Budgeting and Finance* 6: 25–37.

Taylor-Gooby, P. (1985). *Public Opinion, Ideology and State Welfare.* London: Routledge and Kegan Paul.

Tellier, P. M. (1990). Public Service 2000: The Renewal of the Public Service. *Canadian Public Administration* 33: 123–32.

––––– (1991). A New Canadian Public Service. *Business Quarterly* 55 (4): 93–98.

Terry, L. D. (1995). *Leadership of Public Bureaucracies: The Administrator as Conservator.* Thousand Oaks, CA: Sage.

Thain, C., and M. Wright (1992a). Planning and Controlling Public Expenditure in the UK, Part I: The Treasury's Public Expenditure Survey. *Public Administration* 70: 3–24.

––––– (1992b). Planning and Controlling Public Expenditure in the UK, Part II: The Effects and Effectiveness of the Survey. *Public Administration* 70: 193–224.

Theakston, K. (1992). *The Labour Party and Whitehall.* London: Routledge.

Thomas, J. C. (1993). Public Involvement and Government Effectiveness. *Administration and Society* 24: 444–69.

Thompson, V. A. (1975). *Without Sympathy or Enthusiasm: The Problem of Administrative Compassion.* University: University of Alabama Press.

Tiebout, C. M. (1956). A Pure Theory of Local Public Expenditure. *Journal of Political Economy* 64: 416–24.

Timsit, G. (1988). *Les autorités administratives indépendentes.* Paris: Presses Universitaires de France.

Tomkys, R. (1991). The Financial Management Initiative in the FCO. *Public Administration* 69: 257–63.

Tonn, B. E. and D. Feldman (1995). Non-Spatial Government. *Futures* 27: 11–36.

Torstendahl, Rolf (1991). *Bureaucratization in Northwest Europe, 1880–1985: Dominance and Government.* London: Routledge.

Tritter, J. (1994). The Citizens' Charter: Opportunities for Users' Perspectives. *Political Quarterly* 65: 397–414.

Tsebelis, G. (1994). The Power of the European Parliament as a Conditional Agenda Setter. *American Political Science Review* 88: 128–55.

Tullock, G. (1965). *The Politics of Bureaucracy.* Washington, DC: Public Affairs Press.

Tully, S. (1995). Finally, Colleges Start to Cut Their Crazy Costs. *Fortune* 131 (8): 110–14.

t'Veld, R. (1992). *Autopoesis and Configuration Theory.* Dordrecht, the Netherlands: Kluwer.

United Nations Development Programme (1988). *Selected Studies on Major Administrative Reforms.* New York.

U.S. General Accounting Office (1995a). *Federal Quality Management: Strategies for Involving Employees.* Washington, DC 18 April, GAO/GGD-95-79.

—— (1995b). *Federal Hiring: Reconciling Managerial Flexibility with Veterans' Preference.* Washington, DC 16 June, GAO/GGD-95-102.

Van Nispen, F. (1994). *Het dossier Heroverweging.* Delft, Netherlands: Eburon.

Vander Weele, M. (1994). *Reclaiming Our Schools: The Battle over Chicago School Reform.* Chicago: Loyola University Press.

Victor, P. (1995). Freedom of Information: It Will Cost You. *Independent on Sunday* (London), 18 June.

Waldo, D. (1968). Scope of the Theory of Public Administration. *Annals of the American Academy of Political and Social Sciences* 8: 1–26.

Walsh, K. (1991). Quality and Public Services. *Public Administration Review* 69: 503–14.

—— (1995). *Public Services and Market Mechanisms: Competition, Contracting and the New Public Management.* Basingstoke, UK: Macmillan.

Walsh, K., and J. Stewart (1992). Change in the Management of Public Services. *Public Administration* 70: 499–518.

Walsh, P. (1991). The State Sector Act of 1988. In *Reshaping the State: New Zealand's Bureaucratic Revolution,* ed. J. Boston, J. Martin, J. Pallot, and P. Walsh. Auckland: Oxford University Press.

Walters, J. (1992a). How Not to Reform Civil Service. *Governing* 6 (2): 30–34.

—— (1992b). Reinventing Government: Managing the Politics of Change. *Governing* 6 (3): 27–37.

—— (1992c). The Cult of Total Quality. *Governing* 5 (8): 38–42.

Warner, N. (1984). Raynerism in Practice: Anatomy of a Rayner Scrutiny. *Public Administration* 62: 7–22.

Weber, M. (1958). Bureaucracy. In *From Max Weber: Essays in Sociology,* ed. H. H. Gerth and C. W. Mills. New York: Oxford University Press.

Wehrle-Einhorn, R. J. (1994). Reinventing the Government Contract for Services. *National Contract Management Journal* 25 (2): 63–72.

Weir, S. (1995). Quangos: Questions of Democratic Accountability. *Parliamentary Affairs* 48: 306–22.

Werth, W. (1973). *Mitbestimmung: Deutsche Reformpolitik auf falschen Weg.* Munich: Politisches Archiv.

West, W. (1985). *Administrative Rulemaking: Politics and Process.* New York: Greenwood.

Wex, S. (1990). Leadership and Change in the 1990s. *Optimum* 21: 25–30.

White, O. F., and J. F. Wolf (1995). Deming's Total Quality Management Movement and the Baskin Robbins Problem: Part 1: Is It Time to Go Back to Vanilla? *Administration and Society* 27: 203–25.

White, S. K. (1988). *The Recent Work of Jurgen Habermas: Reason, Justice and Modernity.* Cambridge: Cambridge University Press.

Wildavsky, A. (1969). Rescuing Policy Analysis from PPBS. *Public Administration Review* 29: 189–202.

——— (1978). A Budget for All Seasons? Why the Traditional Budget Lasts. *Public Administration Review* 38: 501–9.

——— (1992). *The New Politics of the Budgetary Process.* 2d ed. New York: HarperCollins.

Willetts, D. (1994). *Civic Conservatism.* London: Social Market Foundation.

Williamson, O. E. (1975). *Markets and Hierarchies.* New York: Free Press.

——— (1985). *The Economic Institutions of Capitalism.* New York: Free Press.

Wilson, D. (1995). The Quango Debate. Special issue, *Parliamentary Affairs* 48, no. 2.

Wilson, G. (1994). The Westminster Model in Comparative Perspective. In *Developing Democracy,* ed. I. Budge and D. McKay. London: Sage.

Wilson, J. Q. (1989). *Bureaucracy.* New York: Free Press.

——— (1994a). Can the Bureaucracy Be Deregulated? Lessons from Government Agencies. In *Deregulating the Public Sector,* ed. J. J. DiIulio. Washington, DC: Brookings Institution.

——— (1994b). Reinventing Public Administration. *PS: Political Science and Politics* 27: 667–73.

Wilson, S. V. (1988). What Legacy? The Nielsen Task Force Program Review. In *How Ottawa Spends: 1988/89, the Conservatives Heading into the Stretch,* ed. K. A. Graham. Ottawa: Carleton University Press.

Wilson, W. (1887). The Study of Administration. *Political Science Quarterly* 2: 197–222.

Wiltshire, K. (1988). *Privatization: The British Experience.* Melbourne: Longman.

Wolff, C. (1988). *Markets or Governments?* Cambridge: MIT Press.

Wright, V. (1994). Reshaping the State: Implications for Public Administration. *West European Politics* 17: 102–34.

Wright, V., and B. G. Peters (1996). Public Administration: Change and Redefinition. In *New Handbook of Political Science,* ed. R. E. Goodin. Oxford: Oxford University Press.

Zifcak, S. (1994). *New Managerialism: Administrative Reform in Whitehall and Canberra.* Buckingham, UK: Open University Press.

Zussman, D., and J. Jabes (1989). *The Vertical Solitude: Managing in the Public Sector.* Halifax: Institute for Research on Public Policy.

Index